# Common mental disorders

Unique in combining insights from social psychiatry with recent findings in biological psychiatry, this book provides a new and invaluable model for common mental disorders. The authors, one a physician, the other trained in the social sciences, survey a wide field to describe the physical basis of common mental disorders and the way in which events in an individual's life can bring about an episode of mental disorder. This is the first model to give equal emphasis in determining susceptibility to mental disorder to social and psychological events on the one hand, and to factors affecting physical health on the other.

David Goldberg and Peter Huxley expand and develop their earlier successful and widely-quoted book, *Mental Illness in the Community* (1980), to define three important components:

*vulnerability* – factors which make some individuals more susceptible than others to episodes of mental disorder
*destabilisation* – the process of beginning to experience symptoms
*restitution* – factors which determine how long an episode of illness will last in a particular individual.

They describe the physical processes which underlie states of depression and anxiety, and show how environmental factors can exert direct effects upon these processes. They take a public health approach throughout, and conclude by discussing the implications of recent findings both for the future pattern of services and for training needs of mental health professionals.

Essential reading for all those who work in the specialist mental health services, *Common Mental Disorders* will also be useful to GPs, primary health care workers and the interested layman.

**David Goldberg** is Professor of Psychiatry and Director of the Mental Illness Research Unit at the University of Manchester.

**Peter Huxley** is Professor of Psychiatric Social Work at the University of Manchester, where he is also the Director of the Mental Health Social Work Research and Staff Development Unit.

# Common mental disorders

## A bio-social model

David Goldberg and Peter Huxley

Tavistock/Routledge
London and New York

First published in 1992
by Routledge
11 New Fetter Lane, London EC4P 4EE

Simultaneously published in the USA and Canada
by Routledge
a division of Routledge, Chapman and Hall Inc.
29 West 35th Street, New York, NY 10001

Typeset in Times by LaserScript Limited, Mitcham, Surrey
Printed and bound in Great Britain by
Biddles Ltd, Guildford and King's Lynn

*British Library Cataloguing in Publication Data*
Goldberg, David *1934–*
  Common mental disorders
  1. Mental disorders
  I. Title II. Huxley, Peter
  616.89

*Library of Congress Cataloging in Publication Data*
Goldberg, David P.
  Common mental disorders: a bio-social model/David Goldberg and
  Peter Huxley.
  p. cm.
  1. Affective disorders. 2. Anxiety. 3. Somatoform disorders.
  4. Social psychiatry. I. Huxley, Peter. II. Title.
  [DNLM: 1. Mental Disorders. 2. Models, Psychological. WM 100
  G6168c]
  RC537.G645 1992
  616.85'27 – dc20
  DNLM/DLC
  for Library of Congress                                    91-457
                                                                CIP

ISBN 0–415–06100–8
     0–415–05987–9 (pbk)

# Contents

# Illustrations

## FIGURES

## TABLES

# Foreword

This splendid monograph is informed by epidemiological intelligence. What makes this feature so noteworthy? *Intelligence* has two primary meanings in the American Heritage Dictionary; that is, as 'a faculty of thought and reason' and as 'received information' or 'news'. The third meaning listed is also particularly apposite in the present context: 'secret information'. Although the studies David Goldberg and Peter Huxley cite have been reported in the open literature, it is not much of an exaggeration to call them 'secret' in the absence of evidence they have influenced the delivery of mental health services. But why *epidemiological* intelligence?

The mode of analysis employed throughout this book is *population-based*; it takes into account *denominators* (populations) as well as *numerators* (cases). The reader is alerted to the importance of the way 'caseness' is defined. Definitions, however arbitrary, can be made operational in order to attain reliability; however, their ultimate justification lies in the consequences they have for particular purposes. Goldberg and Huxley are concerned for the way care is – and should be – delivered in the community; their reference point is patient management.

The authors employ epidemiological intelligence in an analysis of the distribution of illness in the community, the demographic and social correlates of that distribution, and the causal inferences in accord with the observed interrelations. The result is a lucidly presented, closely reasoned and firmly data-based argument which has major implications for health policy.

In contrast, most psychiatric texts start by describing the clinical characteristics of patients seen in specialist practice; these descriptions are used to generate 'ideal types' for a classification scheme. The problem with this approach is that the patients who finally reach the psychiatrist are so skewed a sample of ill persons in the population that the scheme necessarily provides a distorted account of problems in the community. On the documentation summarised in the pages that follow, no more than one in ten to one in fifteen individuals with symptoms of mental illness in the community reach the psychiatric out-patient department. Some fail to attend the general practitioner's surgery in the first place; such persons are identified only when community surveys are undertaken. Others are not recognised as psychiatric problems when they do arrive at the generalist's office; still others are managed (more or less well) at this level in the system.

Less than 10 per cent of symptomatic 'eligibles' make their way to the specialist. As would be expected, they are on average the sickest patients; they suffer from the less common ailments. Because traditional psychiatric studies are based on so unrepresentative a sample, it is not surprising that specialist nosology does not meet the needs of generalist practice. It was not until research psychiatrists, taking their lead from Michael Shepherd, undertook to examine patients in the GP's consulting room that psychiatrists became aware of how far short our classification schemes fall in dealing with the more common mental illnesses.

## THE RELEVANCE OF DIAGNOSIS

The fact is that patients do not arrive in the doctor's office neatly packaged and pre-sorted. It is not only that each patient exhibits unique particularities; it is also that the patient's idiosyncracies shape his illness manifestations. This interaction between an unique history and a shared biology is both the bane and the joy of general medical practice: the bane in that the variability in the ways similar illnesses present necessitates a meticulous search for the pathology underlying the patient's complaints; the joy in that each new encounter is a challenge to the practitioner's ingenuity. Medical practice, conscientiously undertaken, defies routinisation!

Making the diagnosis (that is, identifying the diabetes or the depression underlying the complaint of weight loss) only starts the process. The goal is to help *this* patient to understand the nature of *his* problem and to weigh the benefits and the costs of the available therapeutic alternatives. It demands of the doctor a sensitivity to the nuances of cultural meaning as they are refracted through individual experience; it demands the flexibility and the imaginativeness to tailor standard regimens to fit the particularities of the patient's situation.

Naming the problem matters to the patient as well as the doctor. Patients seek more than remission of their symptoms; they search for relief from the anxiety aroused by the threat to their integrity. They want the doctor to interpret the meaning of their misfortune. The medical label given and the explanation provided not only legitimate the illness experience but shape its very expression.

For the doctor, 'making the diagnosis' matters in so far as it informs treatment and forecasts the likely course of the illness. At least, that is what should matter. The process can become an academic exercise, pursued without regard to the hazard for the patient or the likelihood it will lead to benefit. For the dedicated clinician, the point of diagnosis and classification is to enhance the physician's ability to help the patient. That is, its goals are both pragmatic and compassionate. The doctor wants a guide to action, one whose elegance and tightness of logic are far less important to him than its utility in guiding management. Goldberg and Huxley provide just such a structure for evaluating mental illness in general medical practice. The simplicity and straightforwardness of their scheme make it easy to underestimate the profundity of the insights they provide.

## A PRAGMATIC APPROACH TO DIAGNOSIS

All too often, dimensional and categorical models of illness are counterposed as though they were mutually exclusive and demand the choice of one or the other. To the contrary, the one to be preferred depends upon the conditions to which it is to be applied and the purposes of its use. Goldberg and Huxley grant the utility of categorical models for psychotic conditions, even though existing models are imperfect, for the less severe but more common complaint patterns seen in office practice, they demonstrate quite convincingly that a dimensional model provides a far more comprehensive account of clinical reality.

As an example of the utility of a categorical model with careful definitions, the US/UK study of the psychiatric diagnostic process made it clear that the marked differences in the rates at which schizophrenia and depressive illness were being reported from the two countries were due to differences in diagnostic criteria and in modes of assessment rather than in actual prevalence (Cooper *et al.* 1972). A mixed example is provided by the St Louis Diagnostic Criteria (Feighner *et al.* 1972), a major step on the way to *DSM-III*; this scheme proved quite useful for research purposes in separating out unequivocal cases of disorder; however, it did so at the very real cost for use in clinical practice of leaving many cases in a residual unsorted scrap-bin. In primary care, the categorical model just doesn't meet the needs of the generalist physician. The coexistence of anxiety and depression in many patients, the fact that response to treatment is not effectively predicted by assignment to a disorder category, and the fact that many distressed persons 'fail' the category standard despite suffering from major morbidity, all make a dimensional approach much more sensible.

Additional strong evidence for the position advocated in this monograph has come from an unexpected source: studies by American investigators employing *DSM-III*, the Bible of the categorical camp. Klerman *et al.* (1991) report extensive morbidity as well as excessive health care utilisation in individuals with panic attacks *not* meeting full *DSM-III* diagnostic criteria for panic disorder. The source of their data is the National Institute of Mental Health Epidemiological Catchment Area study (Robins and Regier 1991). Averaged across the five study sites, the lifetime prevalence for panic disorder was 1.5 per cent, that for panic attacks was 3.6 per cent. Although individuals with panic disorder report more symptoms, more frequent symptoms, and more co-morbidity than individuals with panic attacks, the important finding is the serious impairment in health, in work performance and financial dependency among the latter. Their illness burden is considerable; they are in need of care even though they do not meet criteria for a 'disorder'; yet a recorded diagnosis of an 'official' disorder is required (in the US, at least) before third party payors will legitimate payment for care.

Recent research findings *vis-à-vis* the impact of depressive symptoms echo the same themes. Wells *et al.* (1989) evaluated more than 11,000 patients who were enrolled in three different US health care systems. The investigators found quite considerable morbidity among patients who did not 'make' full criteria for the diagnosis of depression although they had prominent depressive symptoms. The extent of the dysfunction associated with depressive symptoms, *with or without depressive disorder*, was, in the authors' words, 'comparable with or worse than that uniquely associated with eight chronic medical conditions'. Similar results have been reported by Coulehan *et al.* (1990) among medical patients who fall into a class they labelled 'depressive symptoms only' (that is, without major depressive disorder). Those patients 'had more medical diagnoses, were prescribed more medications, and had a greater burden of mental illness' than a comparison group of non-depressed medical patients.

In both instances (panic disorders and depressive disorders), the operational criteria for 'disorder' identify cases which are more severe but do not differ in kind from 'missed cases' associated with significant impairment. What gets counted in epidemiologic surveys of panic and agoraphobia is very much a function of the way the conditions are defined, as Eaton and Keyl (1990) have shown in the instances of: *DSM-III* agoraphobia, 'situational' agoraphobia, 'classic' agoraphobia, and agoraphobia with panic disorder. Disorders, though more severe, occur less often than attacks. Thus, the total illness burden in the community resulting from symptoms not meeting criteria for disorder may exceed the burden associated with the 'disorder' itself. All of this argues for the importance of a dimensional approach in general medical practice where the goal of the physician is to restore function and to classify only in so far as classifying contributes to better care.

My conviction that the position taken by the authors can lead to better care rests upon two premises: first, that the general practitioner can be taught to recognise common mental disorders and, more importantly, that he or she can learn to treat such problems effectively. Happily, research at Manchester, as well as elsewhere, has shown clearly that the diagnostic skills of the generalist can be improved by short training schemes. The benefits for patients' care from this step alone are not inconsiderable; recognising the locus of the problem avoids resort to unnecessary, invasive and costly test procedures; it reduces the likelihood of fixating the patient in a somatising pattern by the fruitless pursuit of yet one more laboratory test.

More recent studies, many still unpublished, including research by David Goldberg and Peter Huxley, provide a growing body of evidence that brief courses of psychological treatment given by trained general practitioners can accelerate restitution. Treatment need not be medical; it can be given by social workers and psychologists. Psychotherapy is far preferable to routine medical prescription of psychotropic drugs; but it does require time and time is a precious resource in a busy office practice. Whether public authorities will be persuaded to provide the funds needed to make brief psychotherapy widely available remains to be seen.

I must stop. I was invited to write a Foreword, not another book. Having reached the end of the space allotted me, I have failed to comment on the exciting new ideas on vulnerability, destabilisation, restitution and the mind/body problem to be found in this volume. If I have limited myself to public health issues, that is because of my preoccupation with them.

*Common Mental Disorders: A bio-social Model* is a major contribution to psychiatry and medicine. It is destined to become a classic. I wish I could claim credit for it. I shall have to content myself with the reflected glory of having been invited to write the Foreword.

Leon Eisenberg
Harvard Medical School, Boston, MA
1991

## REFERENCES

Cooper, J.E., Kendall, R.E., Gurland, B.J., Sharpe, L., Copeland, J.R.M. and Simon, R. (1972) *Psychiatric Diagnosis in London and New York*. London: Oxford University Press.

Coulehan, J.L., Schulberg, H.C., Block, M.R., Janosky, J.E. and Arena, V.C. (1990) 'Depressive symptomatology and medical co-morbidity in a primary care clinic', *International Journal of Psychiatry in Medicine*, 20, 335–347.

Eaton, W.W. and Keyl, P.M. (1990) 'Risk factors for the onset of diagnostic interview schedule/DSM III agoraphobia in a prospective, population-based study', *Archives of General Psychiatry*, 47, 819–824.

Feighner, J.P., Robins, E., Guze, S.B., Woodruff, R.A., Winokur, G. and Munzo, R. (1972) 'Diagnostic criteria for use in psychiatric research', *Archives of General Psychiatry*, 26, 57–63.

Klerman, G.L., Weissman, M.M., Ouellete, R., Johnson, J. and Greenwald, S. (1991) 'Panic attacks in the community: social morbidity and health care utilization', *Journal of the American Medical Association*, 265, 742–746.

Robins, L.N. and Regier, D. (eds) (1991) *Psychiatric Disorders in America*. New York: The Free Press.

Wells, K.B., Stewart, A., Hays, R.D., Burnam, M.A., Rogers, W., Daniels, M., Berry, S., Greenfield, S. and Ware, J. (1989) 'The functioning and well-being of depressed patients', *Journal of the American Medical Association*, 262, 914–919.

# Acknowledgements

It is a pleasure to record our debt of gratitude to two close colleagues who introduced one of us (DPG) to latent trait analysis, and who helped in the initial data runs on which the whole of our dimensional model rests. Pat Moran and Paul Duncan-Jones were both formidable bio-statisticians, and we are sad that they have not survived to discuss the development of our ideas with us. They made a great contribution to what we have done, although this particular synthesis is our own. We are happy that David Grayson of the University of Sydney – who worked with Pat and Paul in Canberra where the initial mathematical work was done – looked through our description of latent trait analysis in Chapter 5. None of the work would have occurred had it not been for the kindness of Scott Henderson of the NH and MRC Social Psychiatry Research Unit in introducing one of us to his mathematical colleagues, and for arranging several visits to Canberra where many of these ideas took shape. The field work for the latent trait analysis was done by Keith Bridges, working on a grant provided by the Jules Thorn Investment Trust.

We are grateful to many colleagues who have helped us by sending us details of work in progress, and who have answered our questions about their work. We are especially grateful to Bill Deakin and Elemir Szabadi, who were kind enough to read Chapter 5 in several drafts and to save us from many errors. Norman Sartorius of WHO discussed the plan for the book with us, and made comments that were both helpful and penetrating. However, we must be responsible for what we have written. Richard Coaton of the Department of Medical Illustration of Withington Hospital drew all the figures with his usual care. Malcolm Cleverly of the Salford Case Register very kindly ran several computer runs for us, and Richard Gater ran a special analysis of the WHO data-set to answer our query about the 'direct pathway to care'. We are grateful to our publishers for not harassing us, or holding us to deadlines that we should never have committed ourselves to in the first place. Finally, we are both very grateful to our families, who have done without us while we prepared the material for this book.

# 1　Models for mental illness

## MODELS FOR MENTAL DISORDERS

Mental disorders can be studied at two levels: from the standpoint of knowledge about how the brain works, or from knowledge about how man behaves as a social animal. The former approach uses powerful new methods of enquiry deriving from molecular biology, neuropharmacology and immunochemistry, while the latter uses methods derived from epidemiology and the social sciences. Recent technical advances in molecular biology have led to an increased emphasis on the former, so that some psychiatrists approach the subject as though they need to know little more than the way in which cerebral functions can become disorganised during episodes of mental illness. At the other end of the spectrum are those psychotherapists and social workers who believe that abnormal behaviour can be wholly explained in social and psychological terms, and who take little account of accumulating knowledge about disordered cerebral function.

Eisenberg (1986) has argued that neither brainlessness nor mindlessness can be tolerated in psychiatry or medicine, and has pointed out that

> what brings patients to doctors is discomfort and dysfunction, not the pathology which may underlie them. It matters – and matters greatly – to strategies for cure just how far bodily malfunction is causing problems in living and how far the symptoms are the somatic embodiment of problems in living; rarely are they simply one or the other. The doctor's task is to identify their sources when this can be done, to reach agreement with the patient about their significance, to indicate the range of available remedies, and to assist the patient in coping with what is beyond repair. In this process, bio-medical knowledge is necessary but not sufficient; the doctor's transactions with the patient must be informed by the social sciences.
>
> (Eisenberg 1986: 505)

We are not the first to attempt to bridge the gap between the two universes of discourse. The psychobiological school of Adolf Meyer was formulated in the first half of this century as an attempt to oblige psychiatrists to pay attention to both physical and psychological aspects of disorder, and George Engel's (1977) 'bio-psycho-social model' was another step in this direction. The model to be outlined in this book differs in important respects from these similar sounding approaches to the problem.

Meyer (1955) taught that the individual patient was unique, and could neither be broken down into separate aspects nor classified into categories of disease entities. Under his influence a whole generation of psychiatrists learned to take painstaking histories of their patients, and to pay special attention to past habits of adjustment, social influences and immediate stressful experiences. He insisted on the unity of body and mind, and the necessary combination of psychological and biological aspects in all cases of mental disorder. The emphasis on understanding the individual patient is called the *idiographic method*, and it can be contrasted with methods which ask how particular groups of subjects differ from one another – the *nomothetic method*. While the former is indispensable in work with particular patients, knowledge about particular kinds of mental disorder advances by using the latter. Meyer's teachings have led to countless patients being treated with greater understanding, but they have not led to an increase in knowledge about the causes of mental disorder, since if each patient is 'unique' it is difficult to collect information about groups of patients, and so formulate testable hypotheses from the model proposed. Furthermore, where common disorders are concerned it is possible to sympathise with Meyer's aversion to disease entities without abandoning attempts at classifying mental disorders. We will return to the problems posed by various kinds of classification later: at this point we must emphasise that without a classification, we would know little about the causes and best treatment for particular kinds of disorder; nor could we make statements about the interrelationships between social factors and kinds of common disorder.

Engel (1977) claims that the orthodox bio-medical model is reductionist (all behavioural phenomena are physico-chemical) or exclusionist (whatever can't be so explained must be excluded). He argues that schizophrenia and diabetes should be thought of in the same way: psychosocial factors are indispensable for both. In each, the biochemical defect defines a necessary but not a sufficient condition for the human experience of the disorder, and the defect on its own cannot be made to account for all of the illness. Psychological and social factors account for some of the phenomena of each illness, determine whether or not a person with the defect considers that they are 'ill', help to determine the course of each illness, and form a notable part of the treatment offered. The 'bio-psycho-social model' constitutes a plea for the inclusion of social and psychological factors in our formulations about human disorders:

> the scope of the biopsychosocial model is determined by the historic function of the physician to establish whether the person seeking help is 'well' or 'sick'; and if sick ... in which ways ... and to develop a rational [treatment] programme ... boundaries between well and sick are not clear and never will be clear, for they are diffused by cultural, social and psychological considerations .... The doctor's task is to account for the dysphoria and dysfunction which lead individuals to seek medical help, adopt the sick role, and accept the status of patienthood.
>
> (Engel 1977: 132–3)

Engel's argument is stronger as an attack on a view of disease in a rigid bio-medical framework than as a positive statement of a testable theory: as far as it goes, we agree with him, but he has not gone far enough. Although claiming that his theory is a 'blueprint for research', it is difficult to think what precise hypotheses are suggested for testing. It is more a call to arms than a plan of campaign, and one is uneasily aware that the supposed enemy may be a bogeyman.

Although progress in social psychiatry has not been as spectacular as that in biological psychiatry, there have been notable advances in the past ten years, brought about by a combination of a preparedness to use more sophisticated models for ways in which social factors might be implicated in mental disorders, and the availability of new forms of statistical techniques which have allowed data-sets to be analysed in new ways. It is becoming clear that the idea that common mental disorders should be thought of as discrete disease entities with distinct causes, course and treatment is probably untenable, yet there is an accumulating corpus of knowledge about the way in which people's social environment determines both the form and timing of common mental disorders.

The aim of this book is to integrate this knowledge into a common framework in which dimensions defined by common symptoms are related to social variables on the one hand and to underlying biological sub-systems on the other. Inevitably, we can only do this by going somewhat beyond our data, but if the resulting model can be modified by some, and parts of it falsified by others, it will have been worthwhile.

## THE PATHWAY TO PSYCHIATRIC CARE

In a previous book (Goldberg and Huxley 1980) we suggested a framework for understanding the way in which individuals become defined as mentally ill and eventually reach mental illness services. This framework also served to organise epidemiological data about mental illness into groupings which depended upon how far along this pathway individuals had reached. This assisted us by drawing distinctions between, for example, studies on 'depression' which had been carried out on those admitted to hospital, and studies of people found to be depressed in community surveys. We argued in our earlier book that patients admitted to hospital are a highly skewed sub-set of all those in the community with depression, so that statements about the former may be telling us as much about the process by which the sample was selected as they are about the nature of depression itself.

It had long been known that the majority of mental illnesses seen on community surveys have not been seen by the mental illness services. It is clear that there is a filtering process at work between the community and the wards of the psychiatric hospital, which is selectively permeable to those with more severe disorders.

In many countries of the world most patients are referred to the mental illness services by other professionals, so that one can postulate a filter between the community and the referring professional, as well as between that professional and the mental illness service. The framework consisted of five levels at which survey data could be considered, each one corresponding to a stage on the pathway to psychiatric care. We postulated a set of four filters between these five levels, and these are shown in Table 1.1.

*Table 1.1*   Five levels and four filters, with estimates of annual period prevalence rates at each level

| | |
|---|---|
| *Level 1*   The community | |
| **260–315/1000/year** | |
| ..........................................................................................................1st filter | |
| (Illness behaviour) | |
| *Level 2*   Total mental morbidity – attenders in primary care | |
| **230/1000/year** | |
| .......................................................................................... 2nd filter | |
| (Ability to detect disorder) | |
| *Level 3*   Mental disorders identified by doctors ('Conspicuous Psychiatric Morbidity') | |
| **101.5/1000/year** | |
| ..........................................................................................................3rd filter | |
| (Referral to mental illness services) | |
| *Level 4*   Total morbidity – mental illness services | |
| **23.5/1000/year** | |
| ..........................................................................................................4th filter | |
| (Admission to psychiatric beds) | |
| *Level 5*   Psychiatric in-patients | |
| **5.71/1000/year** | |

We also show in Table 1.1 our most recent estimates of the number of people who will suffer an episode of a mental disorder lasting at least two weeks during a calendar year, expressed as a rate per thousand population at risk. These figures will be discussed in greater detail in Chapter 2, when we shall be discussing each level in turn. However, for the present we can observe that episodes of disorder are fairly common in the population, but that only a small minority will be seen by mental health professionals. The majority of distressed people consult their doctor although, as we shall see, they often do so for associated physical symptoms that are causing them distress.

It should not be thought that subjects at higher levels of this framework are all contained within the lower levels, since many of those diagnosed by general practitioners (level 3) do not reach research criteria for a diagnosis, and a small group of those referred for specialist mental illness services (level 4) do not do so either. Figure 1.1 shows the relationships between levels 1 to 4 of the model.

In Figure 1.1, the square represents the population at risk, and circle A the number (71 per cent, in England) who will consult their general practitioner in the course of a year. Circle B represents the 31.5 per cent who will have a distressing episode of psychological symptoms lasting at least one week during the year, and circle C the 10.5 per cent who will be diagnosed by their family doctor as having a definite mental disorder during the year. Circle D represents the 2.35 per cent who will be referred to the specialist mental health services during the year.

The shaded areas within circle B are of special interest, as they indicate what happens to the distressed members of the population. Those who do not pass the first filter (shown in diagonal shading) are distressed, but do not consult; those who do not pass the second filter (shown in speckled shading) consult, but their distress is unrecognised; while those who do not pass the third filter (shown in black) are recognised, but not referred to the specialist services.

## COMMON DISORDERS VERSUS SEVERE MENTAL ILLNESSES

Our starting point for our original suggestion of five levels had been the finding that mental illnesses encountered in community surveys are less severe than those admitted to psychiatric hospitals. In general terms, the former comprise depressive illnesses and anxiety-related disorders, while the latter contain a substantial proportion of more severe illnesses, such as organic mental disorders, schizophrenia and bipolar affective disorders. Such illnesses are associated with much greater social disability and are much less likely to resolve spontaneously with time. However, although we

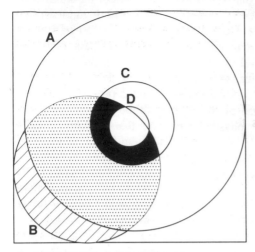

A = Consult their doctor during year
B = Episode of psychological distress during year (level 1)
C = Identified by their doctor as psychiatrically ill (level 3)
D = Referred to mental illness services (level 4)

▨   Do not pass 1st filter (ill, but do not consult)

▦   Do not pass 2nd filter (illness not recognised by Dr.)

■   Do not pass 3rd filter (not referred to mental illness services)

*Figure 1.1*   Venn diagram showing the relationship of disorders at levels 1, 2, 3 and 4. The square represents the population at risk

do not hesitate to describe such disorders as 'severe', this does not imply that the disorders which are common in the community can reasonably be described as 'mild'. They cause enormous suffering, they may be associated with severe disability, and some of them may last long periods of time. Nor are they 'minor' in terms of their financial costs: Croft-Jeffreys and Wilkinson (1989) have calculated that such disorders as are perceived by doctors in primary care settings (level 3) cost the British government £373M at 1985 prices, in contrast to the costs of mental disorders £190M at level 5, and an additional £31M at level 4. These figures should be contrasted with the overall economic costs of hypertension, which were calculated as being £337M annually.

Recent studies have strengthened the idea that mental disorders are by no means homogeneous, and should perhaps be thought of in different ways between the various levels. We showed in our earlier book (Goldberg and

Huxley 1980) that all filters were selectively permeable to severe disorders, so that major mental disorders are more frequent among those seen by the mental illness services, while many of those in the community consist of disorders that might often remit without special care from health professionals.

Hurry, Bebbington and Tennant (1987) have shown that at progressively higher levels of our framework social dysfunction increases, and have also confirmed that clinical severity increases progressively at levels 1, 2 and 4. Bebbington (1988) speculates that moderate and severe depression are different entities, with the age effect in the former arising because of social influences, while ageing probably exerts a biological releasing effect on severe depressions. He points out that the tendency for depression in the community to be more common among those in lower social classes (insisted upon by Brown and Harris 1978a, and now confirmed by many others) is not so strong among severe depressions encountered at level 4.

There is also evidence that those passing the first three filters are more likely to have abnormal personalities than those who do not. Andrews *et al.* (1990) have administered personality tests and other questionnaires to a set of Australian twins with neurotic illnesses in the community (level 1), and contrasted them with neurotic patients seeking treatment in a specialised unit (level 4). The former were only slightly more deviant than non-neurotic controls on such variables as 'neuroticism' assessed by the Eysenck personality inventory and locus of control, whereas the patients seeking care were grossly deviant.

Others have argued that whereas definitions of illness based entirely upon symptoms may be appropriate for more severe disorders, when disorders at lower levels of our framework are considered a triaxial model is more appropriate, consisting of symptoms, personality and social functioning (Williams *et al.* 1986). Those who carry out surveys of mental disorder in community settings are doing a rather peculiar thing: they are taking a concept of mental disorder which has been found to be meaningful among those seeking specialist care, and in effect asking 'how many people are there with similar symptoms – either in the community (level 1) – or among attenders of general medical clinics (level 3)?' It should not surprise anyone that the individuals so identified will, on the whole, be less severely ill and will have different social characteristics.

As we shall see in Chapter 4, it is more reasonable to apply categorical models of disease to more severe illnesses such as schizophrenia, psychotic depression and organic mental states – although even with them, the arguments are by no means conclusive (Crow 1986). However, this book is not about such disorders. We shall be concentrating upon *disorders which are commonly encountered in community settings, and whose occurrence signals a breakdown in normal functioning.* We shall not therefore be concerned with 'personality disorders', since these are ways of describing people who differ from the majority in a stable way – except in fairly rare circumstances, one does not usually suddenly develop a personality disorder; and, once one is present, it is unlikely to go away.

The disorders themselves can be chosen in the way described, but the definitions of each disorder still depend upon the characteristics of similar patients who have presented themselves for medical treatment. In Table 1.2, we have extracted appropriate diagnostic codes from the WHO's (1988) *International Classification of Disease* (now in its 10th revision, so referred to as *ICD-10*) and the *Diagnostic and Statistical Manual* (now in its third edition, and in a revised form – so referred to as *DSM-IIIR*) of the American Psychiatric Association (APA). The latter is of especial interest because workers in the United States have taken the lead in formulating operational definitions of mental disorders. The *DSM-III* system corresponds to the 9th revision of the *International Classification of Disease* in its first four digits, but uses a fifth digit for purely American purposes.

The international coding system was radically revised at the 10th revision, and when the IVth revision of the *DSM* system becomes available it can be expected to come into line with the *ICD-10*. The two systems came about in very different ways, but they are converging quite quickly. The international system has always been somewhat over-inclusive in order to satisfy a wide variety of approaches to medical taxonomy, and has until recently favoured a 'glossary' approach to classification, in which a rater recruits a particular patient to the category that seems most like them. Glossary descriptions of disorders use phrases like 'tend to' and 'will usually be'.

The American classification is an expansion of 14 original, tightly-defined categories of disorder called the Research Diagnostic Criteria. The edges of the categories may well be arbitrary, but there is seldom any doubt whether or not an individual patient has satisfied them. The major categories of *DSM-III* therefore correspond to *ICD* categories, but the APA has resisted undue fragmentation of the system. Where common disorders are concerned, for example, *DSM-III* has 39 diagnoses in Mood, Anxiety, Somatoform and Adjustment disorders; to be compared with no fewer than 99 categories for the *ICD* system. Such complex systems may well strike awe into new recruits, and mystify the general public – but unless they can be shown either to advance knowledge or to improve patient care one must ask whether they are really justified.

In the *ICD-10* system, for example, the 26 varieties of depressive episode allow fastidious distinctions between conditions like F31.11 'depressive episode of moderate severity with somatic symptoms' and

F33.00 'recurrent depressive disorder, current episode of mild severity without somatic symptoms'. It can be seen that these are not really different categories of disorder, they are an attempt to include features such as severity, course and the presence of additional features in a categorical system. The American system is more austere in allowing raters fewer categories, and offers users rigid, clearly stated diagnostic criteria for each category, in contrast to the more flexible 'diagnostic guidelines' of the WHO system. Whereas the WHO classification deals with combined diagnoses by spawning a new category, the US classification declares that two categories are present simultaneously: so, while the WHO might say that someone had 'moderate depression with somatic symptoms' the US classification might have to say that the same person had both 'major depressive episode' *and* 'undifferentiated somatoform disorder'. The latter would only really be reasonable if there was reason to suppose that the individual happened to be suffering from two independent disorders simultaneously – like measles and athlete's foot.

In Table 1.2 we show twelve of the more common diagnoses that are encountered in community settings and in general medical clinics. It can be seen that some quite common disorders – like mixed anxiety-depression and neurasthenia – are not allowed in the *DSM-IIIR* system, but the systems are such that rough comparisons can be made between surveys in different places. In practice, surveys usually compress the disorders encountered in these settings into an even more simple classification of depressive disorders, anxiety-related disorders and somatoform disorders; so the twelve categories have been grouped accordingly in Table 1.2.

In practice there are problems even with the twelve categories shown, because some – like obsessive-compulsive disorder and multiple somatisation disorder – are not that common in community settings; while others like simple phobias are common in all settings, but are not always counted by investigators as mental illnesses. However, the table serves to give some indication of the sorts of disorder which will be addressed in the chapters which follow. We shall be arguing that the taxonomy could be greatly simplified with advantage to both health workers and patients.

## Criteria for defining a case

In order to be said to be suffering from a mental disorder, an individual must have experienced more than a critical number of a particular constellation of symptoms for more than a critical time. There appears to be a rough relationship between the number of symptoms an individual has and the likelihood that the symptoms will remit spontaneously. Studies with the General Health Questionnaire have shown that spontaneous remission

*Table 1.2*  Diagnostic classification of some common mental disorders, showing current International and United States diagnostic codes

| World Health Organisation: *International Classification of Disease*, 10th Edition (ICD-10) | | American Psychiatric Assocn.: Diagnostic and Statistical Manual – IIIR (DSMIIIR) | |
|---|---|---|---|
| *Depression:* | | | |
| F31 | Depressive episode | 296.2x | Major depression, episode |
| F33 | Recurrent depressive disorder | 296.3x | Major depression, recurrent |
| F34.1 | Dysthymia | 300.40 | Dysthymia |
| *Anxiety-related disorders:* | | | |
| F40.0 | Phobic disorders | 300.29 | Simple phobia |
| F41.0 | Panic disorder | 300.01 | Panic disorder |
| F41.1 | Generalised anxiety disorder | 300.02 | Generalised anxiety disorder |
| F41.2 | Mixed anxiety-depressive disorder | | (not allowed) |
| F42 | Obsessive-compulsive disorder | 300.30 | Obsessive-compulsive disorder |
| F43.2 | Adjustment disorder | 309.90 | Adjustment disorder |
| *Somatoform disorders:* | | | |
| F45.0 | Multiple somatisation disorder | 300.81 | Somatisation disorder |
| F45.1 | Undifferentiated somatoform disorder | 300.70 | Undifferentiated somatoform disorder |
| F48.0 | Neurasthenia | | (not allowed) |

of symptoms is a function of the number of symptoms experienced at a particular time: those complaining of more than 20 symptoms on the 60-item questionnaire are much more likely to be symptomatic 12 months later than those with scores in the 'mild case' range of 12 to 20 symptoms (Johnstone and Goldberg 1976; Brodaty 1983).

It is clear that very transient states of distress which are likely to remit spontaneously should not be thought of as mental disorders. By common consent, researchers have required mental disorders to last at least two weeks, and have described disorders that may have lasted less than this and which are in understandable relationship to some stressful event as 'adjustment disorders'.

Depressive illness is only required to last two weeks in recognition of both the degree of suffering entailed by the symptoms and the threat to life: it would not be reasonable to expect people to endure such symptoms for a month before doctors seeing the patient were able to diagnose depressive illness, and therefore initiate a treatment; however, other diagnoses usually have longer time frames. This becomes important when different systems use different frames: for example, the *ICD-10* system requires a person to have a certain constellation of anxious symptoms for 'at least several weeks' before describing him as a case of 'generalised anxiety disorder', whereas the *DSM-IIIR* system required similar symptoms for six months.

In Figure 1.2 we show the diagnostic breakdown at all five levels, from which it can be seen that whereas depressive illnesses and anxiety states form at least 90 per cent of the illnesses in community settings, they form only one quarter of those admitted to psychiatric beds.

Severity of disorder may also be measured by counting the number of key symptoms that patients report on a standardised research interview, and expressing the result as an 8-point scale. The 'index of definition' (ID) is derived from the Present State Examination, and expresses an increasing degree of certainty that a diagnosable mental disorder is present (Wing *et al.* 1978). Respondents with non-specific symptoms will score ID2 or 3; sub-threshold disorders score ID4; definitely diagnosable disorders at the threshold score ID5; and above that ID scores represent increasing severity of undoubted mental disorders. The ID levels are also shown in Figure 1.2 at four of the levels, and they also show a progressive increase in the severity of disorders seen at each level. At levels 1 and 2 the corresponding diagnoses shown are for those subjects at ID5 and above, so they represent a somewhat more severe degree of disorder than the figures already given in Table 1.1 and Figure 1.1, which are derived in a different way. At level 2, the figures shown are for new episodes of illness only, and this probably accounts for the otherwise paradoxical finding that the proportion with severe disorders drops at this level. Had a survey been available which related to all disorders rather than new disorders, it is likely that there would have been a greater proportion of severe illnesses, since these tend to last longer than mild disorders.

## VULNERABILITY, DESTABILISATION AND RESTITUTION

Most patients who begin to experience symptoms in community settings do so for understandable reasons. There are two factors to take into account, the *vulnerability* of an individual, and the magnitude of the impinging stressor. Thus a vulnerable individual may be pushed over the edge by a minor stress, while a more phlegmatic individual may require a major life stress before experiencing symptoms. Most people will experience symptoms, given sufficient stress – but the degree of stress necessary to release symptoms varies enormously from one person to another. Whether the

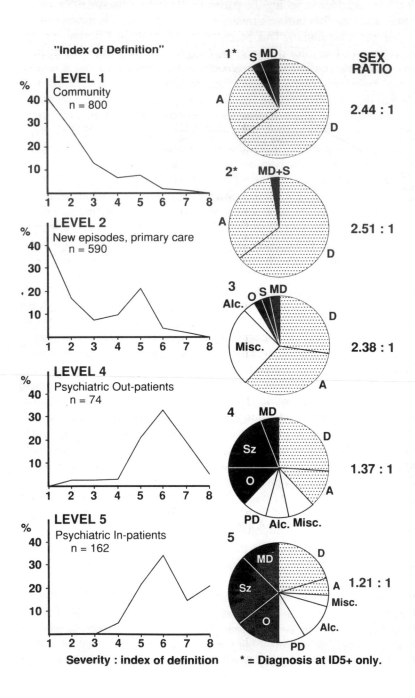

"Index of Definition"

**LEVEL 1**
Community
n = 800

**LEVEL 2**
New episodes, primary care
n = 590

**LEVEL 4**
Psychiatric Out-patients
n = 74

**LEVEL 5**
Psychiatric In-patients
n = 162

SEX RATIO

1*   2.44 : 1
2*   2.51 : 1
3    2.38 : 1
4    1.37 : 1
5    1.21 : 1

**Severity : index of definition**   * = Diagnosis at ID5+ only.

symptoms are about to last for a short time or a long one, we shall be
arguing that the factors that cause people to begin to experience symptoms
are basically similar.

We term the process of beginning to experience symptoms *destabilisation*, and will be describing what is known about such stressors in detail.
Once symptoms have developed, another set of factors determine how long
they will last. The process of losing symptoms is termed *restitution*.
Although there is some overlap between the factors which cause destabilisation and those which determine restitution, we shall argue that the two
sets of factors are by no means identical (Goldberg *et al.* 1990). It is clear
that if restitution can occur quickly enough, an individual will not have
experienced symptoms for long enough to qualify for one of the definitions
of being a 'case'. In contrast, conditions like *DSM-IIIR* 'dysthymia' or
'generalised anxiety disorder' – which require symptoms to have been
present for long periods of time – are ways of denoting people who are
unable to achieve full restitution of their symptoms.

## The problems to be addressed

Given this nomenclature, we can now state the problems which will be
addressed in the remainder of the book. In Chapter 2 we consider the *five
levels*. We compare our recent figures at all five levels with two replications
in different European countries. In Chapter 3, we start by considering what
proportion of patients in various countries can be expected to follow a

pathway through each level of the framework. In the remainder of the chapter we restate the main findings about the four *filters on the pathway to care* in the light of important recent work by others which has thrown more light on the characteristics of each filter, and we describe what is now known about levels of unmet need at the first two levels of the framework.

In Chapter 4, we consider the advantages and disadvantages of *categorical models* for common disorders. We conclude that categorical models are fatally flawed, and set forth a possible *dimensional model* in Chapter 5. We take the opportunity of seeing how this model might relate to biological sub-systems dealing with depression and anxiety.

In Chapter 6, we summarise existing knowledge about *vulnerability* and *resilience*, and include information about the genetics of vulnerability, the importance of events in childhood for later development, as well as an account of personality variables and later social conditions.

In Chapter 7, we summarise what is known about *destabilisation*, and try to reconcile some of the apparent contradictions in recently published work. We pay great attention to the importance of physical illness as a provoking agent for mental disorders, as we consider that this important variable has been relatively neglected by others who have sought to build models for the aetiology of common disorders.

In Chapter 8, we consider what is known about *restitution*. We contrast characteristics of those disorders which remit spontaneously with those which do not, and identify the factors that are responsible for failure to restitute within one year. We consider the evidence that interventions by health workers ('treatments') hasten restitution.

In Chapter 9 ('Mind and body') we return to studies of how the brain works, in order to understand how social factors can affect both our psychological and our physical health. This necessitates an excursion into psycho-immunology, and a description of the three major bodily systems that underlie healthy functions and allow us to adjust to changes in our environment. We are then in a position to re-state our model with greater clarity, and to show what implications it has both for research and for taxonomy of common mental disorders.

We end in Chapter 10 by considering the *public health implications* of the work presented in this book. We consider prevention of disorder in the light of a dimensional model for common disorders. Finally, we consider the implications of recent findings both for the future pattern of services and for training needs of mental health professionals.

# 2   The five levels

This chapter will start with a description of three studies that have assessed morbidity at all five levels at the same time, and will then give an account of other studies of morbidity at each level in turn. At each level, we will summarise some of the salient characteristics of common mental disorders.

## SIMULTANEOUS ASSESSMENTS AT ALL FIVE LEVELS

In order to construct a set of comparable assessments of morbidity at the five levels, it is necessary for three conditions to be satisfied. The levels of illness should be expressed as rates per 1000 population at risk, the periods over which morbidity is measured should be the same, and the method of case identification at level 1 should be the same as that at level 2. In our earlier book (Goldberg and Huxley 1980) we estimated morbidity at levels 1 and 2 with the General Health Questionnaire, and we chose one year as the time period over which we made our comparisons.[1] We have revised our figures in the table shown below, since it is now clear that our original figure (250) at level 1 was almost certainly an underestimate, and we have quoted more recent figures for morbidity at level 3, using a more up-to-date system for diagnosis.

Two other groups of epidemiologists have tried their hand at replicating our figures at all five levels in their countries, and their results are shown as Table 2.1.

It should be noted that whereas the data from Manchester and Groningen relate to annual period prevalence, the data from Verona relate to *weekly period prevalence*. It should be emphasised that the first 'filter' (i.e. that between levels 1 and 2) is less permeable than the figures for Manchester and Groningen suggest, since although many psychologically disordered patients consult their doctors during the year, the consultations may be for other reasons. Also, many depressed patients do not mention their depressive symptoms, but confine their complaints to the doctor to the associated somatic symptoms.

There are two important public health implications of the rates shown in Table 2.1. Despite the fact that mental illness services are treating the most severe cases, over the course of a year the majority of disordered patients are seen in primary care settings. However, many of these disorders will not be detected by the clinician seeing them. Providing that it can be shown that detection of such disorders actually helps the patient, *training general practitioners and staff of general medical clinics* in the detection and management of the common forms of mental disorder becomes an important public health task.

Since a substantial proportion of the more severe forms of mental disorder will in fact be referred to specialist mental illness services, the second implication is that it is of great public health importance to organise such services so that they are most cost-effective, and so that chronic disability due to severe mental disorder is minimised. It is quite wrong to think of 'mental disorder' as a homogeneous entity, so that all resources are funnelled into primary care. The spontaneous remission rate of disorders seen in general medical settings is high, and those referred to levels 4 and 5 of the model are much more likely to have special treatment needs. However, the figures do argue for better co-ordination of services between primary care and specialised services.

*Table 2.1*  Period prevalence rates for total psychiatric morbidity at all five levels in three European cities. Note that the Verona figures are *weekly*, whereas the other two are *annual* rates

| Level | Greater[a] Manchester (annual) | Groningen[b] (annual) | Verona[c] (weekly) |
|-------|-------------------|-----------------------|---------------------|
| 1:  Community | 250–315 | 250–303 | 227 |
| 2:  Primary care (total) | 230 | 224 | 34 |
| 3:  Primary care (conspicuous) | 101.5 | 94 | 23 |
| 4:  Psychiatrists | 20.8 | 34 | 4 |
| 5:  Psychiatrists (in-patients) | 3.4 | 10 | 0.7 |

*Sources:*
[a] Chapters 2 and 3
[b] Giel, Koeter and Ormel 1990 and personal communication
[c] Tansella and Williams 1989

## LEVEL 1: THE COMMUNITY

In our original book (Goldberg and Huxley 1980) we were able to find only five surveys which had used direct assessment of community respondents by standardised research interview, and showed a range of morbidity from 90 to 241/1000 population at risk per month – the highest figure coming from a study of two Ugandan villages. We are now able to add six further studies, and have calculated means and standard deviations to allow some rough overall statements to be made. It can be calculated from Table 2.2 that the overall rate for both sexes is 164.0/1000 (sd 64.8); with the rate for males being 121.4/1000 (sd 55.3); and that for females being 202.3/1000 (sd 79.5).

It can be seen that with the exception of the African villages – where there was probably a high prevalence of illness whichever means of case identification was used – the studies using the Present State Examination (PSE) generally report lower rates than those using either assessments based upon the *DSM-III* system (like the SADS and the DIS) or upon the Clinical Interview Schedule.

Difficulties arise when monthly prevalence rates are extrapolated to annual rates: in our original book (Goldberg and Huxley 1980) we assumed that the annual inception would be at least one-third the point prevalence, and thus inflated a point prevalence of 180 to a period prevalence of 250. Studies which have appeared since then clearly indicate that these assumptions were too conservative. For anxiety disorders, Sashidharan and his colleagues (1988) have shown that the annual inceptions are equal to the point prevalence, although our original assumptions seem approximately correct for depressive illness (Goldberg and Huxley 1980: Brown *et al.* 1985). In view of the ratio of anxiety to depressive conditions in community samples, our revised estimate for one-year prevalence of disorders diagnosed by the Clinical Interview Schedule or the American *DSM-III* system becomes in the range between 260 and 315/1000/year. It is encouraging that the 'overall rates' reported for the 11 studies shown in Table 2.2 are close to the figure used to make our original estimate of point prevalence.

### Sex ratio

The surveys reported in Table 2.2 show that rates for common disorders are generally higher in females, although it should be noted that the rates reported by Regier *et al.* in the ECA (Epidemiological Catchment Area) study (1988) showed an almost equal sex ratio (females: 16.6 per cent; males 14 per cent) by including drug dependency and anti-social personality – which are more prevalent among males. These diagnoses

*Table 2.2*   Prevalence rates per 1000 population at risk for random samples of the general population for all psychiatric illness in the past month; recent surveys based on direct assessment by standardised research interview

| Investigator | Place | Method | Sample size (2nd stage) | Male rates | Female rates | Total rates |
|---|---|---|---|---|---|---|
| Hodiamont et al. 1987 | Nijmegen Holland | GHQ/PSE | 486 | 72 | 75 | 73 |
| Duncan-Jones and Henderson 1978 | Canberra Australia | GHQ/PSE | 157 | 70 | 110 | 90 |
| Bebbington et al. 1981 | London England | PSE | 800 | 61 | 149 | 109 |
| Regier et al. 1988 | 5 sites USA | DIS | 18,571 | 76[a] | 145[a] | 112a |
| Vazquez-Barquero et al. 1987 | Cantabria Spain | PSE | 425 | 81 | 206 | 147 |
| Mavreas et al. 1986 | Athens Greece | GHQ/PSE | 489 | 86 | 226 | 160 |
| Weissman et al. 1978b | Newhaven USA | SADS/RDC | 511 | 164 | 189 | 178 |
| Dilling 1980 | Bavaria W. Germany | CIS | 1231 | 160 | 218 | 193 |
| Vazquez-Barquero et al. 1981 | Baztan valley Spain | CIS | 415 | 191 | 283 | 239 |
| Orley and Wing 1979 | 2 villages Uganda | PSE | 191 | 194 | 291 | 241 |
| Cheng 1988 | 3 areas: Taiwan | CHQ/CIS | 489 | 180 | 333 | 262 |
| Overall rates | | | | 121 | 202 | 164 |

*Note:*   [a] These rates exclude cognitive impairment, substance use and anti-social personality (as these are not included in any of the other surveys quoted). Had they been included, the rates rise to 140 (males) 166 (females) and 154 (total). Abbreviations: GHQ = General Health Questionnaire; CHQ = Chinese Health Questionnaire; PSE = Present State Examination; DIS = Diagnostic Interview Schedule; SADS = Schedule for Affective Disorders and Schizophrenia; RDC = Research Diagnostic Criteria; CIS = Clinical Interview Schedule.

were removed from Table 2.2 to allow a fairer comparison with other surveys, since these diagnoses are not included in the other research interviews. Jenkins (1985) has shown that if samples of male and female subjects are chosen who are closely comparable from the standpoint of social adjustment the sex difference completely disappears.

In the Cantabria survey, Vazquez-Barquero and his colleagues (1987) showed that in those without physical disease, the sex ratio was almost equal, but there were high rates in women with physical illness. Females are more willing to acknowledge illness, to make contact with a doctor, to present psychological complaints, and to remember having had psychological symptoms. The tendency of males to *forget their symptoms* is well shown in the work of Angst and Dobler-Mikola (1984), in which although there are no differences between the sexes in the prevalence rate for depressive illness lasting for longer than two weeks recalled during the previous four weeks or the previous three months, there is a 2:1 difference in rates for illnesses remembered during the previous year.

## Age

Generally speaking, rates for common mental disorders peak in the middle years – an effect which is pronounced for mood disorders. As might be expected, drug dependency peaks in the 18–24 age group, while cognitive impairment peaks in old age (see Regier *et al.* 1988).

## Social class

With few exceptions, most studies show greater rates for common mental disorders in those of lower social class (see, for example, Hesbacher *et al.* 1975). Brown and Harris (1978a) argue that working-class women have higher rates of depression than middle-class women because they have higher rates of severe life events and major social difficulties.

## Employment and unemployment

Finlay-Jones and Ekhardt (1984) found that 49 per cent of a sample of 401 unemployed young adults were cases according to the PSE. Costello (1982) in a partial replication of Brown and Harris (1978) found that lack of intimacy and 'life events and difficulties' are associated with depression, but unemployment was not. Similar results were found by Campbell and her colleagues (1983). However, Surtees and his colleagues (1983) found that social class, unemployment and the marital status of either 'separated, divorced or cohabiting' each made independent contributions to the prediction of caseness in their survey of Edinburgh women. An additive model accounted for their findings with each factor acting independently: no interaction terms were needed. In a study of unemployed men Eales (1988) found that unemployment was far more likely to lead to depression among men who had had a history of employment difficulties.

Unemployment has a substantial effect on self-reported physical health, somatisation, anxiety and depression (Kessler *et al.* 1987), and causes a decline in marital support, with the number of weeks unemployed related to the decrease in the quality of the marital relationship (Atkinson *et al.* 1986). It may result in great financial strain which leaves the individual more vulnerable to the impact of unrelated life events. When the adverse financial impact of unemployment is controlled unemployed people without additional life events in the previous year are no worse (on the SCL-90) than those with stable employment. Men returning to work after a period of unemployment have elevated levels of psychological symptoms for periods as long as two years which are unrelated to their new jobs, and should probably be thought of as residual effects of unemployment (Kessler *et al.* 1987). Such residual effects of unemployment may be worse in those who have had little social contact with others outside the work setting (Bolton and Oatley 1987).

A small scale study in the USA (Rosenfield 1980) compared households where only men worked, with those where women also worked and found higher depression scores for women in the former and higher depression scores for men in the latter. A larger study failed to replicate these results, finding instead a higher rate of depression in women irrespective of household type (Roberts and O'Keefe 1981). Aneshensel and others (1981) also found more depressed women than men, but that the rates differed by family and work roles. Having a family (or being married) or being employed is associated with lower levels of depression, but having both a family and work role does not produce any additional reduction in rates. Gore and Mangione (1983) also observed that the absence of employment or marriage is associated with depression for men and women, but that female sex and parenthood produce a higher rate of psychophysiological complaints in women.

In a community sample of 1026 people Cleary and Mechanic (1983) observed higher rates of psychological distress in women than men, higher rates of distress in employed married men than in housewives, and employed married women also had higher rates than housewives – especially if they also had small children. Cheng (1989) reports higher rates of minor psychiatric morbidity in women in employment rather than out of it, and Lennon (1987) in a study of psychological distress in a community sample found that the features of work which contributed to higher rates in women were having to do simple jobs and having to work full time. Simple jobs were associated with increased alcohol problems in men. Rosenfield (1989) suggests that employment for women is not consistently positive because taking a job often only trades one situation where she has little control for another one with low control. Employment often fails to improve women's general well-being because it simply imposes even more demands. In a re-analysis of three previous data sets involving over 2000 respondents she found that when familial demands on men and women are equal employed women have the same symptom levels as men, but that when job or family demands are low, employed women are lower in symptom levels than housewives.

These studies show that being unemployed is associated with elevated rates of disorder and has a residual effect which is felt particularly by those with poor marital relationships or a lack of support. Under certain circumstances being employed may be associated with increased levels of disorder.

## Race

While non-whites are over-represented among involuntary hospital admissions (Rosenfield 1984) the picture is not so clear at lower levels of the model. Hirschfeld and Cross found that differences between rates of depression for blacks and whites disappeared when social class was controlled (1982). Kessler and Neighbours (1986) re-analysed the data from eight major epidemiological surveys (involving 22,000 responders) and found that race and income combined non-additively to create psychological distress. In contrast to Hirschfeld they suggest that race is related to mental ill health even when social class is held constant. Ulbrich and others (1989), in a community survey in Florida, found that social class and race interacted to increase psychiatric symptoms. Lower status blacks were more vulnerable than lower status whites to the impact of undesirable events, but less vulnerable than lower status whites to the impact of economic problems. Lower status blacks were more vulnerable than higher status blacks to the impact of both events and economic problems. It is important to recognise that the impact of life events may be different in different cultures and religions (Obeyesekere 1985).

## The physical environment

Birtchnell and his colleagues (1988) examined the relationship between depression and the physical environment in which women on a housing estate lived: it was found that those types of dwellings with the highest disadvantage scores had the highest proportion of depressed women.

Gabe and Williams (1987) have shown a J-shaped relationship between crowding and psychological health as assessed by the GHQ. An index of crowding was calculated with a person-to-room ratio, and the lowest GHQ scores were found for those with an index between 0.5 and 1.00. Below this scores were somewhat higher, and above this as crowding increases rates rise very sharply.

## Diagnosis

Individual diagnoses are shown for each survey in Table 2.2. In order to allow comparison between surveys all anxiety diagnoses (see Chapter 1, Table 1.2, p. 10) have been grouped together. It can be seen that with only one exception depression is the most common diagnosis in the community (mean 67/1000; sd 51.7; range 22–189) and anxiety states the second (mean 35/1000; sd 18.9; range 18–78).

Two studies provide more detailed information about individual neuroses. Andrews and his colleagues (1990) studied a sample of 892 Australian twins, and report 'lifetime' diagnoses for 243 individuals who had reported sufficient symptoms for a neurotic diagnosis at some point in their lives, while Vazquez-Barquero and his colleagues (1981) report a random community sample of 1,156 individuals in rural Spain, with diagnostic information about 275 who reached criteria for a mental illness diagnosis in the month before interview. In both studies, female rates were generally very much higher than male rates, and in the latter study 'social phobias' were almost confined to females.

### Rural areas and diagnosis

Three groups of investigators – Vazquez-Barquero in Cantabria, Mavreas in rural Greece, and Brown in the Hebrides – have found that in rural areas anxiety states are more common than depressive illnesses in women.

## LEVEL 2: PRIMARY CARE – TOTAL MORBIDITY

This refers to the total psychiatric morbidity, irrespective of whether or not it has been detected by the health care staff, among attenders in primary care settings, per 1000 population at risk. This needs a word of explanation. It does *not* refer to the rate per 1000 consecutive attenders – but to the number of psychiatrically disordered individuals who attend from a population of known size, over a stated time period. For example, if one carried out a survey for a week among attenders in a practice serving a population of known size, and managed to identify all those with a psychiatric disorder using an appropriate two-stage strategy, then it would be a simple matter to calculate a weekly rate of mental disorders per 1000 at risk. There is an alternative, easier way of making an approximate estimate of this rate. If one knows the size of the population at risk and the proportion of this population that will attend during one year, then one can calculate the rate at level 2 by multiplying this proportion by the percentage of consecutive attenders who are found to be cases.[2]

*Table 2.3* Prevalence rates per 1000 population at risk for random samples of the general population for selected diagnoses in the past month; recent surveys based on direct assessment by standardised research interview

| Investigator | Anxiety states | Depression | Schizophrenia, paranoid states | Bipolar mania | Total |
|---|---|---|---|---|---|
| Hodiamont et al. 1987 | 20 | 53 | 7 | 2 | 82 |
| Duncan-Jones and Henderson 1978 | 35 | 48 | 7 | 2 | 91 |
| Bebbington et al. 1981 | 29 | 70 | 6 | 8 | 109 |
| Vazquez-Barquero et al. 1981 | 40 | 47 | – | – | 133 |
| Vazquez-Barquero et al. 1987 | 78 | 38 | 7 | 2.4 | 147 |
| Regier et al. 1988 | 18[a] | 22 | 7 | 4b | 154[c] |
| Weissman et al. 1978 | 26 | 68 | 0 | n/a | 178 |
| Dilling 1980 | <113> | | 4 | 13 | 186 |
| Orley and Wing 1979 | 34 | 189 | 5 | 19 | 253 |
| Cheng 1988 | 157 | 74 | 4 | 4 | 262 |

*Notes:*
a This rate excludes generalised anxiety disorder, as this was not assessed in the ECA survey. The rate quoted is for 'panic disorder' and obsessive-compulsive disorder, but *excludes the 62/1000 with phobias.*
b The rate quoted is for mania only. Other figures in this column include psychotic depression.
c This overall rate includes substance abuse, anti-social personality, and cognitive impairment, but excludes generalised anxiety disorder.

*Table 2.4* Rates for individual neuroses reported in two community studies

| | Depression | Dysthymic disorder | Obsessive-compulsive disorder | Social phobia | Panic disorder | Generalised anxiety disorder |
|---|---|---|---|---|---|---|
| Andrews | 7.3 | 5.8 | 2.4 | 3.7 | 3.8 | 18.8 |
| Vazquez-Barquero | 3.8 | n/a | 0.1 | 3.35 | n/a | 4.4 |

Our own early estimate of 230 per thousand at risk per year has now been repeated by Giel and his colleagues (1990) in Holland, who found the rate to be 224/1000/year using the PSE as the case-finding interview. Tansella and Williams (1989) carried out an intensive survey for a week in Verona, and found a weekly rate of 34/1000 at risk.

Although there have been many other recent papers describing psychiatric surveys in primary care, none of the others have expressed their results per 1000 at risk – but they can nonetheless be used to examine for sociodemographic and diagnostic characteristics of patients seen in primary care settings and assessed with a standardised interview. By and large, recent surveys have confirmed our earlier findings: in consulting settings, patients with diagnosable psychiatric disorders most commonly consult for physical symptoms, and it is useful to use classifications of complaint which take into account the relationship (if any) between their presenting complaint and the psychiatric disorder found by standardised assessment. Bridges and Goldberg (1985) used an expanded version of an earlier classification, and produced the figures shown in Table 2.5.

We require four conditions to be satisfied in order to describe a patient as a case of 'somatisation':

1 the patient must be seeking help for somatic symptoms;
2 the patient must attribute these symptoms to some physical disorder;
3 a specific mental disorder as defined by *DSM-III* or *ICD-10* must be present; and
4 the somatic symptoms are not due to physical disease, but can be thought of as part of the mental disorder.

The majority of the mental disorders satisfying criterion 3 in consulting settings are depressive illnesses and anxiety states, and these also make up the majority of cases which are presenting with psychological complaints. However, in the case of somatisation the patient does not consider that they have such a disorder: they are seeking help for the somatic symptom which is part of the mental disorder.

## LEVEL 3: PRIMARY CARE – IDENTIFIED MORBIDITY

Once more, this refers to identified psychiatric morbidity among attenders per 1000 population at risk. It is a simple matter to measure this during any survey in which a level 2 estimate is to be made, simply by asking primary care physicians to identify those individuals whom they consider to be psychiatrically disordered. This is often referred to as *conspicuous psychiatric morbidity* (CPM) – 'conspicuous', because it has been seen. Shepherd and his colleagues (1966) estimated the morbidity at level 3 to be

*Table 2.5*  Relationship of mental disorder to reason for consultation in 590 new onsets of illness in primary care settings in Manchester

|  | *All patients* | *Psychiatric cases only* |
|---|---|---|
|  | n = 590 | n = 195 |
| Not mentally ill | 67% | n/a |
| Physical illness with secondary mental disorder | 1% | 3.2% |
| Unrelated physical and mental disorder | 8% | 24.0% |
| Somatisation | 20% | 57.0% |
| Entirely mentally ill | 5% | 15.0% |
| Total | 100% | 100% |

140/1000 at risk/year in a general morbidity survey carried out in Greater London, of which 102 were 'formal psychiatric illnesses', and the remainder were vaguer conditions like 'psychosomatic' and 'psychosocial problems'. These figures can be compared with the rather lower rates varying between 27 and 125/1000/year shown by Regier and his colleagues (1978) in a variety of comprehensive health schemes which had enrolled populations, and could therefore provide rates. The lower rates in the latter survey may be because those enrolled in 'Health Maintenance Organisations' are positively selected for health, or it may be due to insensitivity to psychiatric disorder by these physicians. The latter possibility is certainly partly true, since the scheme with the lowest rate was the Marshfield Clinic at Wisconsin – where Hoeper and his colleagues (1979) have shown that the physicians are remarkably insensitive to such disorders, and seem incapable of using help when it is offered (Hoeper *et al.* 1984).

The most recent British estimate of morbidity in primary care comes from the third national study (HMSO 1986), which gives an annual period prevalence for episodes of mental disorder diagnosable by *ICD-9* as 101.4/1000; a figure strikingly similar to Shepherd's earlier estimate of 102/1000 in 1966. We have seen that Giel and his colleagues (1990) have shown an annual rate of 94/1000 in Groningen, and Tansella and Williams (1989) have calculated a rate of 34/1000 at risk *per week* in Verona.

Many studies have been conducted on consecutive attenders, without calculating population risks. Ormel and Giel (1990) review sixteen well conducted studies in primary care settings, in which over half show rates in the 20–39 per cent range, but the spread is wide, so that it is clear that physicians vary widely in their diagnostic practices. Lobo (1990) reviews eight studies carried out in hospital medical clinics, with rates somewhat higher than in primary care. Once more, the range is very wide, with over half being in the 23–39 per cent range.

## Psychiatric morbidity among the clients of social workers

Corney (1984a) and Huxley and colleagues (1988) report two-stage studies in clients attending social service departments: interestingly, such populations seem to have rates of psychiatric disorder just as high as those seen in medical settings. Newly referred clients (n=141) in two inner city social service department settings were interviewed using the PSE after screening by the GHQ. No less than 53 per cent of the sample were found to be cases at ID5 or above, and of these 73 per cent had high scores on the screening questionnaire. Using a straightforward 'present/absent' assessment of 'caseness' social workers misclassified more than a third of the PSE cases and correctly identified half of the non-cases.

## LEVEL 4:  MENTAL ILLNESS SERVICES – ALL PATIENTS

This refers to all those receiving care from the specialised mental health services per year, per 1000 population at risk. It is most readily derived from areas with case registers, and includes both out-patients and in-patients. In areas where community psychiatric nurses see patients in primary care on their own, such patients should only be included if the nurse is working as part of a multi-disciplinary team. Gibbons *et al.* (1984) show that for eight psychiatric case registers between 1.5 per cent and 1.6 per cent of the population were known to the mental illness services, and the rates were remarkably stable between 1976 and 1981. However, by 1989 the treated rate at Salford had increased to 2.35/1000, partly due to a great expansion in psychogeriatric services, but also to the activities of mental health professionals in primary care clinics.

### Diagnoses at level 4

Information about the diagnoses of all those known to psychiatric case registers is hard to come by (Gibbons *et al.* 1984; and Wing 1989), but fortunately such information is still available from the Salford Case Register, and it is given in the next chapter (see pp. 47–8). Low (1988) has compared the kinds of patient seen by mental illness services in Edinburgh at various locations for care, and these are shown in Table 2.6. It can be seen that patients seen in special clinics in general hospitals are comparable to those seen by psychiatrists in primary care clinics, but that clinics in

*Table 2.6*  Diagnoses made in three consulting settings in Edinburgh (after Low 1988)

|  | Health centres n = 1292 % | General hosp clinic n = 2945 % | Mental hosp clinic n = 7717 % |
|---|---|---|---|
| Schizophrenia, affective psychosis, organic brain syndrome } | 13.2 | 16.2 | 29.3 |
| Miscellaneous diagnosis | 7.2 | 9.3 | 18.9 |
| Neurosis | 36.3 | 39.5 | 21.9 |
| Adjustment disorders, no diagnosis | 25.0 | 15.0 | 10.4 |
| Alcohol, drugs | 5.6 | 7.3 | 9.8 |

mental hospitals attract a higher proportion of patients with severe mental disorders and with rarer diagnoses, at the relative expense of patients with neuroses and adjustment disorders.

## LEVEL 5: MENTAL ILLNESS SERVICES – ADMISSIONS ONLY

Once more, the best source of data for in-patient treatment comes from case registers, since these offer unduplicated counts of treatment in hospital. The last ten years have seen a drastic reduction in in-patient beds, so that in parts of England where these reductions have been most noticeable in-patient units now offer very short stays to quite disturbed psychotic patients. Wing (1989) reports data from eight British case registers, and shows that admission rates vary between a low of 3.8/1000/year (Oxford) to a high of 6.7/1000/year (Southampton). National data confirm that the rates for the whole of England and those for Scotland, are between these extremes. Three of the areas show substantial increases in admission rates between 1977 and 1983, and the rest show no change. Depressive illnesses accounted for about one-third of admissions, schizophrenia and delusional illnesses about one-quarter, alcohol and drug dependence about 20 per cent: the remainder were a miscellaneous group, mainly personality disorders.

It has been shown that admission rates are strongly related to social disadvantage. Jarman (1983, 1984) has devised a numerical score to express the extent to which a place should be considered an underprivileged area (UPA score), and this takes account of eight census variables which are indicative of social deprivation: elderly living at home, under 5s, one-parent families, unskilled workers, unemployed people, overcrowded homes, people recently moved house, and ethnic minorities. Within one London health district, the UPA score of electoral wards correlated with admission rates +0.82, while between fourteen different health districts comprising the North West Thames Regional Health Authority admission rates correlated +0.76 (Hirsch 1988). A more ambitious study by Jarman and others (1990) relating admission rates to selected social variables in each district across the country showed a correlation of +0.87, the social variables being percentage illegitimacy, number of notifications of drug dependency, and the standardised mortality ratio for that district. These variables should be regarded as proxy measures of social disadvantage, rather than as independent variables of direct causal significance.

In Italy, there are many fewer beds available for severe mental illnesses – de Girolamo and his colleagues (1988) compare two areas where there are only about 0.07 beds/1000 population. The area where there is an active community service was able to lower its admission rate to 1.52/1000, whereas the more hospital-based service admitted 2.98/1000 – not far short of the rate for Oxford, where there are 0.35/1000 for acute illnesses. These rates are achieved by using short admissions – since one notes that the 15 beds in one of these units coped with a total of 565 admissions in the course of the year.

### Compulsory admissions and race

Dunn and Fahy (1990) report an excess of black people among police admissions to psychiatric hospital (15 per cent in the population but 22 per cent of admissions). They did not find as others report (Rwegellera 1980) that they were more violent than white people. Although blacks were more likely than whites to be treated with drugs, to stay longer and to be detained compulsorily, this was related to the higher prevalence of psychotic disorder. Harrison and others (1984) reported that West Indians living in the inner city were more likely to be referred to psychiatric services through the police, but that West Indians were not more likely to be violent. Schleifer and others (1968) report that the police did not refer black prisoners in gaol to psychiatrists until they were more disturbed than their white counterparts. Bolton (1984) found that patients on a high secure unit did not have above average rates of Indian and African patients.

Burke reports lower rates of attempted suicide among West Indian immigrants to Birmingham than among natives, but greater rates than in the West Indies, and that depression is more common among older members of the black community (Burke 1976, 1984). Asian immigrants in Manchester have higher first admission rates of neurotic and personality disorder (Carpenter and Brockington 1980). However, the latter study found that first admissions immigrants displayed significantly lower rates of some depressive symptoms and anxiety than UK born residents. Lower than expected rates of neurotic disorders have been found among New Commonwealth Asian and Pakistani immigrants, for both men and women (Dean *et al.* 1981).

## NOTES

1   In order to estimate morbidity in the community we used a formula (Goldberg 1981) to convert the proportion with high scores in a cross-sectional community survey into a 'predicted point prevalence' (a point prevalence rate is the number of persons with a specified condition per 1000 population at risk at a particular point in time), and then made the assumption that at any particular time one-third of those with high scores are likely to be new cases, so that the period prevalence rate is likely to add at least one-third to the predicted point prevalence: period prevalence = point prevalence + inception rate; or the rate per 1000 at risk with a specified condition over a stated time period.

  Since the point prevalence was 18 per cent, we estimated the period prevalence to be at least 25 per cent – but recognised that this was likely to be a crude approximation. See text p. 17 for more recent data. The period prevalence at level 2 was derived by calculating that the proportion of consecutive attenders who were predicted cases (using the same formula), and then predicting the likely period prevalence at level 2 by multiplying it by the proportion of people who were known to attend that practice in the course of a year, following the procedure described by Regier *et al.* (1978). This produced a figure of 23 per cent, which was also recognised to be a crude approximation to the actual rate. We therefore published our figures with some diffidence, in the hopes that we might encourage others to make their own estimations of these rates.

  Since we did so there have been a number of studies which have made direct assessments of morbidity at level 1, which have not relied on the vagaries of a pencil and paper test like the GHQ. It is reassuring to find from Table 2.2 (p. 18) that the point prevalence rates found in these surveys ranged from a low of 84 to a high of 241/1000 at risk, so that our estimate of 180/1000 does not seem unreasonable. Our estimate that the inception rate would be about one-third of the point prevalence can now be compared with Regier *et al.*'s (1988) Epidemiological Catchment Area Study, from which we find that while the one-month period prevalence was 15.4 per cent, the six-month prevalence was 19.1 per cent – leading one to predict that the one-year prevalence should have been slightly over 21 per cent: once more, our estimates seem to have been approximately right.

2   An example may make this clearer. Suppose that a two-stage survey finds that 20 per cent of consecutive attenders may have a diagnosable disorder, and it is known that 2000 people are served by the practice, and that during any one year 80 per cent of them will attend their doctor. During a calendar year 1600 (2000 × 80 per cent) will attend, and of these 320 (1600 × 20 per cent) will be cases. The rate per 1000 at risk per year is therefore 160 (320/2). (In practice this can be simplified – just multiply the proportion attending by the proportion who are found to be cases.)

# 3 Filters on the pathway to care

## THE INTERNATIONAL PATHWAY TO CARE STUDY

It is clear that the five levels model represents an over-simplified picture of the pathway to psychiatric care, since in some countries patients may refer themselves directly to mental health professionals, while others will be referred by longer, less direct pathways – perhaps involving multiple carers. Gater and his colleagues (1991) have carried out a collaborative study on behalf of the World Health Organisation concerned with the pathway taken by patients on their way to care by the mental illness services (levels 4 and 5) in eleven countries. Pathways in countries well provided with mental health staff were dominated by general practitioners and to a lesser extent by hospital doctors, while less well resourced centres like those in Pakistan, India and Indonesia showed a wide variety of pathways with native or religious healers often playing an important part. The four European centres (England, Portugal, Spain and Czechoslovakia) as well as Cuba were the countries containing the better resourced centres, and these all showed a straightforward pathway from community to primary care, and from there straight on to the mental illness services, for between two-thirds and four-fifths of the patients, with most of the remainder coming from hospital doctors, as shown in Figure 3.1.

This figure is derived from studying all patients receiving care for the first time by the specialised mental illness service over a calendar month. The figures shown are percentages of those seen for the first time, and the size of the arrow indicates the relative importance of the pathway. If an individual saw more than one GP before being sent on for specialist care this is shown as a 'recursive pathway'.

The two centres with the fewest patients coming from primary care physicians were Pakistan and India, where a substantial proportion come as direct referrals from the community, or from native healers, as shown in Figure 3.2. The other countries tended to be intermediate between these positions.

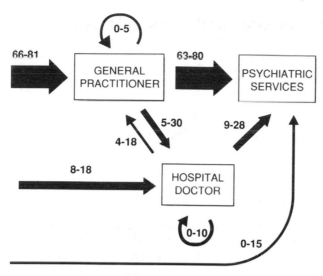

*Figure 3.1* The international pathways study: four European centres and Havana. The community is shown on the left, and the size of each arrow indicates the relative importance of the pathway. Numbers shown are percentages of those receiving care from the psychiatric services over a calendar month

Delays on the pathway to care were found to be remarkably short regardless of the level of manpower resources, although in some centres longer delays were found related to native healers. Illnesses initially presenting as somatic symptoms were common in all centres, and were sometimes associated with longer delays than those illnesses initially presenting with depression or anxiety.

## THE DIRECT FILTER: FROM THE COMMUNITY TO THE MENTAL ILLNESS SERVICES

In our previous book we described direct referrals as 'the American By-pass' (Goldberg and Huxley 1980: 53–55), but the WHO Pathways Study now shows that in five countries – Spain, Portugal, Mexico, Pakistan and India – there were sufficient numbers of people seeing the psychiatrists as their first port of call to enable comparison to be made between such individuals and those referred from other carers. As might be expected, somatic presentations of distress were much less frequent among the direct referrals, and it was of interest that direct referrals were more likely to have had the referral initiated by a member of their family in all five centres. In three centres (India, Spain and Portugal) the complaints of those coming

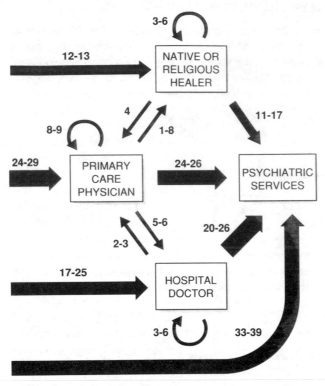

*Figure 3.2* The international pathways study: pathways in Pakistan and India (see note on Figure 3.1)

directly were of shorter duration, but there were no differences in the other two centres. In Spain, Portugal and Mexico the direct referrals were more likely to be female and younger, but in India and Pakistan males were more likely to be in the direct group, and there was no age difference.

We have seen that in many countries the majority of those seen by the mental illness services have been referred from other care-givers, most usually general practitioners and hospital doctors. Since we know that only a small proportion of mental disorders at level 1 find their way to the mental illness services, the remainder of the chapter will be devoted to considering the factors that determine passage from being in the community experiencing symptoms to occupying a bed in a psychiatric unit. In the interests of clarity, we will consider a patient moving along the 'direct pathway', and we will consider each of the four major filters in turn.

## THE FIRST FILTER: ILLNESS BEHAVIOUR

The term 'illness behaviour' was suggested by Mechanic (1968) to refer to any behaviour relevant to a condition that causes individuals to concern themselves with their symptoms and to seek help. Transient episodes of malaise, pains and dysphoria are widely distributed in the population. When an individual experiences such symptoms they first ask themselves why they are doing so – this is an effort after meaning. Severe headache and nausea after a drunken party will be readily interpreted as a hangover, but the same symptoms coming out of the blue will be emotionally disturbing. At this stage if the patient is alone illness may be denied, but if someone close to the patient is available the patient may attempt 'provisional validation' of the sick-role. This discussion may be for information and advice; and the advice will often include the other person's agreement for the sick individual to suspend their normal obligations. The sort of advice given by the other person is often critical in deciding whether or not the sick-role will be adopted – and it is at this stage that the many cultural influences described by Mechanic as illness behaviours may have a decisive effect. Lonely people may go directly to doctors for this 'provisional validation'.

With certain notable exceptions – like prison doctors, works doctors and army medical officers – most doctors will agree with their 'sick' patients that they are unable to function, and will provide certification to excuse them from work. The provision of such certification reinforces illness behaviour and confirms their inner conviction that all is not well. Thus, once a doctor is consulted the transition to the sick-role is ensured, at least temporarily. In a later paper Mechanic (1980) argues that neurosis – which he calls a 'distress syndrome' – is part of a learned pattern of illness behaviour involving an intense focus on internal feeling states, careful monitoring of bodily sensations, and a high level of self-awareness.

Andersen and his colleagues (1975, 1978, 1983) have proposed a 'structural model' to account for utilisation of health services, consisting of three sets of factors: societal, system and individual. *Societal determinants* include the current state of medical knowledge and prevailing attitudes towards health and illness; these either act directly on the individual or indirectly via the system determinants. *System determinants* include the availability of health services resources and ease of access to them, and *individual determinants* which are subdivided into predisposing, enabling and illness level variables. Predisposing variables include socio-demographic characteristics and health beliefs; enabling variables include such factors as income, ability to pay for care, local facilities and nature of the community; while illness variables include perceived symptoms, disability and general health and the individual's evaluations of meaning of such perceptions.

A number of large-scale surveys (Wolinsky 1978; Berkanovic *et al.* 1981) have shown that virtually all the variance detected is accounted for by the effects of illness-related variables. Such surveys do not give the whole picture however, since as Mechanic (1968) has pointed out such large-scale studies may use crude proxies to measure subtle social processes, and the dependent variable – 'illness' – is usually a summary measure including several psychological and attitudinal components. However, such major surveys do underscore the importance of distress as a major determinant of help-seeking. Williams, Wilkinson and Arreghini (1990) conclude their review of this field by asserting that

> a person's decision to seek care is influenced by four main factors: the severity of the problem, the individual's propensity to seek help, the accessibility of the services and the availability of alternative resources. Help seeking for mental disorders in primary care may reflect patient's help-seeking behaviour history as much as their current clinical need.
>
> (Williams *et al.* 1990)

### Some numerical data

In our earlier review we concluded that 'most patients with marked psychiatric disorders, and the majority of those with mild disorders, do contact their doctor' (Goldberg and Huxley 1980). Part of the evidence for this assertion was our calculation that the annual period prevalence at level 2 was only slightly lower than that at level 1 (230 versus 250/1000/year). This turns out to have been an optimistic conclusion, and it is now clear that although such patients may consult their doctor, they may do so for other reasons than their psychological symptoms, or at other times of the year when they are not in fact symptomatic. It also seems likely that our estimate of morbidity at level 1 may have been too low (see p. 17).

If periods much shorter than one year are taken as a time frame, it is clear that the first filter is less permeable than we had suggested (see Table 2.1, p. 18). Simultaneous measures in the community and in primary care have now been undertaken by Finlay-Jones and Burvill (1977) in Perth, West Australia; by Williams and his colleagues in the West London Survey (1986); by Tansella and Williams (1989) in Verona, Italy; and by Vazquez-Barquero and his colleagues (1987) in Cantabria, Spain. All these surveys show much the same thing. Patients with high scores on the GHQ are twice as likely to consult their GP as those with low scores, and 20 per cent of all consultations in primary care can be attributed to psychiatric disorder.

Vazquez-Barquero (1990) also showed that 15.5 per cent of the male, and 20.3 per cent of the female attributable risk of consultations could be attributed to psychiatric morbidity in Spain. The probability that someone with a high score would consult during two weeks was 21 per cent in Perth, and 27 per cent in London.

## Effects of gender

In our earlier book (Goldberg and Huxley 1980) we speculated that the first filter might be less permeable to women since the female rates at level 1 were approximately double the male rates, while the sex ratio of high GHQ scorers at level 2 was approximately 1.2:1. Although both observations were correct, the conclusion was unwarranted, since like was not being compared with like. A confirmed case is one thing, and a high score on a pencil and paper test is another. The sex ratio of confirmed cases at level 2 is approximately the same as that of confirmed cases in the community; and the sex ratio of high GHQ scorers is also approximately similar in the two settings. In the West London Survey, for example, the sex ratio of high GHQ scorers was 1.2:1 at level 1, and 1.17:1 at level 2. The relationship between GHQ score and probability of consulting a doctor in the previous two weeks was almost identical for each sex, ranging from +0.10 for those with GHQ scores of zero to +0.40 for those with scores in the highest range (Williams *et al.* 1986: Fig. 5, p. 22). This confirms an important claim in our earlier book (Goldberg and Huxley 1980), that there was a direct relationship between the degree of psychological distress and the probability of consulting. However, women are more likely than men to consult doctors at all levels of distress, but the effect of this is additive to the effect of high GHQ score. There is no interaction between sex, psychological distress and the probability of consulting a doctor. Thus, sex affects the permeability of the first filter in the same way across the whole range of emotional distress: the female excess for those with high GHQ scores is the same as the female excess for those without psychological distress. Williams and his colleagues (1986) have presented data which suggests that this excess is largely accounted for by consultations undertaken on behalf of others.

## Other 'additive' variables

Gender is not the only example of a variable which increases permeability of the first filter, but does so independently of psychological distress measured by the GHQ. Unemployment makes consultation more likely for men only across the whole range of emotional distress, but once more there is no interaction between GHQ score and unemployment. Unemployment has no significant effect on consultations for women.

Self-assessment of health status, and the presence of chronic physical disease, are also important variables which help to make consultation more likely, but do so equally across the whole range of distress.

### 'Interactive' variables

No consistent findings have emerged. In the West London Survey some variables showed a significant interaction with GHQ scores: thus, social impairment increases the probability of consulting in women with low scores, and men between the ages of 30 and 64 are more likely to consult in the presence of high scores. However, Burvill and Knuiman (1983) showed that men – but not women – with high scores became more likely to consult with increasing age.

Corney and Williams (1987) measured both social problems and GHQ scores in a sample of married women, and showed that high GHQ increases the probability of consulting only in the absence of social problems, while social problems increase probability of consulting only in those with low GHQ scores.

### Effects of diagnosis

There are no striking differences between the Catego diagnoses reported in the community and at level 2. Bebbington and his colleagues (1981) show that almost two-thirds of those receiving an ID-Catego diagnosis received one of a depressive illness, and Bridges and Goldberg (1985) showed that a similar proportion of new illnesses at level 2 were either neurotic or retarded depression. Only a small minority of patients in either setting report psychotic illnesses.

The most obvious difference between the clinical states of patients in the two settings is that diagnosable patients seen in consulting settings are commonly complaining of somatic symptoms which are the focus of their consultation, and often do not consider themselves to be psychologically unwell despite admitting to many symptoms which cause a research psychiatrist to make a diagnosis of a mental disorder. They are also often complaining of neurasthenic symptoms – fatigue, irritability and lack of energy – which cause them to seek medical care.

### Unmet need at level 1

Bebbington (1987) reported that only 45.3 per cent of those receiving PSE diagnoses in London had actually attended their family doctor for treatment, and an additional 9.4 per cent had seen a psychiatrist; the remainder had seen no one. The situation seems even worse in the United States, but the DIS generates 'diagnoses' which are not very reliable indicators of need for care. Thus Shapiro and his colleagues (1984) showed that of those with *DSM-III* diagnoses only between 15.6 per cent to 19.8 per cent sought care for their disorders over the previous six months. However, the *DSM-III* disorders included in the ECA study (Regier *et al.* 1984) included mild phobias and personality disorders. They therefore decided that in addition to a formal diagnosis from the DIS a respondent should also have a high score on a distress scale (the GHQ-30), and at least one day of disability caused by the problem (Shapiro *et al.* 1986). Put in this way, 15 per cent of the population of Baltimore could be said to be 'in need', and this need had been met (in the sense that the person had seen a care-giver) for 55 per cent of these. However, a longitudinal study of these subjects showed that many of these conditions were not long-lasting: only one-third of those with needs unmet originally were still in a state of unmet need at 12-month follow-up.

In Switzerland, Angst and Dobler-Mikola (1985) showed that only 20 per cent of those with anxiety or phobias had discussed their problem with a doctor, although nearly all had discussed it with a friend or relative.

## THE SECOND FILTER: ABILITY TO DETECT DISORDER

In our earlier review we concluded that the inability or unwillingness of care-givers to acknowledge psychological distress was a major reason why so many patients did not receive help for their psychological problems. We showed that in Greater Manchester family doctors picked up only about 54 per cent of the psychological disorders among their patients: subsequent work has shown that the population of Manchester is relatively well-served by its doctors.

There are two kinds of research designs for investigating the second filter. Our original work (Marks *et al.* 1979; Goldberg *et al.* 1980a) consisted of administering a psychiatric screening questionnaire – the GHQ – to consecutive patients seeing a family doctor, and to ask that doctor to make ratings about how psychologically distressed each patient was thought to be. The second kind of study actually confirms that a patient has a mental disorder by direct assessment using a standardised research interview, and looks to see how many cases of confirmed disorder were actually detected by their doctor.

When comparing a doctor's assessments with those of a questionnaire, it is possible to derive a number of measures of the doctor's performance. One of these, *accuracy*, does not involve dichotomising the population into 'cases' and 'non-cases', since it merely examines the relationship between the doctor's ratings on a six-point scale, with the total number of symptoms about which the patient complains. It is measured by Spearman's rank-order correlation, which takes a value of 0 if there is no relationship between the two measures, and 1 if agreement is perfect. However, the *identification index* is more important for our present purposes, since this measures the ability of the doctor to identify probable cases correctly. The number of high scorers identified as cases (the 'observed true positives') is compared with the 'expected true positives', itself calculated by using a formula which takes account of the probable number of false positives in a particular run of patients. Thus, a doctor with an identification index of 54 per cent is correctly identifying 54 per cent of the cases that are probably there.

However, the identification index is affected by the frequency with which a doctor identifies people as psychiatrically ill. A doctor with a low threshold for case identification who considers that the majority of his patients are 'cases' will inevitably have a higher identification index than another doctor with a high threshold, even if the total number of patients misclassified is the same in each case (the former by incorrectly stating that non-cases were cases; the latter by stating that cases were non-cases). The proportion identified as cases is called the *conspicuous psychiatric morbidity* (CPM) of the practice. We now need some measure that assesses the tendency of the doctor to either over-identify, or to under-identify, psychiatric illness. This can readily be measured by dividing the CPM by the probable prevalence predicted by the screening test, and is called the doctor's *bias*. Table 3.1 shows these four measures for 4 multi-practice studies.

*Table 3.1*   Four characteristics of family doctors relating to their ability to detect mental disorder among their patients

| Investigator, Location | No. of Drs; Screen test | CPM | Bias | Accuracy | Identification index |
|---|---|---|---|---|---|
| Goldberg et al. Charleston, USA 1980a | 45 residents GHQ-28 | 39.7 | 1.46 | 0.33 | 0.80 |
| Marks et al. Manchester, UK 1979 | 91 GPs GHQ-60 | 31.1 | 0.79 | 0.39 | 0.54 |
| Wilmink Groningen, Holland 1989 | 30 GPs GHQ-30 | 25.7 | 1.84 | 0.41 | — |
| Boardman London, UK 1987 | 18 GPs GHQ-28 | 19.3 | 0.62 | 0.19 | 0.36 |
| Schein Philadelphia, USA 1977 | 32 GPs GHQ-30 | 17.6 | 0.45 | — | 0.31 |

We may draw a number of conclusions from these surveys. First, the numbers given in the table are means, which hide considerable variation between doctors – yet it is clear that considerable variation exists between doctors in different places in the amount of mental disorder that they identify among their patients. A comparison between the figures for CPM and bias reveals that much of this variation is accounted for by differing standards of case identification. However, the family practice residents in Charleston, with a bias of 1.46, are identifying far more patients as sick than the questionnaire, and this partly accounts for their high identification index. In contrast, the 32 family practitioners in West Philadelphia are under-diagnosing relative to the screening test, and this partly accounts for their low identification index. Secondly, the figures for accuracy are really very low. In the first two studies, about one-third of the doctors did not have significant correlations between their ratings and the GHQ – so that a monkey with a pin would have done as well as they did in making accurate assessments of their patients' distress. These doctors were counterbalanced by family doctors so good at detecting disorder that their correlations with the GHQ were as good as research workers with unlimited time and assisted by a research interview.

In our earlier book (Goldberg and Huxley 1980) we considered the determinants of overall accuracy and bias. As one might expect, doctors with a high bias towards making psychiatric diagnoses ask many questions relating to psychological distress and ask about the patient's home; they are empathic and sensitive to verbal cues relating to emotional distress, and in one study they tended to be low status doctors working in busy clinics (Schein 1977). Accurate doctors shared two characteristics with high bias doctors – they are sensitive to verbal cues and are rated as showing more interest and concern for their patients – but otherwise the determinants of accuracy are dissimilar, and fall into three groups:

first, they had superior interview techniques: they tended to start the interview well (looking at the patient more, being good at clarifying the main complaints, and using directive rather than closed questioning techniques);

second, they had higher knowledge scores concerning internal medicine (in Manchester, they were more likely to have additional qualifications); and

third, in their personality and attitudes, they were less 'conservative' on the Wilson-Patterson Social Attitude Inventory (and in Charleston, more self-assured and sensitive to their own needs and feelings).

It should be noted that 'overall accuracy' is even more influenced by the ability to identify asymptomatic patients as normal as it is by the ability to identify distressed patients as sick – since there are almost always more normal people than emotionally distressed people in consulting populations. In both the Charleston and the Groningen studies, there was not a significant correlation between accuracy and bias.

The other kind of study uses a two-stage design to identify actual cases of mental disorder, and then examines the extent to which these syndromes have been detected. There are two advantages to this type of design: one no longer has to use numerical adjustments to predict probable prevalence, and one is able to examine failure to detect mental disorder by specific diagnosis. Schulberg and his colleagues (1987a) conclude that physicians under-diagnose mental disorder with a magnitude of error ranging from 50 to 80 per cent. There is reason to believe that the range is even wider than this.

Three studies have used the PSE as a second stage examination, one with primary care physicians in Holland, the second with social workers in Manchester, and the third with primary care workers in four developing countries. The results are shown in Table 3.2. It can be seen that anxiety states are generally less well detected than depressive illnesses, and the first two studies give detection rates within the range already encountered in Table 3.1.

However, it is worth noting that trained social workers seem to do at least as well as doctors, and that detection rates are low in developing countries. Wilmink and his colleagues (1990) have shown that primary care physicians with a 'family orientation' were no better than doctors with a 'clinical orientation' in this respect.

*Table 3.2*  Detection rates by primary care workers and social workers for specific diagnoses using two-stage research designs

|  | Anxiety state | Phobias | Neurotic depression | Retarded depression | Overall detection rate, ID5 |
|---|---|---|---|---|---|
| Wilmink 1989 Dutch GPs (292 interviews) | 35% | 44% | 62% | 100% | 56% |
| Huxley *et al.* 1987 Social workers (141 interviews) | 58% | — | 66% | 56% | 68.5% |
| Harding *et al.* 1980 4 developing countries (288 interviews) | — | — | — | — | 36.8% |

Two further studies have used American second stage research interviews, and generated diagnoses using the RDC or *DSM-III* systems, but with rather different results. Hoeper and his colleagues (1979) show low detection rates by primary care physicians in Marshfield, but Shapiro *et al.* (1987) have published data from Baltimore suggesting that doctors there are very much sharper at picking up morbidity. Von Korff and his colleagues (1987) report that 100 per cent of panic disorders, 75 per cent of depressions and even 70 per cent of anxiety states are detected. However, their results are less impressive when one notices that they also falsely identify 27.7 per cent of non-cases as cases, and that their overall rate of identified cases (CPM = 33.1 per cent) is very much higher than the prevalence found by the DIS interview, so that the bias of these physicians is no less than 3.9! Hoeper's results from Wisconsin are more comparable with those found by others, and here the doctors are missing 81.5 per cent of the cases found by research interview (see Table 3.3).

*Table 3.3* Discrepant results on detection from two US studies

|  | CPM | Actual prevalence | Bias | % detected by GP |
|---|---|---|---|---|
| Hoeper *et al.* 1984 | 16.8% | 27.0% | 0.62 | 18.5% |
| Von Korff *et al.* 1987 | 33.1% | 8.4% | 3.94 | 83.0% |

## The determinants of the ability to identify emotional distress

### The doctors

It follows from Table 3.1 that the ability to identify emotionally distressed patients accurately ('identification index') will be a composite of the factors determining overall accuracy and bias; and so it turns out to be. In the Charleston study (Goldberg *et al.* 1980b), identification index was correlated with accuracy +0.51, and with bias +0.83. In Marks *et al.*'s (1979) study, doctors with a high identification index were rated by an independent observer as having more interest and concern for the patient, having a greater interest in psychiatry, as well as tending to be older and more experienced. More detailed analysis showed that such doctors asked more questions with a psychosocial content, avoided technical jargon, were more settled in their practice, and tended to possess additional qualifications.

Goldberg and his colleagues (1980a, b) replicated this study in Charleston, South Carolina in a Department of Family Practice, and were able to show that a brief set of videotaped feedback sessions succeeded in modifying the doctors' interview behaviour over the next six months, and that this in turn caused them to become more sensitive in detecting emotional distress in their patients. The interview skills which could be modified by training and which are each related to identification index are shown below, and can be seen to be an amalgam of the factors that were earlier shown to relate to overall accuracy and bias:

*Start of the interview:*
  makes eye contact with patient
  is able to clarify complaint
*General interview skills:*
  picks up verbal cues
  picks up non-verbal cues
  can deal with over-talkativeness
  deals with interruptions well
  isn't buried in the notes
*Types of question:*
  asks directive 'psychiatric questions'
  asks closed 'psychiatric questions'
  makes supportive comments
  asks about home

More recently, Davenport and her colleagues (1987) have been able to show that doctors themselves influence the way in which patients behave during the interview. When patients are chosen with the same degree of emotional distress, those interviewed by doctors with a high identification index (high II) make it easier for the doctor, by emitting more verbal cues relating to distress, and by having more distress in their voices. Put another way, when a distressed patient is being interviewed by a poor detector of illness they will manage to control themselves and emit few signs of distress.

Goldberg and his colleagues (1991) have extended these findings, and shown in addition to the earlier findings the able identifiers of emotional illness have the following features:

– more eye contact throughout interview
– less avoidant, more relaxed posture
– make facilitatory noises while listening
– less urgency and hurry initially
– don't give information early

However, the characteristics of the doctor that are associated with cue emission by the patient are somewhat different. These cues include abnormal movements, posture, the quality of the patient's voice as well as what the patient actually says. Asking directive rather than closed questions, making empathic statements, asking directive social questions, and asking questions with a psychological content are all behaviours which facilitate the release of cues by the patient. Asking questions that follow from what the patient has just said (being 'patient-led') leads to increased cue release, while asking questions derived from theory (being 'doctor-led') leads to a reduction.

There are significant interactions between the ability to detect emotional disorder and the effects that certain behaviours have on cue release. Thus, only doctors poor at detecting disorder inhibit cues when they ask closed questions, and directive social questions only lead to increased cue release when they are asked by doctors good at detecting disorder. It is all a matter of timing.

Millar and Goldberg (1991) have shown that the ability to identify emotional distress is itself part of a generally superior set of communication skills. Able identifiers of emotional distress are more likely to offer patients information, advice and treatment relevant to their illness, and they are significantly more likely to do these things well with patients with low distress scores, as well as those with many symptoms. They are more likely to negotiate information and advice to the patient, and thus more likely to obtain co-operation and produce satisfaction.

### Characteristics of the patient that influence identification of distress by the care-giver

In our earlier book (Goldberg and Huxley 1980) we argued that female sex, the middle of the age range, those living apart from their spouse or widowed, being unemployed, having had a minimum education and having been seen many times before all made detection more likely (Marks *et al.* 1979). These findings were obtained by comparing GHQ scores with ratings made by family doctors, and they have been replicated and extended by Boardman (1987) in London. In addition to confirming all the earlier findings, he showed that social class exercises no clear effect, and that case identification was good with patients from Eire, but extremely poor with patients from the West Indies, Africa and India.

It is not clear how much should be made of these findings, since a pencil and paper test is being compared with ratings by a clinician, and we saw that this led us into error in the matter of the effects of sex on the first filter (see p. 35).

*The patients*

The findings concerning the determinants of identification index were obtained by watching many videotapes of real doctor–patient encounters in family practices. After one has watched an encounter where a doctor has failed to respond to repeated verbal and vocal cues relating to emotional distress, it is striking to note that the patient does not appear to leave the consulting room in a dissatisfied way. The patient has typically presented some somatic symptom as his or her main complaint, and this has been taken seriously by the low II doctor. The patient is happy with the physical examination, the physical investigation which may have been ordered, and the symptomatic medicine prescribed. Indeed, the high II doctor may have a hard time persuading such a patient that their emotional distress is related to their main complaint – since they will not have been offered much help in medical school or in later training helping them with this difficult skill. It is clear to the detached observer that failure to detect emotional distress is thus often a *collusive phenomenon*, affecting both doctor and patient. When an emotional disorder is avoided, both participants have opted for an easier path. The doctor does not have to elicit and then manage emotional distress, and the patient does not have to face up to their distress, and perhaps their own partial responsibility for their current predicament. Both take refuge in safer roles: the doctor as a fighter of supposed organic disease, and the patient as a victim. Faced with such mutual satisfaction with a professional encounter, it ill behoves an outsider to declare that anything is wrong.

## Does detection of emotional distress actually help the patient?

Two influential studies from the United States suggest that detection of emotional distress may not be helpful, although it is important to note that neither measured outcome in the patients. Hoeper and his colleagues gave family physicians feedback of GHQ scores in Wisconsin (1984), and Shapiro and his colleagues (1987) gave both GHQ feedback and feedback of the results of a research assessment and a diagnosis in Baltimore, and neither were able to show that overall detection by the physicians improved. However, Shapiro was able to show that detection of emotional disorders did improve among the elderly, the black patients and among males – all groups which ordinarily have low rates of detection. A problem with both these studies was that the family doctors did not really use their feedback in any constructive way with the patients; for example, in the latter study the doctors were uninfluenced in their treatment by feedback of either GHQ or research assessment. Unless the doctor translates any feedback provided into some constructive dialogue with the patient, no one should hope for a better outcome.

In contrast, there are many studies which suggest that detection may hold real advantages for patients. Johnstone and Goldberg (1976) randomised patients with high GHQ scores to an index condition in which the doctor was given feedback, and a control condition in which it was withheld. It was shown that treatment – in the form of counselling and psychotropics – was offered to index patients in an exactly similar way to those with conspicuous illnesses in the practice at that time. At three months, significantly more of the index group had improved, and at twelve months those in the index group had had to endure their symptoms for 2.1 fewer months over the year. Zung and her colleagues (1983) randomised patients with high scores on a self-report depression scale and re-assessed patients four weeks later. Of those detected and given a psychotropic 68 per cent had improved, compared with 28 per cent of those detected but untreated, and 18 per cent of the undetected control group.

Rucker and his colleagues (1986) gave feedback of a depression scale to 32 residents who had participated in Shapiro's study (Shapiro *et al.* 1987), but this time allowed residents to discuss the feedback with the patients at a subsequent interview (Dr Johnstone had also been able to do this). The residents indicated that 17 per cent of the patients were indeed more depressed than they had supposed, 21 per cent of the clinicians changed their plan of treatment, and 58 per cent found the feedback useful. Rand and her colleagues (1988) had the idea of randomising residents, rather than randomising patients. Residents in the index group were provided with training about how to interpret the GHQ results. GHQ feedback resulted in a two-fold increase in psychological diagnoses, with statistically significant differences for depression.

Two naturalistic studies have shown that depression which is recognised by family doctors has a better outcome than depression which has been missed. Freeling and his colleagues (1985) showed that undetected depressive illness lasted longer, while Ormel and Giel (1990) showed that the better outlook in the detected group was not because they had received a particular treatment.

Taken together, these studies suggest that it is pointless providing family doctors with feedback that they have not asked for and do not perhaps know how to use anyway. On the other hand, there is a great deal to be said for providing them with training which will sharpen up their own skills in both detection and management of common mental disorders. We return to this theme in Chapter 10.

## Detection by social workers

As Table 3.2 shows Huxley and his colleagues (1987) found social workers able to recognise the presence of psychiatric disorder when they were given the chance to say whether they thought it was present or absent in their clients. This unsophisticated judgement enabled the social workers to 'detect' psychiatric illness in 58 per cent of the anxiety states and 66 per cent of the neurotic depressions, but only 56 per cent of the psychotic depressions. In no diagnostic category did the social workers perform better than chance, but the social work rating of caseness and the client's PSE scores were significantly correlated.

## THE THIRD FILTER: REFERRAL TO MENTAL ILLNESS SERVICES

The third filter stands between primary care and the specialist mental illness services, and reduces an overall morbidity of just over 10 per cent to one of about 2 per cent. It is therefore an extremely important filter, since it keeps so many patients from passing it. The arrival of mental health professionals in primary care settings will mean that significant alterations may be expected in this filter, since patients who would be reluctant to see a psychiatrist in a hospital setting are often prepared to see a specialised worker at their doctor's surgery.

It is possible to compare the morbidity at levels 3 and 4 of our model by examining data from the Morbidity Statistics in General Practice for 1982 (HMSO: 1986) with data prepared from the Salford Case Register in 1983.

### Time trends

Since 1983, community-based services have expanded in Salford, so that the rate for all those known to the register has increased from 20.87 to 23.5/1000 by 1989; while the rate for admissions has risen from 3.3 to 5.71/1000. The third filter therefore became slightly more permeable, while the fourth filter remained about the same. These changes may not be typical, since Salford has a contracting population, and the increased rate at level 5 is partly due to greater admissions for the over 65s associated with an expansion of psychiatric services for the elderly.

### Clinical severity as a determinant of permeability

The first point to make concerns the percentage distribution of cases at the two levels. As one might expect, conditions such as adjustment disorders

*Table 3.4* Rates per 1000 population at risk per year, by diagnosis, for levels 3, 4 and 5, showing percentage distribution of diagnosis at each level. Level 3 from Morbidity Statistics in General Practice, 1981–1982 (HMSO 1986); levels 4 and 5 from Malcolm Cleverly of the Salford Case Register; data for 1983

|  | Level 3 Primary Care | | Level 4 Mental Illness Services all patients | | Level 5 in-patients | |
|---|---|---|---|---|---|---|
| Organic, dementia | 2.2 | (2.2%) | 2.75 | (13.2%) | 0.50 | (15.3%) |
| Schizophrenia | 2.0 | (2.0%) | 4.08 | (19.6%) | 0.72 | (22.1%) |
| Affective psychosis | 3.0 | (3.0%) | 1.47 | (7.0%) | 0.41 | (12.6%) |
| Depression | 28.0 | (27.6%) | 5.35 | (25.6%) | 0.69 | (20.3%) |
| Other neurosis | 35.7 | (35.2%) | 2.46 | (11.8%) | 0.17 | (5.1%) |
| Alcohol, drugs | 2.7 | (2.7%) | 1.37 | (6.6%) | 0.39 | (11.9%) |
| Personality disorder | 1.1 | (1.1%) | 1.62 | (7.8%) | 0.30 | (9.2%) |
| Adjustment, other diagnoses | 26.7 | (26.3%) | 1.74 | (8.4%) | 0.11 | (3.5%) |
| All diagnoses | 101.4 | (100.0%) | 20.87 | (100.0%) | 3.30 | (100.0%) |

and psychophysiological disorders such as insomnia and tension headache account for over a quarter of cases seen by family doctors, but are rarely seen by the specialised mental health services. The same is true of 'other neuroses', which in primary care are largely accounted for by anxiety disorders (29.6/1000 at risk). In contrast, more severe disorders such as organic states, schizophrenia and affective psychosis are more commonly seen by the specialist services.

When we consider rates per thousand at risk, we see that mental illness services are seeing only a very small proportion of cases of depressive illness and neurosis, and of adjustment disorders. However, in the course of a year the absolute number of schizophrenics, organic states and personality disorders will be greater among those seen by mental illness services than by primary care, and the rate for affective psychosis and alcohol and drug problems is about two-thirds as high as the rate seen by primary care physicians. The findings for schizophrenia are particularly striking, and appear to indicate that many cases of schizophrenia are in contact with the specialist services, but are either not in contact with their family doctor or not recognised as schizophrenics when they are in contact. We may conclude that severity of disorder is an important determinant of passage through the filter.

The arrival of clinical psychologists and community psychiatric nurses with direct attachments to primary care means that the case-mix seen by these workers is changing.

It can be seen from Table 3.5 that cases seen by social workers and CPNs on their own contained a greater proportion of cases of non-psychotic depression and neurosis than cases seen by the whole service, and contained fewer cases of more severe disorders such as schizophrenia and organic states. These changes may be expected to gather momentum as the old multi-disciplinary team breaks up, leaving each mental health profession free to make its own arrangements in primary care.

## Other factors determining permeability of the third filter

There now seems to be good evidence that, in England, men are more likely to be referred for specialist care than women. The National Morbidity Study shows a sex ratio of 2.38:1 for all psychological diagnoses combined, while the five case registers that publish data broken down by sex show that the ratio at level 4 is 1.37:1. This difference is so substantial, and is based on such large data-sets, that one is justified in concluding that the third filter is less permeable to women. This finding echoes an earlier findings by four independent European groups summarised in our earlier book (Goldberg and Huxley 1980: 115).

Where age is concerned, the age specific rates per 100,000 population at risk for Salford closely resemble the age structure of the base population

*Table 3.5* A comparison between cases seen only by CPNs and social workers, and all cases known to the Salford Case Register, for selected diagnoses during 1983. Rates per 1000 at risk, and percentages (from Malcolm Cleverly)

|  | All patients known to case register | | Seen only by CPN or social worker | |
|---|---|---|---|---|
| Dementia, organic | 3.63 | (13.2%) | 1.68 | (8.7%) |
| Schizophrenia etc. | 5.39 | (19.6%) | 0.77 | (11.4%) |
| Affective psychosis | 1.94 | (7.0%) | 0.24 | (3.6%) |
| Other depression | 7.04 | (25.6%) | 2.21 | (32.6%) |
| Other neurosis | 3.25 | (11.8%) | 1.16 | (17.0%) |
| Alcohol, drugs | 1.81 | (6.6%) | 0.41 | (6.0%) |
| Personality disorder | 2.14 | (7.8%) | 0.58 | (8.5%) |
| All diagnoses | 27.50 | (100.0%) | 6.79 | (100.0%) |

between the ages of 25 and 65; however there are fewer cases known to the register in the 15–24 age group, and many more in the over-65 group, than would be expected from the distribution in the population at risk. However, direct studies of referral all show that younger patients are more likely to be referred than older patients, so that the under-representation of young people in the case register reflects the fact that such registers are cumulative, and it is bound to take some years before the members of a particular age cohort have percolated through the first three filters.

Practices in urban areas are more likely to refer patients for specialist care than those in rural areas, perhaps partly due to the higher rates in depressed urban areas, but also because travel times are shorter and so specialist care is more readily available (seven studies, summarised in Goldberg and Huxley 1980: 114) and older doctors are more likely to refer than younger ones (Shepherd *et al.* 1966; Shortell and Daniel 1974; Robertson 1979). Doctors with readily available mental health services providing primary care clinics have very much higher referral rates than those without such facilities: Jackson and her colleagues (1991) showed that introduction of such services more than doubled the rate at which new cases were seen.

The reason most frequently given by GPs for a referral is that the patient has failed to respond to treatment by themselves; after this, there has been a need for a diagnostic opinion or some further investigations or the request has come from the patient or his family. Less common reasons are the wish for the specialist to take over the treatment and the risk of suicide.

Balestrieri and his colleagues (1988) have reviewed eleven studies in which referral to a mental health professional was compared to treatment by the family doctor, and showed that, in general, specialist treatment has a success rate about 10 per cent greater than routine treatment; and counselling, behaviour therapy or general psychiatry were generally equally effective.

## A study of the first three filters

It is of interest to compare morbidity at level 4 with that encountered in the community, and this has been carefully carried out for Edinburgh women by Sashidharan and his colleagues (1988). They comment that 'for every 100 women identified in the community with a psychiatric disorder, 3 are in hospital care. However, the majority of the hospital cases (56 per cent) are given diagnoses which were *not* applied to the community sample ... when only those with a diagnosis of affective disorder were considered, 1 out of every 100 women with the disorder in the community was found in the hospital setting' (see Table 3.6).

*Table 3.6* A comparison between prevalence and inception rates for mental disorders for Edinburgh women in the community, and those seen by the mental illness services (after Sashidharan *et al.* 1988)

*Level 1: The community, women only*

| Diagnosis: | Prevalence | Inception |
|---|---|---|
| Major depression | 54.0 | 20.0 |
| Panic disorder | 7.0 | 3.0 |
| Generalised anxiety disorder | 36.0 | 36.0 |
| All diagnoses (includes minor dep) | 156.0 | 115.0/1000/year |

*Level 4: Cases known to Edinburgh Case Register, women only*

| Diagnosis: | Prevalence | Inception |
|---|---|---|
| Affective psychosis | 1.07 | 1.96 |
| Neurotic disorders | 0.66 | 4.23 |
| Organic brain syndrome | 0.27 | 0.27 |
| Mental handicap | 0.06 | 0.09 |
| Schizophrenia | 0.46 | 0.68 |
| Alcoholism | 0.30 | 1.69 |
| Drugs | 0.11 | 0.14 |
| All diagnoses | 3.87/1000 | 14.00/1000 |

These investigators went on to compare the ratio of rates between level 4 and level 1 by age and marital status, and show that single women, and those older than 55, are more likely to be seen by the mental illness services. The impermeability of the filters for women below the age of 35 is particularly striking (see Table 3.7).

Tischler and his colleagues (1975) carried out an ingenious study on the determinants of consulting a community mental health centre from the community in the United States, by comparing new patients seen over the course of a year with data from a community survey. A variable was said to be 'concordant' when actual utilisation reflects the variable's distribution among impaired people in the community. For example, the proportion of non-whites attending for treatment was the same as the proportion among symptomatic people in the community. The same was found for low social class, those on welfare, and the separated and divorced. 'Over-utilisation' occurs for those who are isolated and lack social support: for the

*Table 3.7* Ratio of cases seen by specialist services to cases existing in the community among Edinburgh women (after Sashidharan *et al.* 1988)

|  |  | *Prevalence* | *Inception* |
|---|---|---|---|
| Age | 18–34 | 1:140 | 1:26 |
|  | 35–54 | 1: 77 | 1:16 |
|  | 55–65 | 1: 59 | 1: 7 |
| Marital status | Married | 1: 94 | 1:18 |
|  | Single | 1: 20 | 1: 7 |
|  | Divorced, cohabiting, widowed | 1:230 | 1:40 |

unemployed, the unmarried, women over 50 and those without religion. In contrast, 'under-utilisation' occurred for women between the ages of 30 and 50, and those on low incomes.

## THE FOURTH FILTER: ADMISSION TO HOSPITAL BEDS

Despite the proliferation of services in the community, admission rates to in-patient facilities in England have increased by 6 per cent between 1977 and 1983. There has been an overall slight reduction in admissions for those aged under 65 (from 451 to 418/100,000/year), but this has been more than made up for by the increase in those aged above 65 (from 608 to 830/100,000/year) (Jennings *et al.* 1989). There are quite wide variations in admission rates between health districts, although much of this variation can be accounted for in terms of social differences of the sort derived from Census indicators and measured by the Jarman Index (Jarman 1983, 1984; Hirsch 1988).

The number of beds available to the mental illness service has been progressively declining, so that increased admission rates are obtained by shortening the mean duration of stay in hospital. In 1977 the median duration of stay for patients aged less than 65 was between 15 days and 22.5 days in seven of the eight case register areas; these figures had dropped to between 10 and 20 days by 1983 (Wing 1989).

### Direct comparison between level 4 and level 5

It is not easy to make direct comparisons between total patients seen by the service and in-patient admissions, since reliable diagnostic information is hard to come by. We have seen in Table 3.4 (p. 47) that the percentage distribution between major diagnostic categories in Salford during 1983 were much the same, except that a greater proportion of depressives admitted to hospital had severe forms of the illness, and there were rather fewer alcoholics and more neurotics among out-patients. None of this is very surprising. It is also clear that in-patient admission is more likely for those beyond the age of 65, which once more is what one might expect.

The progressive reduction in in-patient facilities has meant that patients with non-psychotic and non-organic illnesses are less likely to receive in-patient treatment, although admission rates for the more severe disorders are not decreasing. The evidence that provision of community services leads to a reduced demand for admissions is not easy to show for severe disorders, although there have been some well-publicised studies showing that treatment in the community can be an alternative to in-patient treatment for patients with acute psychoses. However, such studies tend to exclude those with organic disorders, with drug dependency, with suicidal or homicidal tendencies, and those without community support – and these are important groups. Furthermore, most studies have allowed very short admissions followed by treatment in the community, so that they should be seen as demonstrations that admissions can be made much shorter if proper community support services are available.

In a controlled study in which mental health services were introduced into primary care settings, Jackson and her colleagues (1991) show that the reduction in the need for hospital services was mainly confined to out-patient and day-patient services: the need for in-patient services was not reduced for those with severe disorders.

# 4 Common mental disorders as categories

The English physician Thomas Sydenham (1682) observed that

> Nature, in the production of disease, is uniform and consistent; so much so, that for the same disease in different persons the symptoms are for the most part the same; and the self-same phenomena that you would observe in the sickness of a Socrates you would observe in the sickness of a simpleton.

It is notable that he called unusual symptoms 'hysterical' if they could not be accounted for by any known disease, and noted that there was usually a preceding disturbance of the mind, which he regarded as the cause of the disease. There was a firm belief in the existence of disease entities at the time: diseases were to be reduced 'to certain and determinate kinds with the same exactness as we see it done by botanic writers in their treatises of plants'.

His arguments were taken further by nineteenth-century psychiatrists like Kahlbaum and Kraepelin, who concluded that the various forms of madness consisted of a finite number of disease entities, each with its own distinct cause, psychological form, outcome and cerebral pathology. These workers receive an echo in our century when the DSM-III system was introduced; for each DSM-III category there were thought to be 'organismic dysfunctions which are relatively distinct with regard to clinical features, aetiology and course' (Spitzer *et al.* 1977). These remain pious hopes, as it is in fact not possible to produce a system which completely fulfils these requirements, admirable though they may be in their intention.

Indeed, these views have always been controversial. The young Virchow argued that 'diseases have no independent or isolated existence ... they are only the manifestations of life processes under altered conditions'. Psychiatrists like Adolf Meyer (1955) argued that mental disorders were reactions of the whole organism to its total environment, rather than being produced by some discrete inner lesion produced by some definable external cause. However, as more becomes known both about the biological underpinnings of common symptoms, and the way in which environmental variables relate to different symptom-clusters, Meyer's views become less attractive. However, a view which regards symptoms as existing on several independent dimensions seems worth exploring.

## ADVANTAGES OF HAVING A CLASSIFICATION

Kendell (1975) observes that classifications – which are collections of categories – are much more widely used than dimensional systems, and indeed the structure of our language and of all verbal thinking is based upon classifications. Indeed, we need some form of classification for knowledge to advance at all. Without a concept of depression, we would never have learned what we have about the various causes of depression, or about how it can be most effectively treated. We could not know how depression varies with social class, or how it relates to stressful life events – because we would have no concept of depression to use to advance our knowledge. Clinicians need some form of classification, unless – like psychoanalysts – they are to use essentially the same treatment approach with everybody that they see. A classification is also essential if any statements at all are to be made about the future, because all prognostic statements are implicitly recruiting the individual patient to a class of similar patients. Finally, some form of classification is necessary in order to communicate with others about particular mental disorders, and it also facilitates communicating about individual patients.

A simple categorical model would consist of a finite series of categories which were mutually exclusive and jointly exhaustive. Such a model is not on offer where mental disorders are concerned: not only do the various syndromes often co-exist, but a system can only be 'exhaustive' by having large residual categories. A possible alternative would be a multi-dimensional system of classification, where one produced pseudo-categories for research purposes and for treatment purposes by declaring that any individual beyond some arbitrary point on, say, the depression dimension was declared a 'depressive'. This is straightforward when only single dimensions are concerned, but becomes cumbersome when several dimen- sions are used. To be told that someone has scored 0.80 on anxiety and 0.22 on depression is more cumbersome than saying that the person 'has' an anxiety state.

The advantage of a categorical model is that it simplifies three tasks: carrying out clinical work, producing homogeneous groups for research purposes, and the book-keeping of health administration. The clinician likes to say he has just seen a 'case' of hysteria, the researcher that she has collected 50 'cases' of depressive illness, the administrator that his unit has found a more economical management for agoraphobics, and the father may find it helpful to be told that his daughter is suffering from anorexia nervosa. It may have a specious simplicity, but it is certainly seductive.

It should be observed that present allegedly categorical systems – like the American *DSM-IIIR* system – are in any case effectively not all that different from pseudo-categorised dimensional systems. The ponderous statement that a particular patient is displaying 'co-morbidity for major depressive episode and generalised anxiety disorder' can be translated into the statement that this individual is above a certain threshold on an anxiety dimension, as well as being above another threshold on a depression dimension.

It therefore turns out that the choice between a categorical model and a multi-dimensional model is hardly a hanging matter, since each can effectively be reduced to the other. In any case, models cannot really be said to be right or wrong; one has to ask which fits the data better, which is the more useful, and which might suggest more testable hypotheses?

Kendell (1975) concluded his discussion on categorical versus dimensional models by asserting that the advantages of a categorical model were greater than a dimensional model for psychosis, but that the reverse applied to neuroses and personality disorders. Maxwell (1972) had earlier shown why dimensional models won't work with psychotic illnesses, since many symptoms have such low incidences. He wrote

> we have a sample of patients, broadly labelled as 'neurotic' for whom clustering techniques fail, but whose symptomatology can be satisfactorily described in terms of several dimensions of abnormal behaviour ... the majority of patients tend to have a basic core of symptoms, neurotic in type, which lend themselves to a dimensional description, but one whose prominence decreases somewhat as we pass from neurotics through affective psychotics to schizophrenics.
>
> (Maxwell 1972)

## REQUIREMENTS FOR A CATEGORICAL MODEL

1 Kendell (1975) argued that in order for a disease-category to have any meaning, there should be a *natural boundary* or discontinuity between the condition in question and its neighbours. 'In terms of the familiar aphorism that classification is the art of carving nature at the joints, it should imply that there is indeed a joint there, and one is not sawing through bone.' In practical terms, he was seeking 'points of rarity'

between adjoining syndromes in the distribution of symptoms, as was shown by Cloninger and his colleagues (1985) where schizophrenia was concerned. Grayson (1987) has argued that points of rarity as demonstrated by bimodality of test scores cannot be used as a criterion of 'category-ness', since it can easily arise from data that are undoubtedly dimensional. Another related requirement would be that consistent syndromes should be identified by cluster analysis with different data-sets, as was done for mania, depression and schizophrenia by Everitt and his colleagues (1971). We would not wish to regard apples and bananas as different categories of fruit if there were in nature an unbroken continu- um between them, or if there was no really reliable way of distinguishing the structure of one fruit from that of the other.

2  By the same argument, there should also presumably be *discontinuities between a syndrome and normality*. We should be able to tell where the branch ends and the fruit begins.

3  Categories should be reasonably *robust*, both between different categorical systems, and between observers. If one system identifies a fruit as a banana, we would hope that the other system would not say it was an apple. And within one system, different observers should agree about which fruit was the banana.

4  Categories should remain reasonably *constant over time*. There would be little point in distinguishing between apples, bananas and cherries if they were constantly turning into one another whenever one took one's eyes off the fruit-bowl.

5  One would expect that the *genetics* of different categories were distinct. It would be disquieting if the same genetic factors accounted for two different categories: it would be like noticing that apples and bananas always grew on the same tree.

6  Different categories should require different *treatments*. Stretching the metaphor somewhat, some recipes should suit some fruit more than others!

Severe mental illnesses – such as organic mental states, schizophrenia, mania and depressive psychosis – at least partially fulfil many of these criteria; although the case for a unitary psychosis still has its adherents even with psychotic illness (Crow 1986). However, in the remainder of this chapter we will consider to what extent these criteria can be met for the common forms of mental disorder.

## PROBLEMS WITH A CATEGORICAL MODEL

### The existence of points of rarity between categories, and the structure of categories

Aubrey Lewis (1934) wrote that anxiety was a common, and probably integral part of the depressive reaction; and this certainly accords with clinical experience, both among depressives treated by psychiatrists, and in those encountered on community surveys. It is a tribute to the power of the categorical model that so many psychiatrists somehow manage to avoid recognising this fact. Angst and Dobler-Mikola (1985) founds that over one-third of their community cases of both major and minor depression also had anxiety states, and found that the overlap was even greater at the symptom level, or on scales of anxiety and depression administered to the respondents. Angst and his colleagues (1987) calculated how many more times than chance expectancy one would encounter combined syndromes in the community: they found the odds ratio to be 3.5 for anxiety and depression; and to be between 5 and 9 for panic and depression. Prusoff and Klerman (1974) had previously shown that depressed out-patients scored higher on anxiety than did out-patients with anxiety disorders.

Eaton and Ritter (1988) extracted scales for anxiety and depression from the DIS interview used on 2796 respondents at the Baltimore site of the Epidemiological Catchment Area (ECA) study, studied on two occasions one year apart. They were unable to provide any data to support a noso-logical distinction between anxiety and depression: the sociodemographic characteristics of high scorers on each scale were similar; the associations between scale scores and diagnoses of alcohol dependence, drug abuse, schizophrenia and anti-social personality disorder were the same, and so were the relationships between scale scores and various life-events. (In view of arguments to be advanced in Chapter 7, it is of interest that after a relationship ended, depression scores tended to increase more than anxiety scores.) They found that the two scales correlated +0.42 with one another.

In our own work we have consistently found correlations between anxiety and depression that are even higher than this. Factor scores on depression and anxiety from the GHQ, ratings for observed anxiety and observed depression on the Clinical Interview Schedule, and the latent traits for anxiety and depression derived from the Present State Examination, are correlated at levels between +0.65 and +0.75 in patients assessed in primary care settings.

Blazer and his colleagues (1988) have tried a different approach in their analysis of the 2993 ECA respondents in Piedmont, North Carolina. They extracted the 406 respondents from this sample who had at least two depressive symptoms, and used a form of multi-variate analysis called 'Grades of Membership analysis' (GOM) in order to study the natural groups which emerged of patients with particular constellations of symptoms, so that these could then be related to *DSM-III* categorical diagnosis. The GOM analysis of symptoms produced five 'fuzzy' types of patient:

| | | |
|---|---|---|
| 1 | A mild, dysphoric group | 197 |
| 2 | An elderly cognitively impaired group | 83 |
| 3 | A predominantly depressed group | 44 |
| 4 | A group with pre-menstrual symptoms | 39 |
| 5 | A predominantly anxious group | 43 |
| | Total | 406 |

It is of interest that the fifth group emerged despite the fact that in order to be selected for the study subjects had to have at least two depressive symptoms. The *DSM-III* diagnoses of major depression and dysthymic disorder both load on group 3 *and* group 5, while generalised anxiety disorder loads only on group 5. The authors observe that many patients in the community have symptoms near the threshold for these diagnoses, and tend to move randomly between the diagnoses as time passes.

## The existence of discontinuities between categories and normality

There is no hard and fast line between where normality ends and mental disorders begin. The careful longitudinal studies by Angst and his colleagues (1984; 1985) show how common brief episodes of anxiety and depression are among a probability sample of young adults, and how few of those affected seek professional help. The investigators show a continuum both for the severity of symptoms (measured by their number) and for duration of symptoms. If a disorder was required to last a month rather than two weeks, this would therefore clearly have the effect of greatly reducing the reported rates for that condition. When comparisons are being made – either between different places or between different levels in the same place – it is clearly of great importance that the same definitions are used about what constitutes a disorder.

It would be tedious to enumerate the surveys which have shown that symptoms are continuously distributed in populations: rather than attempt to do this, we will observe that we are unaware of a single survey which shows anything else.

Irrespective of whether one is using a categorical or a dimensional model, there are excellent reasons for drawing arbitrary lines for both severity and duration in order to demarcate cases. As we have seen, health professionals like to treat cases, researchers like to compare rates, and administrators like to know what the service is doing, and how much it costs. There are ways of deciding between different ways of defining thresholds so that one produces a grouping of schizophrenics with high genetic loadings; or a way of defining depression so that there are significant drug/placebo differences in outcome; or a way of defining anxiety disorders so that one excludes transient disorders that remit spontaneously – but none of them depend on there being some natural discontinuity in the data.

## The reliability of the categories between diagnostic systems, and between observers

If the categorical systems at present in use were fairly robust, then the group of individuals identified as 'depressed' by one system should roughly correspond to those identified by the other. Of course there would be disagreement at the margins because of different rules for the respective categories, but we should be talking about essentially the same group of people. Unfortunately, we are not.

Surtees and his colleagues (1983), who interviewed 576 Edinburgh women at level 1 using a research instrument that was capable of making diagnoses using either the *DSM-III* system or the *ICD* system, found that of those identified by either system, only 61 per cent are identified by both systems as cases. Agreement was therefore poor about what constituted a case, but it was worse still about individual categories: only 56 per cent of cases of depression, and 16.7 per cent of cases of anxiety, were labelled by both systems in the same way.

Grayson and his colleagues (1990) studied 426 patients at level 2 with new episodes of illness with a research interview capable of making diagnoses on either system: of those thought to be a case by either system only 65 per cent were identified by both; and only 50 per cent of cases of depression, and 25.6 per cent of cases of anxiety, were labelled in the same way by both systems.

Finally, Van den Brink and his colleagues (1990) interviewed 175 psychiatric out-patients (level 4) and found agreement about caseness in 72.8 per cent; of those thought depressed by either system there was agreement on 57.5 per cent, and in those thought anxious there was agreement on 47.5 per cent. The greater degree of severity of disturbance at level 4 probably accounts for the greater degree of agreement relative to the other studies. In order to produce comparable prevalence rates with the two systems the latter investigators found it necessary to lower the criterion for a case to 'ID4' on the PSE, which is lower than the level usually recommended (ID5). The investigators noted that of 37 patients said to be a case by *DSM-III* but a non-case by *ICD*, in 11 cases this was due to restricted coverage of symptomatology by the *ICD* system, and observed that the ICD failed to diagnose 50 per cent of the cases of somatisation disorder.

The reliability between observers using one particular system is acceptable providing that raters are assisted by a standardised research interview, but become rather poor when the systems are used in naturalistic settings at level 3. Jenkins and her colleagues (1985, 1988) invited 27 prominent family doctors to watch videotapes of actual consultations between doctors and patients and rate what they saw using two systems with which they were familiar: the *ICD-9* system and the International Classification of Health Problems in Primary Care (ICHPPC) (WONCA 1979). Agreement coefficients between the raters was very poor using either system (0.1 for *ICD*, 0.3 for ICHPPC), and it appeared that the GPs did not have their own 'common language' for communication. The investigators experimented with their own quadraxial system (Psychological axis; Social axis; Personality axis and Physical axis) and were able to report very much more satisfactory agreements between raters within each 'domain'.

It must be concluded that the two systems agree with one another poorly at level 4, and very poorly indeed at level 1 and level 2. Furthermore, even though the systems used by GPs can be made reliable in standardised settings, as they are used in the field the categories appear to have very little meaning.

### The temporal stability of categories

In an early study using diagnostic returns to the Mental Health Enquiry, Kendell (1974) looked at the records of 2000 people admitted (level 5) in 1964 and then re-admitted before 1969; of those receiving diagnoses of reactive depression, anxiety states, hysteria or personality disorder the proportion receiving similar diagnoses at their next admission varied between 32 per cent and 41 per cent; the corresponding figure for schizophrenia was 75 per cent, and for all forms of depressive illness grouped together 69 per cent. In Eaton and Ritter's study (1988) mentioned earlier, the stability of both anxiety and depression scores with time were disappointing, with regression coefficients of only 0.15 for depression, and 0.29 for anxiety, over a period of one year.

Angst and his colleagues (1990) followed up a cohort of 39 patients who had had anxiety states, and of 58 patients who had had depressions in 1979 and assessed their status seven years later.

It can be seen that the overall outlook for each group is similar, although there is some tendency for movement to be in the direction of depression; however, the numbers are small. In this study the investigators also reported that there was no tendency for the three syndromes shown in Table 4.1 to

*Table 4.1*  7-year follow up of anxious and depressed patients (Angst *et al.* 1990)

| Status in 1979 | STATUS AT FOLLOW–UP | | | |
|---|---|---|---|---|
| | Anxiety only | Anxiety and depression | Depression only | Non-cases |
| Anxiety states | 10% | 31% | 18% | 41% |
| Depressions | 16% | 17% | 28% | 40% |

aggregate in the parents of their patients, and that phobias had little overlap either with panic disorders or with generalised anxiety disorder.

Lee and Murray (1988) followed up 89 level 4 and 5 depressives seen by Kendell eighteen years later, and found that no fewer than 63 per cent had attracted other diagnoses since their initial illness, in contrast to only 4 who had experienced typical histories of recurrent depressive episodes.

Andrews and his colleagues (1990) studied a group of 892 Australian twins from the National Twin Register (level 1) and 165 people seeking help for anxiety-related problems (level 4). They looked at the 'lifetime' prevalence (i.e. experience of all illnesses from birth to the time of the interview) of six common neurotic syndromes: depression, dysthymia, obsessive-compulsive disorder, social phobia, panic/agoraphobia, and generalised anxiety disorder and found that all the syndromes tended to co-occur, and that the rate of co-occurrence did not vary between syndromes. The mean number of diagnoses per person was 1.6, and the number of people receiving single diagnoses was always less than would have been expected by chance. The mean age of those with a single diagnosis was only 35, and of those with two or more diagnoses 39, so that the twins had many risk-years left to live, during which rates of co-occurrence would presumably increase still further.

It must be concluded that stability of categorical diagnosis within the group of common disorders is very low.

## The genetics of the categories

Slater (1943) studied 2000 neurotic soldiers, and concluded that the evidence favoured a generalised predisposition to neurosis, which was responsible for the appearance of various neurotic syndromes under stress. Slater and Slater (1944) then compared neurotic diagnoses among parents and sibs of six groups of neurotics, and showed no tendency for the syndromes to 'breed true'. They concluded that the neurotic constitution was determined by a large number of genes of small effect.

*Twin studies*

Slater (1966) showed that anxiety states showed a higher concordance than other neuroses, while in a later paper Price (1968) showed that in 24 twin pairs in which the proband suffered from a reactive depression, not a single co-twin suffered in the same way. Marks (1986) agrees that twin studies support a genetically determined vulnerability to anxiety, and points out that MZ concordance exceeds DZ concordance for degree of fear of a stranger shown by babies at 22 months, and separation stress and fearfulness by the age of 7.

Torgersen (1983a) has shown modest evidence for a genetic vulnerability factor for panic disorder (MZ 31 per cent versus DZ 0 per cent), but a zero MZ concordance for the *DSM-III* category 'generalised anxiety disorder – (GAD)' (the latter finding may merely indicate that GAD was not well defined in *DSM-III*). In 1985 Torgersen separated 150 twins with mood disorders into three groups using discriminant analysis: anxious, mixed anxiety/depression, and depressed. Only pure anxiety neurosis seems to be influenced by genetic factors, and this finding holds whether clinical diagnosis is used, or a diagnosis derived from the discriminant analysis. Among anxious probands, MZ concordance is higher than DZ concordance both for the anxious group and the mixed group.

Kendler and his colleagues (1987) have carried out an impressive study on the genetics of common disorders using the Australian twin register. Nearly 3800 twins were sent a symptom questionnaire (Foulds' DSSI), and clusters of anxious and depressive symptoms were derived from this. Multi-variate genetic analysis shows that genes act largely in a non-specific way to influence the overall level of psychological symptoms. No evidence could be found for genes affecting symptoms of depression without also strongly influencing anxiety. By contrast, the environment was shown to have specific effects – so that certain features of the environment strongly influence symptoms of anxiety while having little influence on symptoms of depression. The results are replicable across sexes, and show that separable symptom clusters in the general population are largely the result of environmental factors. These findings fit very well with the model set forth in this book.

*Family studies*

Illnesses can run in families for two reasons: either because the illness is genetically determined, or because the illness is somehow transmitted within the culture of the families in some unknown way. As will become clear, most common disorders do in fact tend to run in families. The list of conditions shown to be familial includes obsessive-compulsive disorder, agoraphobia, panic disorder, anxiety states and depressive illnesses.

Marks (1986) points out that anxiety disorders, alcohol dependence and secondary depression are commoner among the relatives of patients with anxiety-related disorders than among controls, and this effect is especially strong for female relatives and first degree relatives. The risk of anxiety disorders is increased to 24–42 per cent if one parent is affected, and to as much as 35–44 per cent if both parents are affected.

McGuffin and his colleagues (1988a, b) showed that the relatives of patients with depression in the Camberwell survey had a higher incidence of depression than non-depressed controls (17.2 per cent vs. 10.9 per cent). The age-corrected risk of hospital treatment for depression, assuming survival until the age of 65, was calculated to be 24.6 per cent for relatives of depressives, to be compared with only 8.9 per cent for controls. However, they also showed that relatives of depressed patients had a higher rate for life events, showing that the tendency to manage one's life in such a way that stressful life events are experienced is also strongly familial (41.8 per cent of depressives' relatives had experienced life events, versus only 7.3 per cent of controls). The highest life-time prevalence for depression is seen among the relatives of patients who have both stressful life events and high social adversity. Since it hardly seems likely that the tendency to experience life events is genetically determined, the evidence points to events within the culture of the family determining both whether it is likely that stressful events are experienced, and whether or not one becomes depressed.

Crowe and his colleagues (1983) provide convincing evidence that panic disorder is familial, by showing that it occurs among 17.3 per cent of relatives of patients with panic disorder, compared with only 1.8 per cent among the relatives of surgical controls. Generalised anxiety disorder was equally common among both groups. Leckman and his colleagues (1983) compared illnesses among the relatives of two groups of patients: those with depression and panic, and those with depression only. Relatives of the former had twice the risk of depression, panic, phobias and alcohol dependence.

## Response of different categories to pharmacological treatment

In an orderly, categorical world it would be a simple matter to demonstrate that patients with anxiety states respond to anxiolytic drugs but not to anti-depressants; while depressed patients respond to anti-depressants but not to anxiolytics. That is, after all, what the names of the drugs imply. However, no survey that has randomised drugs to assorted patients with common mental disorders has been able to show that this is so. Johnstone and her colleagues (1980) gave non-psychotic level 4 patients treatment with two drugs simultaneously. One of these drugs was either diazepam or placebo, and the other either amitriptyline or placebo. The patients had therefore been effectively randomised into four groups, one with both active drugs, two with one active drug and one placebo, and the fourth with double placebos. The only effects better than placebo were obtained by using the sedating anti-depressant, which is effective on both depression and anxiety. Kahn and his colleagues (1986) also showed that diagnoses of anxiety or depression did not provide a sound basis for choice of drug treatment.

Tyrer and his colleagues (1988) randomised 210 non-psychotic level 4 patients to diazepam, dothiepin, placebo, cognitive behaviour therapy or a self-help group. All treatments were for six weeks, and follow-up was for ten weeks. Dothiepin, behaviour therapy and self-help all emerged as better than placebo; only diazepam was worse than placebo. Of those initially given placebo 31 per cent had to be offered active medication. The treatment effects were completely independent of diagnosis, 'thus removing one of the main planks supporting such diagnostic distinctions'.

## Comment

'For the forseeable future', wrote Kendell in 1975, 'clinicians are likely to continue to prefer [categorical models of common illnesses] for historical and practical reasons'. It looks as though times may be about to change. Tyrer (1985) and Andrews and his colleagues (1990) have both marshalled arguments against the categorical model for common illnesses, and we leave readers to make their own judgements about the arguments we have collected in this chapter. It is quite clear that the categorical model provides a poor fit to the data on all six grounds we have considered here, but it remains to consider whether an alternative model would fit the data better, and whether it could be expressed in such a way that it was found useful by working clinicians, as well as by researchers.

# 5 A dimensional model for neurosis

Dimensional models for symptoms are fraught with quite as many problems as categorical models. Using conventional multi-variate statistical techniques, the number and form of the dimensions produced will depend upon the size and nature of the pool of symptoms being used, and the particular population of subjects on which the test is being used. Thus the various scaled symptom inventories all contain different numbers of scales, and scales found in one are not necessarily found in another. Some scales even include test items that are not symptoms at all in the conventional sense: thus the Psychiatric Epidemiology Research Interview (PERI) includes scales which reflect personality traits like rigidity, approval of rule breaking, distrust and low self-esteem (Dohrenwend *et al.* 1980). Even when the same item pool is used with different test populations, the dimensional structure of symptoms may vary between cultures: thus Goldberg and Williams (1988) show that the dimensions of symptomatology measured by the General Health Questionnaire differ between blacks and whites, and between developing and developed countries. Furthermore, even when a particular scale which recognisably measures something clinically important – like depression – can be found in all studies, the items which load on this scale are not identical in different places (Goldberg and Williams 1988: 33).

Difficulties become still greater when multi-variate analysis is applied to patients receiving care for relatively rare disorders like psychotic illness, since such patients represent highly selected sub-samples of the general population, and it is not known to what extent the clinical sample represents even those members of the general population that possess the disorder in question.

Next, most symptoms are not distributed in the population in a normal manner, and the most extreme examples of non-normality occur with relatively rare symptoms. Maxwell (1972) showed that patients with psychotic illnesses characterised by rare symptoms also tended to possess a common core of 'neurotic' symptoms, and this point was confirmed by Sturt (1981) when she observed that 'symptoms that are rarer in the general population are associated with the presence of many other symptoms or with other symptoms present to a severe degree'. Maxwell argued that the symptomatology of common 'neurotic' disorders can be satisfactorily described in terms of several dimensions of psychopathology.

There is no general agreement about the kind of multi-variate analysis which is most appropriate for dimensional modelling; any statistical model represents a simplified picture of reality, and each model has its adherents. The particular form of statistical analysis to be described here has an important advantage over more conventional procedures, in that it assumes that symptoms are dichotomously distributed in populations; thus, you are either hearing voices, or you are not. It does not assume underlying 'sick' and 'well' categories of patient (as for example, cluster analysis or latent class analysis does), and it has been carried out on reasonably large samples of the general population, using only those symptoms that define common mental disorders.

## LATENT TRAIT ANALYSIS

This form of analysis was developed by Rasch (1960) as a way of analysing the attainments of Danish schoolchildren, and has been applied to problems in psychiatric epidemiology by Duncan-Jones and others (1986). The latter authors point out that in latent trait modelling it is assumed that responses to a particular test instrument are all reflections of one or more underlying variables that cannot be observed directly. We can observe symptoms of depression, but we must infer the illness itself, and the latent trait model provides a mathematical picture of the relationship of the symptoms to the illness. This underlying variable is assumed to be normally distributed in the general population, with a mean of zero and a standard deviation of one. It is assumed that any common property possessed by symptoms can be taken to be a measure of the underlying latent trait: the specific or error component of any symptom is assumed to be independent of every other symptom. Neither of these assumptions may be reasonable; for the present we should note that this is what the model assumes.

If we start by considering a set of symptoms which are measuring a single latent trait, then the analysis provides two measures about any particular symptom. The *threshold* of the symptom represents a measure of *severity*, and can be thought of as that point on the underlying illness dimension where 50 per cent of the population will possess that symptom. The *slope* of the symptom represents the *discriminatory power* of the symptom to distinguish between individuals who are close to the level of severity of illness measured by that particular symptom.

A form of latent trait analysis which allows for several dimensions (or latent traits) to be fitted simultaneously was fitted to data derived from interviews by a psychiatrist using the Psychiatric Assessment Schedule with patients attending general practitioners in Manchester (Goldberg *et al*. 1987). At the time the study was carried out, this interview consisted of the short (40-item) version of the Present State Examination, together with 19 additional symptoms which allow diagnoses to be made using the American *DSM-III* system. The analysis was therefore confined to only those symptoms which are used to make diagnoses of common disorders using two of the most widely used systems for categorical diagnosis.

It was found that two dimensions provided a somewhat better fit for the data than a one-dimensional solution, but that three dimensions offered no additional advantages over two. These two dimensions were by no means independent of one another, and in this particular data set were found to correlate with one another +0.70. The analysis therefore provided a two-dimensional space that had been defined by the symptoms themselves, and in which any individual symptom could be located. Many of the symptoms clustered into two reasonably distinct groups, which could easily and meaningfully be associated with anxiety and depression. Two corresponding axes were therefore chosen to define two-dimensional space.

In view of the substantial correlation between the two dimensions, they have been drawn at an angle to one another in Figure 5.1. However, the figure also shows that an equally valid representation of the relationship between symptoms is to conceptualise two dimensions, one which corresponds to illness severity, and another independent axis running from anxiety to depression. This second axis would represent an 'anxiety–depression imbalance'.

The symptoms described in our original paper (Goldberg *et al*. 1987) could be thought of in four groups: first, an anxiety group; second, a depression group; third, a group intermediate between the axes with substantial slopes on the 'severity of illness' dimension; and finally a group which is intermediate and which has rather low slopes, so that its members must be thought of as having little connection with the major axes of mental illness encountered in primary care settings. Items representing the anxiety group and the depression items that lie closely on the depression axis are shown in Table 5.1; we have omitted poor concentration, neglect due to brooding, loss of libido, frequent thoughts of death, poor appetite and depressed mood, since although these symptoms are nearer to the depression axis, they are all well on the 'anxiety side' of

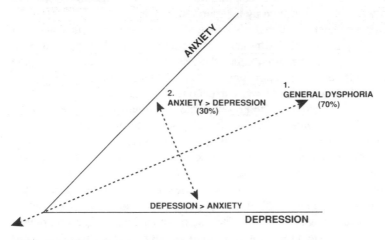

*Figure 5.1*    The two latent traits for anxiety and depression

this axis. The '*severity of illness*' group of symptoms were tiredness and exhaustion; restlessness; ideas of reference and lack of energy. The non-specific symptoms were situational anxiety; anxiety when meeting people; specific phobias; increased appetite and weight gain.

Three points should be made about Table 5.1. First, the symptoms loading on the two dimensions are intuitively reasonable both in terms of their nature and in the order in which they appear. Second, it is inevitable that symptoms which occur infrequently and which are poor indicators of the underlying illness will have low slopes together with high thresholds. Such a combination indicates that the symptom is occurring rarely among people at all levels of the latent trait (symptoms which have a high threshold and a high slope may also occur, and these can be interpreted as more reliable indicators of severe illness).

Finally, it is of interest that the four most severe depressive symptoms are neurovegetative phenomena[1] rather than purely psychological symptoms.

In view of the controversy that has occurred concerning the classification of depression, we carried out a two-dimensional analysis in which we constrained the seven neurovegetative symptoms to lie on one dimension, and the seven psychic symptoms on the other: the goodness of fit was not improved by this procedure, and the two axes were found to correlate +0.94 with one another. Thus, for the common forms of depressive symptoms, it would seem more parsimonious to consider that the two kinds of symptom lie on a single dimension.

*Table 5.1* Latent traits for anxiety and depression; showing the slopes and thresholds for each symptom. On each latent trait, symptoms have been arranged in order of increasing severity. The higher the threshold, the more 'severe' the symptom

| | Threshold (Severity) | Slope (Discriminatory power) |
|---|---|---|
| *Latent trait: anxiety* | | |
| Subjective nervous tension | 0.36 | 4.47 |
| Worrying | 0.38 | 6.06 |
| Irritability | 0.50 | 2.13 |
| Muscular tension | 0.75 | 1.71 |
| Poor sleep | 0.76 | 1.65 |
| Tension pains | 0.85 | 1.71 |
| Free-floating anxiety | 1.01 | 1.54 |
| Health worries | 1.24 | 1.09 |
| Delayed sleep | 1.24 | 1.34 |
| Observed anxiety | 1.88 | 0.98 |
| *Latent trait: depression* | | |
| Anergia | 1.09 | 1.18 |
| Loss of interest | 1.23 | 2.65 |
| Loss of libido | 1.29 | 1.15 |
| Observed depression | 1.32 | 1.96 |
| Self-depreciation | 1.42 | 1.34 |
| Low self-confidence | 1.60 | 1.68 |
| Loss of appetite | 1.67 | 1.07 |
| Hopelessness | 1.74 | 1.50 |
| Subj. inefficient thinking | 1.92 | 1.06 |
| Social withdrawal | 1.93 | 1.05 |
| Weight loss due to poor appetite | 2.43 | 0.76 |
| Early waking | 2.48 | 0.88 |
| Slow, underactive | 3.18 | 0.90 |
| Diurnal variation; worse morning | 5.23 | 0.44 |

These results have been replicated by Wilmink (1989) in a sample of 297 attenders in general practice in Holland. The interview used was the Present State Examination, which means that some of the symptoms in the Manchester study were not available. However, this was compensated for by the fact that some symptoms which had been rare in Manchester and had thus been excluded from the analysis, were sufficiently frequent for inclusion in Holland. Wilmink also found that three dimensions offered no advantages over two, and that the two dimensions represented anxiety and depression, and were correlated +0.61 with one another. It is of interest that 'depressed mood' was, once more, intermediate between the axes, and that 'panic attacks' (which had not been available in the Manchester data-set) were also intermediate between the axes. However, the symptoms which loaded on each axis were not identical in Holland, even though there were broad similarities. The two-dimensional model explained 52 per cent of the total variance in the Manchester data, and 53 per cent in Holland.

In the remainder of the chapter, we will assume a two-dimensional model for common symptoms, while recognising that the precise symptoms that load on each dimension are likely to vary somewhat between different clinical and cultural settings.

## THE DIMENSIONAL MODEL PROPOSED

Most people, by definition, are to be found near the intersection between the two axes. Had we included items that measured well-being (calmness and serenity on the anxiety axis; happiness and contentment on the depression axis), then our two-dimensional space would have been able to assign individuals to positions on the left hand side of the point of intersection of the axes shown in Figure 5.1. However, clinical interviews are concerned with dysfunction on both axes, and are measuring best in the area shown.

Individuals do not have fixed positions in two-dimensional space; they move about it in response to environmental stresses. It is possible to assign diagnostic concepts to positions in two-dimensional space, and these are shown for common diagnoses in Figure 5.2. (from Grayson *et al.* 1987).

In this figure, the further an entry is from the intersection the more 'severe' the disorder: thus while any *DSM-III* case is approximately as severe as a case at the Index of Definition (ID) 4/5 level, one can see that ID5/6 is much more severe, and canted over away from anxiety. The size of the dot represents the discriminatory power of the diagnostic construct at that point in bivariate space: thus Catego's 'retarded depression' is better than, say, the old *DSM-III* concept of 'generalised anxiety disorder'. It can be seen that Catego's 'neurotic depression' and *DSM-III*'s 'major

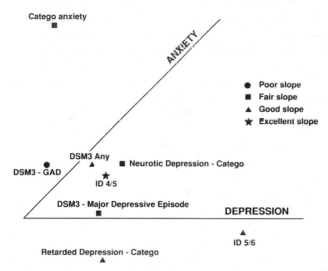

*Figure 5.2* Position of common diagnostic concepts in two-dimensional space

depressive episode' are approximately equivalent concepts, but that the Catego 'anxiety state' is superior to 'generalised anxiety disorder' on three grounds: it is more severe, it loads less on depression, and it discriminates better between subjects. Catego's 'retarded depression' emerges as an interesting construct, since it loads hardly at all on anxiety.

## A dimensional framework for conceptualising social variables

We will be referring to the acquisition of symptoms as *destabilisation*. An individual who occupies a deviant position in symptom-space for less than two weeks will be said to have an 'adjustment disorder', but if symptoms last longer than this, the individual is likely to be recruited to the nearest diagnostic category to that point in two-dimensional space. Those with adjustment disorders have clearly been able to lose symptoms and regain their former position (*restitution*) more quickly than those who receive diagnoses; while those with chronic disorders are those who cannot restitute at all.

It is known that some individuals develop symptoms more readily than others for a given degree of environmental stress. The factors that render some individuals more liable than others to develop symptoms in the face of a given stressor are described by us in Chapter 6, on *vulnerability*. In this chapter we will ask whether vulnerability is best thought of as a unitary concept, or whether there is evidence that different factors account for vulnerability to anxious symptoms on the one hand, and depressive symptoms on the other.

The factors that cause individuals to develop symptoms at particular points in their lives are described by us in Chapter 7 as destabilising factors. Once more, we shall ask whether different factors of the environment are responsible for developing anxious rather than depressive symptoms. For our own data-set, we shall do this by taking each social variable which we have studied, and considering the effect that each variable has in determining the position of individuals in two-dimensional space. We will examine existing literature to find to what extent this supports our findings that different environmental variables determine the development of each kind of symptom.

Next, the factors that determine rate of loss of symptoms are described in Chapter 8 on restitution. We shall ask whether the variables which determine loss of symptoms discriminate between loss of anxious symptoms one the one hand, and depressive symptoms on the other.

## Types of restitution

The possession of symptoms of depression and anxiety is so uncomfortable that people naturally try to lose their symptoms more quickly than they would by just waiting. We can distinguish three main ways of speeding restitution up: we will call these psychological, chemical and neurotic.

*Psychological restitution* is more likely when we are surrounded by friendly, caring people and we are allowed to rest in a secure environment – like at home in bed. We lose symptoms more quickly if we have an *expectation* that we will improve: faith-healers, charlatans and ordinary doctors all make use of hope and the expectation of improvement in hastening symptom loss. In one controlled experiment a family doctor randomised people who had symptoms that could not be accounted for by a definite physical diagnosis to two groups: in one, it was predicted that he would improve in a few days, while in the other no such assurance was offered. Two weeks later, 64 per cent of the former group had lost all their symptoms, to be compared with only 39 per cent of the controls (Thomas 1987).

*Chemical restitution* occurs by self-medication with alcohol, tobacco or recreational drugs, or by the prescription of sedatives or anti-depressants by doctors. The latter tend only to be used when it is clear that other means of restitution have not been effective.

Perhaps the most interesting phenomenon is *neurotic restitution*, since this has given rise to the many categories of mental disorder which we considered in the last chapter. At its most obvious, if a special feature of the environment produces symptoms, one can deal with this by simple avoidance; this is perhaps the most 'normal' of the methods, and is seen in patients with agoraphobia and with specific phobias. Gray (1988) regards such patients as having high anxiety, and dealing with this by behavioural inhibition, which he sees as one of the ways of coping with anxiety.

Other neurotic symptoms have been developed as ways of *reducing anxiety*, and include obsessional symptoms, depersonalisation and hysterical dissociation. Whereas avoidance works (except that it is at a price of opportunities foregone), the other methods are each maladaptive in a particular way, and none of them are successful in producing a state of normality. However, rather than being thought of as different categories of disease, it seems more useful to see them as different mechanisms for trying to remove distressing symptoms.

### Other neurotic syndromes

One of the commonest sorts of psychologically distressed patients seen in primary care and general medical settings is a patient who is complaining of somatic symptoms for which there is either no apparent cause, or where the severity of the somatic symptom is greater than would be expected from any physical disease that is present. Such patients do not consider that they are psychologically ill, but they will describe enough psychological symptoms to justify a diagnosis of mental disorder. These patients have been described as *somatisers*, and they have been shown to constitute the commonest kind of new psychological disorder seen in these settings (see Chapter 2, p. 19; Bridges and Goldberg 1987; Bridges *et al.* 1991). In the latter paper latent trait analysis was used to show that whereas such patients are equally anxious as those psychologically ill patients presenting with psychological symptoms, they are significantly less depressed. It was also shown that they have more negative attitudes to the idea of mental disorder and are less likely to be prepared to disclose psychological information about themselves. One possibility is that somatisation allows those who are unsympathetic to the idea of mental disorder to occupy the sick-role while they are under stress, and the fact that they do not feel responsible for their predicament may account for the fact that they do not blame themselves for being unwell, and are thus able to occupy a position in two-dimensional space that is less depressed than their counterparts who admit the psychological component to their illness.

Another common kind of mildly disordered patient has symptoms that are described as *neurasthenic*, consisting of fatigue, irritability, lack of energy and mild dysphoric symptoms. Viewed in the framework of two-dimensional space, these symptoms represent a mild degree of disorder, since they are all intermediate between the two axes yet have rather low thresholds. Thus, such symptoms could either represent a partial destabilisation, or, more likely, an incomplete restitution of a mixed anxiety/depression.

### The nature of categorical diagnoses

Viewed from a dimensional standpoint, a categorical diagnosis is merely a hypothetical construct, or a way of labelling an individual who has spent more than a specified time in a deviant position in two-dimensional symptom space. In terms of our model, the individual has destabilised, and has been unable to restitute spontaneously. Sometimes the categorical label will just reflect the *general position of that individual* (e.g. 'major depressive episode', 'dysthymic disorder', 'anxiety state' or 'anxious depression') but at other times the label will reflect the *way in which the individual is attempting to reduce their symptoms*, as in 'obsessive-compulsive disorder', 'conversion hysteria' or 'somatisation disorder'.

It is not sensible to ask which of these two models is correct; only what are the uses of each model, and how well do they fit the data? We have seen that there is great overlap between the symptoms of patients in different categories, and use of a dimensional model helps us to understand why this might be so. A dimensional model is also helpful in allowing us to test hypotheses about the way in which social and environmental variables might relate to affective illness, since such models allow us to extract what different categories of patient in fact have in common with one another.

Categorical models are most useful when they suggest particular interventions: so that the label 'depressive illness' may help to attract interventions specific to depression, whereas 'obsessive-compulsive neurosis' may remind the clinician to ensure that a particular individual has been considered for specific psychological and pharmacological interventions which have been shown to help those who are coping with anxiety in this particular way. They are also useful in predicting outcome and long-term prognosis, since particular methods of neurotic restitution like somatisation and obsessive-compulsive disorder may have different outcomes from those with uncomplicated mood disorders.

## BIOLOGICAL SUBSYSTEMS FOR DEPRESSION AND ANXIETY

We have seen that it is plausible to conceptualise the common symptoms of mental disorder as manifestations of two underlying dimensions of symptomatology which are related to one another, and which can be identified as anxiety and depression. It remains to ask what the biological sub-systems might be that correspond to these dimensions. It is worth reminding ourselves about what is known from the study of animal behaviour, since it would be surprising if the biological sub-systems with which we shall be concerned turned out to be unique to humans. It is usual to relate anxiety to threat, and depression to loss: we are therefore dealing with processes of punishment and reward, which have of course been studied intensively by psychologists. We shall first summarise some recent findings about animal models for anxiety and depression, before going on to consider the neurochemical basis for these processes.

### Animal models for anxiety, neurosis and depression

Gray (1982) has defined anxiety as a state produced by exposure to threats of pain, or by stimuli associated with non-reward, or by novel stimuli; *and* which gives rise to behavioural inhibition, increased arousal and increased attention. In simple English, one stops, looks, listens and prepares for vigorous action. The somatic and behavioural accompaniments of high anxiety have been well documented in experimental animals, and can be brought about by threats of electric shock, or by stimuli which are either perceived as unfamiliar and threatening, or are associated with failure. An example of the latter would be an experiment by Pavlov in 1921, in which a dog is given food after being shown a circle, but not when shown an ellipse. After the dog has learned this discrimination, the experimenters then show it ellipses that are progressively more like circles. By the time the two axes of the ellipse are almost equal, the dog can no longer carry out the task, and his behaviour becomes progressively more disrupted. Instead of coming readily to the apparatus as in the past, the animal now shows signs of extreme distress, and both struggles and howls. He is said to have an 'experimental neurosis'. Gray points out that this remarkable effect had been produced without the dog having been subjected to any painful stimuli other than the experience of not having been rewarded. In some quite basic way, it is evident that there is a parallel between the effects of punishment, and that of non-reward. This is a point to which we shall return.

However, most fear responses are acquired through punishment rather than through non-reward. Some animals are quicker than others to become anxious when subjected to painful stimuli, and it is known that this differential vulnerability is genetically determined. It is possible to breed strains of rats which are called 'Emotional' or 'Reactive' rats, and it has been shown by ingenious experiments that these characteristics of general fearfulness are not due either to the intra-uterine environment or the post-natal environment of the rat (for a full account, see Gray 1982: 35–51). It is clear that there are excellent animal models for anxiety; that vulnerability to anxiety is constitutionally determined; and that anxious traits can be conceptualised largely in terms of sensitivity to punishment.

It is less easy to demonstrate a convincing animal model for depression, although Seligman (1975) comes close to having done so. Seligman and his colleagues showed that if dogs were subjected to electric shocks which they could not escape or do anything to avoid, they would later fail to escape shock when in a situation in which escape was possible – although dogs who had not had the earlier experience of helplessness readily learned to avoid such shocks. They termed the failure of the former dogs to escape 'learned helplessness', and also showed that an animal which had prior experience of escapable shock before the inescapable shock was 'immunised', and did not display helplessness when escape became possible at a later stage. This suggests that experience of a successful coping response has long-lasting beneficial effects on an animal's ability to withstand stressful experience.

Interesting as these results are, it would be mistaken to make too much of them. The fact is that experimental animals do not appear to suffer from a disorder which corresponds to human depression, and the animal work modelling depression is very much less robust than that for anxiety. Nor does the human evidence favour the idea that repeated inescapable punishment causes depression – it seems likely that loss of reward is important. It seems certain that humans have greater cognitive elaborations of the basic punishment and reward systems than those inferred in animal studies. However, the relationship between the uncontrollability in the face of noxious stimuli and later helplessness is an illuminating one, and the suggestion that coping mechanisms might prevent helplessness has parallels with work with humans.

## Neurotic personality, anxiety and depression in humans

### The nature of neurotic personality

A neurotic person can be thought of as someone with an increased sensitivity to reinforcing events, whether rewarding or punishing. Thus their emotions tend to be labile and strong, as well as easily aroused — they may be described as moody, irritable or anxious. Results of factor analyses of personality tests can be used to produce two major, uncorrelated, dimensions of 'neurotic/stable' and 'introversion/extraversion'. Whereas introverts tend to be more susceptible to punishment, extraverts are more susceptible to reward. Sensitivity to the effects of reward and punishment are greater for more neurotic individuals. Put another way, stable introverts are insensitive to the loss of reward, while stable extraverts are insensitive to the threat of punishment (see Figure 5.3). Those with common mental disorders such as anxiety-related disorders and reactive depressions tend to be both neurotic and introverted, or 'dysthymic'. Just as in animals, the available evidence suggests that genetic factors have an important part to play in determining the 'reactivity' of the nervous system in the face of aversive stimuli.

*Anxiety as a dimension*

The psychological axis of 'manifest anxiety' can be drawn at 45° to each of the other axes, so that it runs from stable extraversion to neurotic introversion (see Figure 5.3).

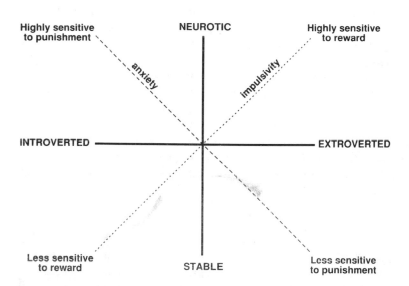

*Figure 5.3* The relationship of Eysenck's dimensions of neuroticism–stability and extraversion–introversion to Gray's dimensions of anxiety and impulsivity (after Gray 1971)

As Gray (1971) has pointed out, those with clinical neuroses are especially sensitive to punishment; so that the 'anxiety axis' runs from cheerful, calm individuals who are relatively insensitive to punishment, to fearful moody individuals who are highly sensitive to it. At right angles, the axis of 'impulsivity' runs from phlegmatic individuals who are relatively insensitive to reward, to histrionic impulsive people who are reward-driven. (In Sjobring's theory of personality, the former axis is called 'validity', and the latter 'solidity' (Hirschfeld and Klerman 1979).)

## The interdependence of depression and anxiety

It has been argued that depression can be regarded as a state induced by loss of important sources of reward, so that one would expect those with highly reactive punishment systems (who are therefore vulnerable to various kinds of anxiety disorder) to be especially vulnerable to loss of reward, since the loss of an accustomed reward – as we saw with Pavlov's dog – has aversive effects mediated by punishment systems. Thus those who tend to be anxious might be expected to be especially vulnerable to loss. The correlation between scales measuring depression and anxiety would therefore be expected.

Reward and punishment processes are in a state of reciprocal inhibition; each inhibits the other. Thus loss of reward is aversive, and chronic aversive stimuli impair sensitivity to rewards. Whichever is released first, the other is therefore likely to occur as a secondary consequence. Loss of a reinforcer (death of a spouse, loss of a lover, retirement from a valued job) may lead to primary depression through loss of reward, but this will lead to secondary anxiety due to a release of punishment systems. (As C.S. Lewis put it in *A Grief Observed*, 'why did no one tell me that grief is so like fear?')

Similarly, an aversive event (being told one has cancer, being mugged, involvement in a severe road accident) leads to primary anxiety through an increased activity of the punishment system, which in turn leads to secondary depression by inhibition of reward systems.

## The neuropharmacology of depression and anxiety

The transmission of nervous impulses in the brain is effected by a wide range of chemical substances, of which three seem to be especially important in understanding the biological underpinnings of common mental disorders related to depression and anxiety. These three substances are referred to as cerebral monoamines, and they comprise the catechol-amines *dopamine* (DA) and *noradrenaline* (NA), and the indole amine *5-hydroxytryptamine* (5HT; or serotonin). The broad functions influenced by monoamines may reflect their roles in general psychological processes such as reward, punishment, attention and memory. They all modulate homeostatic, reproductive and aggressive behaviour – all of which are disrupted in states of anxiety and depression.

Crow (1973) proposed a neurochemical basis for the processes of incentive and reinforcement. 'Incentive' refers to an approach or 'go' mechanism guiding the organism to areas of the environment associated with reward, while 'reinforcers' refer to stimuli which are satisfiers, in that their occurrence following a response increases the probability that that response will occur again. He suggested that 'stimuli which act as incentives do so by activation of the DA approach system, whereas stimuli which are reinforcers activate the NA system, and encourage the organism to repeat the stimulus, or "do it again"'.

### The role of dopamine (DA) and noradrenaline (NA)

It is generally accepted that DA is related to reward systems, but the role of NA is more controversial. There is good evidence that NA is involved in attention and memory, and also evidence that it transmits information about the magnitude of reinforcement (Bradshaw and Szabadi 1989; Morley *et al.* 1987). It seems clear that NA levels first rise with initial stress, but fall if it is prolonged, but the interpretation of these changes is controversial. It has been shown that animals faced with inescapable electric shock in 'helplessness' experiments have depleted stores of central NA. Gray (1982) regards decreased noradrenaline levels as reflecting 'helplessness' associated with anxiety, whereas another view would be that such changes are better thought of as models for depression. It is certainly of interest that both anti-depressant drugs and ECT can be shown to alleviate helplessness in dogs, and this would give some support to the idea that helplessness is an analogue for depression.

When an animal undergoes acute threat there is an increase in both NA and 5HT release that are related both to increased arousal and to symptoms of anxiety. The NA neurons are thought to mediate increased arousal and attention to significant stimuli, as well as influencing defensive and aggressive behaviour.

If stress is continued over a long period there is eventually a decrease in central NA levels, which in animal studies have been found to be associated with exhaustion and helplessness. Helplessness and hopelessness can be identified with insensitivity to reinforcers and incentives, and there is some evidence that NA permits or amplifies DA effects; so that decreased NA leads to decreased DA, which in turn leads to decreased incentive, or hopelessness.

*The role of serotonin (5HT)*

The functions of the third monoamine, 5HT, are more complex. There are two main groups of 5HT receptor, and they each appear to have different functions. $5HT_2$ receptors are widely distributed parallel to the distribution of DA receptors, whereas $5HT_1$ receptors are mainly localised in the hippocampus – a part of the brain thought to be concerned with memory and learning, and also possibly anxiety and punishment systems (Gray 1988).

Deakin (1989, 1990) has argued that 5HT neurons are concerned with *adaptive responses to aversive stimuli*. The acute adaptive response to an aversive stimulus is anxiety or fear, which is adaptive because it inhibits ongoing behaviour and guides the organism away from danger. Where DA is concerned with approach to positive incentives, $5HT_2$ receptors mediate avoidance of negative incentive, or fear stimuli. An enhanced state of $5HT_2$ receptor function may occur either because of endogenous vulnerability producing a super-sensitive $5HT_2$ system, or *because psychosocial stressors* act as negative incentives or fear stimuli and so activate $5HT_2$ systems. Sensitivity of these receptors is decreased by taking anti-depressant drugs, which may explain the anxiety-reducing properties of these drugs.

$5HT_1$ receptors, on the other hand, are thought to be involved in the *longer term adaptive responses to aversive stimulation*. If short-term anxiety responses fail to terminate aversive stimulation, these receptors would be related to *resilience*. Failure of the system results in 'learned helplessness' in animals, or depression in humans, but enhancing transmission through such synapses reverses symptoms of depression and restores resilience. One way that the $5HT_1$ resilience system may break down is if the aversive situation is extreme and prolonged, as this may involve the direct inhibitory influence of $5HT_2$ function on $5HT_1$ neurotransmission, which has been described in a number of biochemical and behavioural experiments. Anti-depressant drugs reverse this imbalance by decreasing $5HT_2$ receptor numbers and by increasing function in $5HT_1$ receptor systems.

According to Deakin's theory, depression can be related either to a deficiency of catecholamines (DA and NA) – and thus an insensitivity to rewards – or as a secondary consequence of overactivity of $5HT_2$ aversion systems leading to a relative underactivity of the DA and NA reward systems. Depression will be related to anxiety because reward and punishment processes are necessarily reciprocally related.

We have therefore described a preliminary framework for the somatic basis of the major dimensions of symptomatology: we shall return to the way in which life stress affects our biological functioning in Chapter 9, on 'Mind and body'.

## NOTE

1   A neurovegetative symptom of depression refers to a disturbance of bodily function known to be associated with depressive illness, like early waking, weight loss and diurnal variation of mood.

# 6 Vulnerability and resilience

People vary in their ability to remain well in the face of environmental stressors. Some individuals develop psychological disorders after little or no discernible environmental stress, whereas others appear able to remain well despite exposure to multiple and severe stressors. Before we turn our attention (in Chapter 7) to the nature of events in the environment which release episodes of disorder, we shall consider what is known about the factors which render one person extremely vulnerable, and another relatively resilient in the face of life stress.

## GENERAL OR SPECIFIC VULNERABILITY

Kleinman (1988) has said that depression and anxiety disorders are 'non-specific forms of bodily distress' and need not be distinguished from one another when, after all, they 'share the same social origins'. He argues that

> demoralisation and despair owing to severe family, work, or economic problems trigger syndromes of distress that have biological as well as social correlates. These correlates are often labelled psychiatric disorder, but they have been reconceived by social scientists as the psychobiological sequelae of social pathology and human misery generally.
>
> (Kleinman 1988)

In this view, social factors are seen as global factors which both make disorder more likely, and indeed are the true causes of disorder, and although he allows that 'genetic predisposition and neurobiological vulnerability convert the experiential effect of social pressure here into depressive disorder, there into panic disorder', he claims that what we are dealing with is simply social distress.

If he is correct, then the same social factors which make one kind of disorder will also make other types of disorder more likely as well. Given the correlation between anxiety and depression which has been described in the previous chapter, even if there are separate vulnerability factors, it may prove difficult to disentangle them. In this chapter, we will start with possible genetic factors which may render individuals more vulnerable to disorder, and then move through the life cycle considering other possible vulnerability factors. For each possible factor, we will consider whether or not there is evidence for vulnerability for a specific form of psychological disorder.

## GENETIC CAUSES OF VULNERABILITY

Although there is good evidence for genetic factors being important for severe forms of depression like manic-depressive illness, for the common forms of depressive illness it is difficult to show that genes have anything more than a non-specific effect in making disorder more likely. There is very good evidence that the common forms of depressive illness tend to run in families (McGuffin *et al.* 1988a,b), but this is by no means the same as showing that it is determined by specific genes. The finding that high rates of stressful life events also run in families focuses attention on the possibility that some families somehow help their members to avoid life events, while others do not.

Kendler and his colleagues (1987), in a study of nearly 4000 Australian twin pairs, showed that there was no evidence for genes affecting depression which did not also affect anxiety. Genetic factors acted in a non-specific way to influence the overall level of psychiatric symptoms, whereas the environment seems to have specific effects, since certain features of the environment strongly influence symptoms of anxiety while having little influence on symptoms of depression.

There is evidence in both rats and humans that emotional reactivity is genetically determined. We saw in the previous chapter that rats can be bred for high or low emotional reactivity. It has been shown by twin studies that by 22 months a human baby's fear of strangers is genetically determined; and by the age of 7 there is a strong genetic component for separation stress, fearfulness and emotionality (Marks 1986). Torgersen (1985) showed that pure anxiety states were genetically determined, although depressive illnesses were not. If one parent is affected the risk of anxiety state rises to between 25 per cent and 40 per cent, whereas if both are affected the risk is as high as 35 per cent to 44 per cent. However, it is possible to define anxiety states in such a way that no constitutional factors can be demonstrated: the original *DSM-III* diagnosis of 'generalised anxiety disorder' could not be shown to be genetically determined, and may have reflected chronic social adversity. Crowe and his colleagues (1983) have shown that panic disorder runs in families, and Torgersen (1986) has shown that genetic factors may indeed be responsible for these symptoms. Where obsessional states are concerned, there is good evidence for raised rates in the families of such patients, but they also have raised rates for other neurotic disorders (Black 1974).

In summary, the available evidence does not favour different genetic factors for determining the two common forms of depression and anxiety states. It seems likely that genetic factors determine a generalised vulnerability towards affective illness, possibly related to one's degree of emotional reactivity, and thus susceptibility to all anxiety-related disorders. It is possible that a susceptibility to symptoms of panic is separately genetically determined, but this remains to be confirmed. However, in our view the available evidence favours an exactly opposite interpretation to that suggested by Kleinman: instead of differing constitutional factors being mediated by social distress as a single variable, we suspect that there is a single genetic vulnerability factor, and that differing syndromes of minor disorder are partly determined by factors learned within the family, and partly by differing environmental factors occurring later in life.

## ENVIRONMENTAL CAUSES OF VULNERABILITY

### Parental separation and death

Studies of parental loss and subsequent illness have produced inconsistent results (Brown and Harris 1978a; Parker 1979; Tennant *et al.* 1980). One possible reason for this inconsistency is that the studies have been conducted on very different populations. Studies involving in-patient and out-patient samples (levels 4 and 5) are least likely to show an association because we know that some of the vulnerability factors for depression in women (loss of mother in childhood) are also associated with a decreased tendency to be seen by a psychiatrist (see, for example, Corney and Williams 1987, on the effects of social adversity on consultation rates).

In community studies positive associations have been found between loss of mother before 17 and depression (Harris *et al.* 1986; Bifulco *et al.* 1987), but these findings have not always been replicated. Tennant and others (1982) found no relationship between childhood separations and adult morbidity in 800 respondents in Camberwell, although between the ages of 5 and 10 separation by parental illness and marital discord was found to be related to depression in adult life. Parental loss before 17 and unemployment were found to be vulnerability factors for depressed men at levels 4 and 5 (Roy 1981), and more common in depression than in other neuroses (Roy 1980).

Parental loss increases risk of psychiatric disorder and delinquency in early adult life (Rutter 1985), but appears to predispose to depression only if it leads to inadequate child care (Birtchnell 1988; Parker 1983; Harris 1988). Harris and her colleagues (1986) show that lack of care defined as neglect rather than simply hostile parental behaviour accounts for a higher rate of depression in later life and that this effect was more frequent after the loss of father rather than mother. Subsequently they showed that it appears to be subsequent lack of care which gives the 'loss of mother' predictive power for depression (Harris *et al.* 1987).

It was not only rejection or abuse that seemed to launch the child onto one of these pathways, but rather more neglect: then she seemed likely to become pregnant before marriage and such a premarital pregnancy was associated with many adversities in adulthood – a greater probability of an 'undependable' spouse who was prone to unemployment, drinking, violence and even criminal activity and with whom an intimate relationship was difficult if not impossible, a lower rate of social mobility out of the working class, and a higher chance of experiencing a provoking agent.

(Harris 1988: 61–62)

The crucial factor seemed to be the quality of care received after the loss – in particular neglect. Adversities in adult life followed from *structural vulnerability* (unemployment, poor housing, etc.) or from *emotional vulnerability* (low self-esteem, inability to confide, etc.). The mechanism by which hopelessness about a specific event leads to depression is that the individual has the tendency to generalise from this specific situation to others – so a general lack of hope develops – a lack of hope in the ability of others to restore sources of value which have been lost and a lack of hope in one's own ability to restore them. This is consistent with Fennell and Campbell's study (1984) in which the factor which distinguished those who had been depressed from those who had not was the tendency to generalise from negative situations.

Maternal death and parental separation and divorce have both been found to be associated with agoraphobia with panic attacks in one of the Epidemiological Catchment Area sites (Tweed *et al.* 1989), and these authors quote three other studies at level 4 which also claim that there is an association between parental divorce and death and anxiety disorders in adult life.

Vulnerability factors linked with common mental illness could be acting through other mechanisms, for instance long-term personality characteristics or early childhood experiences. In Brown's work (Brown and Harris

1978a,b), problems in confiding with a spouse, loss of mother and three children at home were frequently present in the same woman; other predisposing factors could be responsible for this association. In summary, parental loss or deprivation seems only to be pathogenic if it is followed by neglect, and this seems to bring about an increased vulnerability to a range of disorders, rather than to a specific disorder.

## Poor parenting and childrearing

According to Rutter (1985) the risk of emotional and conduct disorders in childhood is mediated by family discord, which has the greatest impact when the quarrelling and hostility involve the child in some way; we know that exposure to hostile behaviour and marital discord is associated with persistent disorder among children (Rutter and Quinton 1984). Tennant and his colleagues (1982) report that marital discord during childhood (between 5 and 10 years) is related to adult depression. Parker (1979) has devised the 'Parental Bonding Instrument' (PBI) to categorise the kind of parental care that adults remember themselves to have had, and has shown that students with neurotic depression remember their mothers as more overprotective and less caring, and their fathers as less caring, than non-depressed students. Gotlib and others report similar findings for puerperal depressives, and show that the abnormal PBI scores stay the same after full remission of symptoms (1988). Birtchnell (1988) has shown that depressed women report poor early relationships with their mothers and report them as less caring and more overprotective than controls using the PBI.

Parker (1983) examined the relevance of 'affectionless control' in the backgrounds of depressed patients and controls. The patients felt that they had been exposed to an 'insufficiency of parental care' and parental overprotection. However, as Parker (1983) and Henderson *et al.* (1981) point out, these findings could be due to the patients' lifelong tendency to have a 'plaintive set' (i.e. to complain; in this case about their parental care) about qualitative aspects of parental care existing before as well as after parental separation. Parker (1983) examined his data for this type of effect and for social desirability and found that the controls exhibited more frequent socially desirable responses; perhaps depressed people no longer experience the need to give socially desirable responses. On the other hand depressed people may actually have a more accurate view of their parental and other relationships because they have lost the 'illusory warm glow' which gives 'normals' a tendency to report an overoptimistic view of their relationships. Abrahams and Whitlock (1969) have shown that hospitalised depressives certainly recall their childhoods as being unsatisfactory or bad, relative to surgical controls.

Some authors favour the view that these parental care characteristics do not on their own predispose individuals to develop depression, but only do so in interaction with provoking agents. When decrements in care are encountered in later life depression may result because 'low care' has acquired cue properties (Becker 1974). If parents disparage a child's worth, such an evaluation will be internalised and depression can be triggered in a vulnerable individual by similar events in adult life (Beck 1967). A long-term (16-year) follow-up study of children from a community sample in Madison, Wisconsin by Mechanic (1980) showed that respondents with depression and anxiety were more likely to come from families in which the mother had been more upset and symptomatic, the child had had more physical symptoms, and attention had been directed to such symptoms by keeping the child at home from school. Mechanic concludes that factors that focus the child's attention on internal states and that teach a pattern of internal monitoring contribute to a distress syndrome in adult life.

Those with severe anxiety disorders also report deviant childhoods. Raskin and his colleagues (1982) have shown that adults with panic disorder have significantly higher rates of disturbed childhood environments than adults with general anxiety and depression. A disturbed environment is defined rather vaguely as being 'grossly deviant from one in which support for the child was consistent and appropriate'. Compared with normal controls patients with agoraphobia and panic have significantly more traumatic events in childhood (58 per cent compared to 16 per cent). They also differ significantly in terms of divorce and separation experiences (Faravelli *et al.* 1985).

Rutter (1985) reports that women reared in institutions are twice as likely to react adversely in a discordant marriage or poor living conditions. Adverse childhood experience makes them more vulnerable to stress; more likely to marry for negative reasons (to escape) and thus marry a man with multiple problems, from a similarly deprived background.

Finally, a community study in New Zealand has presented strongly suggestive evidence that women who have been sexually abused in childhood are more vulnerable to mental disorders in adult life (Romans-Clarkson *et al.* 1988).

In summary, poor parenting and adverse childhood experience do appear to make individuals vulnerable to both anxiety and depressive disorders in adult life, compared to normal controls. There seems to be overlap in the kinds of adverse childhood reported by adults with both groups of disorders, with inadequate care occurring in both groups. However the combination of low care and overprotective parents may favour later depression, whereas parental discord and traumatic events may favour anxiety. On the present evidence there are no clear links between specific experiences and specific disorders.

## Personality

Questionnaires which are designed to measure personality are attempting to assess relatively stable characteristics of an individual in terms of attitudes, habitual ways of behaving and emotional characteristics. They differ in the extent to which each is affected by genetic factors, or represents learned behaviour. Those that have been implicated in vulnerability to common mental disorder range from attributes like 'neuroticism', where there is certainly an important genetic component, to those like 'low self-esteem' which appear to be largely determined by life experiences. The attributes which they measure can therefore be regarded as measuring qualities that have been partly determined by constitutional factors, and partly learned. They are a final common path for genetic factors and the effects of having been brought up in a particular family.

Up to 1982, no studies attempted to relate personality factors to depressive symptoms in community samples (Hirschfeld and Cross 1982), and only a small number examined personality factors in treated populations, where dependency, low self-esteem and obsessionality were found in association with unipolar depression, and obsessionality with bipolar depression (Hirschfeld and Klerman 1979). McKeon and others (1984) in a study of people with abnormal personality characteristics report that, in comparison to controls, they have more life events in the year before the onset of obsessional disorder.

### 'Emotional strength'

'Emotional strength' means that a subject is able to handle stress well and is even-tempered. Those low in this quality are described as being more passive, hypersensitive, over-reactive, self-doubting and emotionally labile. This quality is found in a number of personality scales, including 'neuroticism' on the Maudsley Personality Inventory, and 'Ego-resiliency' on the MMPI. It should be thought of as a quality that overlaps with, but is not identical to, 'neuroticism'.

Hirschfeld and his colleagues (1983) consider various possible relationships between personality and depression, including the possibility that personality features predispose to depression, or that they change as a result of depression. In their study, 31 female recovered depressives were compared with 'normals' and found to be more introverted, submissive, passive, with increased interpersonal dependency but normal emotional strength (ES). Similar results were obtained when they were compared to never ill relatives, however the latter had 'extraordinary emotional strength' compared with population norms. In a later prospective study of relatives of depressives, they measured personality traits associated with affective disorders over a 6-year period, during which 29 of the subjects became ill and 370 did not (Hirschfeld *et al.* 1989). Lower emotional strength and resiliency differentiated the group who became ill from those who were never ill. Over time, the subjects in the 'never ill' group reported increasing emotional strength, while those who became ill did not. Among older subjects, those who became ill also scored highly on 'interpersonal dependency'. The latter qualities reflect a person's desire for emotional support and help from other people, as well as lack of self-confidence in social situations.

Reich and his colleagues (1987) found that people recovered from panic disorder and those recovered from depression both had less emotional strength than controls and significantly more interpersonal dependency. These results seem to suggest that decreased emotional strength is an important risk factor for later depressive illness, but that there is also a strong effect of depressive illness on later measures of personality. Recovered patients in Hirschfeld's study (Hirschfeld *et al.* 1983) had substantially less healthy personality features than relatives of subjects with first onset, who in turn differed little from never ill subjects.

## 'Neuroticism'

A number of studies have examined the extent to which psychiatric disorders occur in people with high neuroticism scores. Long-term vulnerability (measured partly by scores on a brief neuroticism scale) dominated the aetiology of neurosis accounting for about 75 per cent of the variance in a study by Duncan-Jones (1987).

In a study of twins in a community sample Andrews and others (1990) have shown that twins with neurotic depressions do not differ markedly from population norms for depression, but that *among those seeking care* there was a substantial difference, these having higher neuroticism and external locus of control scores. Paykel and others (1976) have also shown that patients seeking care for neurotic depression have high 'n' scores. Wilhelm and Parker (1989) in a prospective study (of students over five years) found that higher dependency and neuroticism scores in women did not lead to depression without interaction with vulnerability factors (such as low social class) or life events.

Although 'n' scores have been shown to be related to mood (Kendell and DiScipio 1968), when Fergusson and his colleagues (1989) controlled for the effects of depression they found that trait neuroticism still related to disorder in a study of 1000 women. Neuroticism has also been found to be related to depression, low self-esteem and high alienation, and to the number of depressive episodes in the past year (Parker 1980). Angst and Clayton (1986) compared the personality profiles of 19 conscripts to the Swiss Army who later developed unipolar depressive illness with those of the total sample of 6284 conscripts who did not develop depression, and found that they had significantly greater scores for autonomic lability (a component of neuroticism) and aggressiveness.

Duncan-Jones and his colleagues (1990) report results of three substantial longitudinal studies that have modelled stability and change in psychiatric symptoms using a longitudinal design. His own Australian study followed 231 subjects on four occasions over one year; a Dutch study followed 246 subjects on three occasions over seven years; while a New Zealand study followed 1053 women on four occasions over three years. Each study measured neuroticism using the Eysenck personality inventory, but measures of psychiatric symptomatology differed between the three studies. Data from all three studies were found to fit a model that assumed that any individual has a stable characteristic level of symptomatology, and to fluctuate about this level as a result of the effect of non-observed environmental events. All three studies found strong correlations (between +0.79 and +0.93) between these stable symptom levels and measures of neuroticism. The investigators conclude that what is called 'neuroticism' is not so much a personality trait as an account of an individual's characteristic level of psychiatric symptoms.

There is therefore good evidence that those who score highly on measures of neuroticism are at greater risk of episodes of common mental disorders, but also people with neurotic personalities tend to seek care more frequently, so that those with higher scores on neuroticism are more likely to pass the filters to care.

*Low self-esteem*

The role of low self-esteem has been given a central place by Brown and his colleagues (Brown and Harris 1978a,b) in the development of depression in women in the community. Harris points out (1988) that each of their four vulnerability factors relates to low self-esteem. Lack of a confidante could be associated with feeling less valued, whether it stemmed from the lack of an approving partner or an inability to confide. Lack of full-time employment and the presence of three children at home constrain women from finding sources of value by experiencing alternative roles.

Those with the loss of mother may not have had 'good-enough parenting', thus lowering their long-term self-esteem.

Ingham and his colleagues (1986) found that among a community sample of Edinburgh women cases of either anxiety or depression had much lower ratings of self-esteem. These workers considered depressive illness to be an important cause of low self-esteem, rather than the other way about. Among non-cases, absence of a confidante and separation from one's parents before the age of 11 were found to be related to low self-esteem. In a prospective community study these workers (1987) found that low self-esteem did not make subsequent episodes of depression more likely, except in those people who had had previous treated episodes of depression. Women who had recovered from illnesses detected at the first interview still had significantly less self-confidence six months later than those who were well throughout. These findings echo Hirschfeld's results (Hirschfeld *et al.* 1983), and suggest that treated episodes of depression are themselves vulnerability factors.

Miller and others (1989) investigated which types of life event are associated with lowered self-esteem, and the additional significance of prior psychiatric consultation in determining onset. Stressors involving impaired relationships with others were the only ones clearly associated with lowered self-esteem. Minor psychiatric illness was predicted by 'stress of uncertain outcome', and, to a lesser extent, by impaired relationship stress. Onset of major depression was best predicted by an interaction between total stress experienced and low self-esteem. There was evidence that such onset involves a pre-existing low level of self-esteem on which life stress impinges, rather than life stress generating low self-esteem and then onset. A small group of subjects characterised by low self-esteem, prior psychiatric consultation and maladaptive coping seemed to be fluctuating in and out of psychiatric illness irrespective of stress.

Alternative candidates for the mediating role between provoking agents and subsequent illness have been proposed, perhaps the main one of which is the role of coping strategies (Pearlin and Schooler 1978; Pearlin *et al.* 1981) which are discussed further below. Wheaton (1983) has proposed an 'external attributional orientation' or 'fatalism' which arises in lower socio-economic groups. Fatalism includes ideas of powerlessness and external locus of control, but does not include concepts like alienation or low self-esteem. It represents a devaluation of coping effort and relative absence of internal coping resources. A similar candidate is Kohn's (1972) 'learned inflexibility' which is a general socialised impairment in coping ability. Wheaton (1983) has been able to show that low fatalism scores and low inflexibility have a positive moderating impact on the effect of stress on symptomatic outcome.

Lewinsohn and his colleagues (1981) have been able to show that depressive thoughts are not antecedents of depressive illness, nor are they necessary consequences of it. A similar study has been reported by Dent and Teasdale (1988) who show that the degree to which women rated themselves in a globally negative way (as 'pathetic' or 'inadequate') when they were depressed, added significantly and independently to the prediction of whether they were still depressed five months later.

## Long-term social adversity

Another factor which may well act as a vulnerability factor is prolonged social adversity. It may predispose the individual to a greater risk of depression and a higher rate of provoking agents. Champion (1990) found an association between lack of intimacy in women and the occurrence of adversity, leading to an increase in the number of life events. Harris (1988) shows that women who lack support have a greater chance of experiencing provoking agents when they also have childhood lack of care. It is not hard to envisage the sort of social circumstances which lend themselves to higher rates of events beyond the control of the individual (nor to the sorts of social policies which result in more people with mental ill health being located in such circumstances). Murphy (1983) suggests there are social class differences in the experience of life events.

The type of housing which women live in is associated with depression (Birtchnell *et al*. 1988). Housing with the highest 'disadvantage scores' – raised walkways – has the highest depression rates. Of women in the raised walkway sample 25 per cent were depressed, and this was twice as many as in tower blocks and six times as many as in brick houses. As the authors say, the various other vulnerabilities of these women may have played a part in their housing location, but the accommodation itself probably played a part in the development and maintenance of their depression. In a study of puerperal depression, previous psychiatric history and housing problems both contributed to the occurrence of depression in the presence and in the absence of life events (Paykel *et al*. 1980). Huxley and others (1987) report an association between housing problems and PSE 'caseness' in a social services sample.

Overcrowding has also been found in association with elevated GHQ scores (Gabe and Williams 1987). Although only 6.6 per cent of the variance in the GHQ score was explained in this study, half of this variance was due to the overcrowding factor, which made an independent contribution.

Murphy (1982) found that major social difficulties predicted the onset of depression in elderly women seen in general practice. The level of neuroticism and adverse social circumstances were the two main vulnerability factors determining the occurrence of life events for women with school-aged children in a six-year longitudinal study conducted in New Zealand (Fergusson and Horwood 1987).

A number of studies, particularly in the USA, have focused on the effect of daily social adversity, which in true North American style is referred to as 'hassles'. Hassles are less dramatic but ongoing problems or strains. Lazarus and DeLongis (1983) found that hassles have a stronger relationship to health outcomes than do life events. They argue that hassles are proximal measures, reflecting the person's immediate experience of the social environment, whereas life events are distal measures which may not carry a common meaning for all persons.

To the extent that hassles are long standing, they are similar to Brown's concept of chronic social difficulties (Brown and Harris 1978a,b) and Pearlin and his colleagues' (1981) concept of role strain. Pearlin and Lieberman (1979) suggest that life events create new role strains or exacerbate existing ones. In Brown's model (Brown and Harris 1978a) life events bring into focus an unfavourable implication of long-standing social problems giving them a stressful new meaning for the individual.

Pearlin and others (1981) agree with Brown and Harris (1978a) in giving major emphasis to the impact of social circumstances on self-esteem as a major mechanism in the production of depression and anxiety, and they also consider 'mastery' to be important. They say that 'persistent role strains can confront people with dogged evidence of their own failures ... under these conditions, people become vulnerable to the loss of self-esteem and the erosion of mastery'.

In summary, there is good evidence that characteristics of the social environment, in particular long-term social adversity, are implicated in the onset of disorder. Harris (1988) calls long-term social adversity such as chronic housing problems or unemployment 'structural vulnerability'. For the most part structural vulnerability exerts an influence when life events occur, and their effect is mediated by lowered self-esteem or a similar mechanism. It is important to note that housing and overcrowding are reported as exerting an independent direct influence in some studies.

## Deficiencies in social support

Henderson and his colleagues (1981) suggest that the lack of social network is an effect and not a cause of neurotic symptoms, because it is only the perceived inadequacy of networks which is related to subsequent neurotic symptoms. Inadequate social relations only predict future morbidity in the presence of social adversity, and may reflect how others have behaved towards the patient. However, the dependent variable in this work is a high

GHQ score. Henderson is predicting not depression but the tendency to have a high GHQ score. Although some of those with high scores will be depressed, others will be anxious, and a substantial proportion will have very transient disorders. All that the patients will have in common is that they have destabilised. In the circumstances it is not unexpected that personality variables play a major part, so that neuroticism and social adversity explain 40 per cent of future variance in GHQ scores of a cohort of patients all of whom have low scores initially.

Henderson and Moran (1983) show that for those becoming symptomatic, there is no difference between them and 'normals' in the availability or adequacy of close or diffuse ties. 'We conclude that when neurotic symptoms arise, there is no evidence that the social network is affected, but rows with close others increase. When neurotic symptoms improve, there is no significant change in social relationships at 4 and 8 months ...'.

There has been a substantial controversy about the extent to which social support is related directly to measures of mental health and the extent to which social support acts to modify the effects of provoking agents (Alloway and Bebbington 1987; Thoits 1983). The studies essentially test the two models described by Williams and others (1981) as the 'additive model' – in which life events and social supports have a direct independent effect on mental health measures (for life events this effect is negative and for social support it is positive) – and the 'interactive model'. In the latter the negative impact of life events on mental health is modified by social supports, and this is the model which is referred to as the 'stress-buffer' or vulnerability model.

Andrews et al. (1978b) found that coping style and social support (in a community sample) have independent relationships with high scores on the General Health Questionnaire (GHQ), rather than a moderating effect between stress and GHQ score. Risks appear 'additive' in that the highest risk lies in those with life event stress, poor support and low coping.

In recent years longitudinal designs have been employed to circumvent the main limitations of cross-sectional studies but some studies continue to confound measures of mental health, life events and social support. Nevertheless, most of the work reported since 1980 reveals that the relationship between social support and disorder is by no means a straightforward one, but takes the form of complex reciprocal interactions.

For instance, Pearlin et al. (1981), in a study of 1106 respondents broadly representative of the population of Chicago, found that while coping and social support measures were unrelated to measures of depression, they did reduce the effect of changes in economic strain since job disruption, and helped to buttress the sense of mastery and self-esteem when changes in economic strain and job disruption are held constant.

Coping does blunt some of the effect of job loss, but social support seems to act by helping job losers to avoid the lowering of positive self-concepts, and by doing this they indirectly rather than directly act to prevent an increase in depression scores over time.

McFarlane *et al.* (1983) in another longitudinal prospective study of 428 subjects from primary care settings in Hamilton, found a reciprocal relationship between social supports and stressful events in that those who suffered from symptoms were more likely to experience stressful events subsequently; the impact of life events was to increase the size but reduce the perceived helpfulness of the social network.

Others have argued that the association between lack of social support and depression is primarily due to respondents' perceptions of the inadequacy of available support rather than any absolute deficiency (Wetherington and Kessler 1986). Henderson (1981) found that reported deficiencies in social relationships explain 30 per cent of the variance of neurotic symptoms. The perception of the relative as being adequate in adversity has the strongest predictive power. Henderson and his colleagues (1981) found patients with high GHQ scores had smaller primary groups but that this had only modest predictive powers and lack of close affectional ties was not associated with high risk.

Another aspect of the reciprocity between social support and depression is the relationship between support and personality. Costello (1982) found that possibly independent events were more closely associated with depression than independent events, and that some of the reasons for this can be found in the subject's own behaviour and personality. One of the consequences of patients' behaviour is that they may have unsupportive social networks. Harris (1988) includes this as one of the possible interpretations of her findings in Islington. She reports that some measures of current unsupportiveness relate prospectively to depression. A confiding relationship relates retrospectively, but 'negative interaction with husband' relates prospectively. Bad marriages rarely turn out to provide unexpected support at the time of crisis, and so negative measures are more stable over time.

Mitchell and Moos (1984) completed a similar study of 233 clinically depressed patients. Positive life events were related to increased family support, while negative events showed no effect. The authors surmise that positive and negative events may be linked in ways that suppress the effects of negative events. Individuals reporting marital separation, legal problems and/or trouble with in-laws are also more likely to report marital reconciliation. Similarly those reporting being fired are more likely to report getting a new job! When positive events were controlled the correlation between negative events and the number of close friends and between negative events and depression both increased. In other words as Brown and colleagues (Brown *et al*. 1988) have suggested, positive events may, in part, be determined by the occurrence of prior negative events, and may be part of the successful resolution of the circumstances engendered by the negative events. It might be productive in future research to retain a distinction between positive events which are brought about partly as a consequence of prior negative events, those which appear 'out of the blue', and those which represent a major new beginning in life ('fresh-start' events as defined by Brown *et al*. 1988).

Positive events may protect an individual's social support network from the impact of negative events. Mitchell and Moos found that, for individuals experiencing few positive events, increases in negative events were associated with decreases in social support, whereas the social support of those experiencing many positive events remained unaffected by negative events. Some events and strains may reduce perceived support because they alter the behaviour of friends and family. For instance, women are less likely to obtain support in dealing with marital problems from those friendships developed through their husbands.

Lin and his colleagues (1985) attempted to see whether, once an event occurs, those receiving help from strong and homophilous social ties had lower rates of depression than those whose help came from people who were unlike the patient. (Individuals are said to be homophilous if they share similar personal and background characteristics.) In general help from closer ties was associated with lower levels of depression, but this result applied only to individuals in stable marriages. For those experiencing marital disruption the social network is disrupted and cannot act in this way. The greater the similarity between the married person's helper in terms of age and to a lesser extent education the fewer the depressive symptoms. For the unmarried the greater the similarity in occupational prestige the lower the level of depression. The actual mechanism by which negative marital interaction operates could be either a cognitive influence on the generalisation of hopelessness, or through a more immediate impact upon self-esteem at the time of the crisis.

Whatever the mechanism involved, Harris (1988) has pointed out that in future one might explore cognitive sets such as hostility, dependency and attitudinal constraints about intimacy. She proposes three relevant hypotheses: more dependent women are more susceptible to depression but also to reporting their relationships as lacking intimacy (a Henderson-type hypothesis); hostile women may alienate their core contacts (a Costello-type hypothesis); women with inhibitions never get round to approaching anyone for support, and the inhibitions make them more likely to suffer onset (a Parker-type hypothesis).

## The Bedford College work

The most sustained and thoughtful contribution to our understanding of the relationship between social support and minor mental illness has been made by George Brown. In a series of theoretically linked pieces of empirical research Brown and his co-workers, most notably Tirril Harris, have attempted to show that severe threatening life events have differential effects upon individuals, in particular women, depending upon the presence or absence of a number of social factors, which have been called 'vulnerability' factors. The main factors for working-class women are a lack of intimacy, death of mother before 11, the presence in the home of three or more children under 14 and unemployment. In replications of Brown and Harris's earlier work (1978a,b) lack of intimacy acted as a vulnerability factor in ten replications (Roy 1978, 1981; Paykel *et al.* 1980; Brown and Prudo 1981; Costello 1982; Martin 1982; Campbell *et al.* 1983; Bebbington *et al.* 1984; Brown and Andrews 1985; Parry and Shapiro 1985; Finlay-Jones (reported in Harris 1988)), and the presence in the home of three children under 14 in three replications (Roy 1978; Brown and Prudo 1981; Campbell *et al.* 1983). Unemployment was not replicated, but loss of mother before 11 was replicated in one study (Roy 1978), and loss of mother before 17 was found to be a vulnerability factor in three studies (Roy 1981; Harris *et al.* 1986; Bifulco *et al.* 1987). Of these studies only one (Roy 1981) found similar factors in relation to depressed men.

The tendency to develop common mental illnesses is a risk through exposure, and is due to a combination of individuals with vulnerability factors (open to attack) encountering risk factors (exposure to mischance – life events). As Harris (1988) points out, people may be open to attack and exposed to mischance because of other factors which predispose both to openness and to the tendency to exposure to events. The recognition that there may be factors which increase the risk of both depression and exposure to provoking agents is now part of the biographical model of Brown and his colleagues (Harris 1988). Other studies provide supporting evidence. McGuffin and others (1988b) examined the relationship between life events and depressive disorder in 83 families ascertained through depressed probands (this is not therefore a community sample, nor is it a sample of level 4 or 5 subjects, it is a study of level 4 or 5 relatives). Comparison with a community sample showed that the first degree relatives of depressed patients had significantly elevated rates both of current depression and recent threatening life events (even when proband related events were removed). This is consistent with Harris's assertions regarding the role of social deprivation and lack of care in childhood leading to an adverse adult lifestyle which in turn leads to a high rate of provoking agents. Similar findings have been reported by Miller *et al.* (1976) who found that lack of support was related to both psychological symptoms and more life events.

It would be wrong to suppose that there is a general consensus about the nature of vulnerability factors and their conceptual separation from provoking agents. Indeed, a good deal of debate has taken place between the proponents and opponents of the Brown model (Tennant and Bebbington 1978; Brown and Harris 1978b) and alternative explanations have been proposed concerning the type of psychological mechanisms at work which do not give such a central role to self-esteem (Kohn 1972: Wheaton 1980, 1983; Norris and Murrel 1984).

Cleary and Kessler (1982) discuss the relevant methodological problems involved in the debate about vulnerability models. They first distinguish between main effects, in which a risk factor has a direct relationship with the dependent variable, in this case depression, and a conditional effect in which the effect of one variable is conditional upon the characteristics of the individual or his environment and an effect is only seen at a particular value of these modifying influences. Many terms are used to describe conditional effects, including vulnerability, modifier and buffer. They point out that problems arise because social science measurements do not have 'true zero' points, producing a situation in which the alteration of the zero point of a scale can produce significant results where none existed previously. Simple changes in the scores obtained by such measures, such as adding a constant, can alter the conditional effects making them significantly positive, significantly negative, or non-existent.

A common solution to this technical problem is to use dichotomous variables, to represent the presence or the absence of, for example, a vulnerability factor. To illustrate their point they examine the data presented by Brown and Harris (1978a), in which they show that women with and without a confidante have low rates of depression (1 per cent and 3 per cent respectively) but that in the presence of a stressful life event the absence of a confidante increases the risk of depression (32 per cent in those without a confidante and 10 per cent in those with a confidante). They say 'this is compelling evidence if one is willing to assume that exposure to life events and access to a supportive relationship can accurately be described as dichotomies'. They show that it is equally possible to argue that events are nothing more than buffers for the relationship between an absence of support and depression, since events are unrelated to depression in the presence of an extremely strong relationship with a confidante (1 per cent) and absence of a confidante increases risk of depression even in the absence of events (10 per cent).

They go on to show that the re-analysis of Brown's work by Tennant and

Bebbington (1978) fails to appreciate that log-linear analysis is a ratio model rather than a linear model, and that the former is based on assessing the relative risk of being depressed in the presence or absence of support, while the latter is based on assessing the absolute level of risk (a point also made in Everitt and Smith 1978). Brown and Harris's (1978a) argument that the difference between rates of depression in women with vulnerability factors and severe life events is substantial is based on the differential probability of being depressed, as shown in the table below.

*Table 6.1*  The relationship between life events and social support in depressed women (after Cleary and Kessler 1982)

|  | Social support | No support |
|---|---|---|
| No life event | 1% | 3% |
| Life event | 10% | 32% |

It can be seen that the difference in probability is only 2 per cent in those without a life event, to be compared with 22 per cent in those with a life event.

The probability ratio, or relative risk of depression is, in contrast, similar at about 3:1 in those with and those without confidantes. Cleary and Kessler (1982) believe that the only way to make a judgement about the correct model to use is to appeal to the theoretical understanding of the nature of the links involved. The problem is that although Brown and Harris's arguments (1978) are the most theoretically convincing, alternative theoretical views are also plausible.

## Protective factors

So far we have considered the way in which social factors can increase vulnerability to common mental disorders. We shall now stand these arguments on their heads and consider factors which decrease vulnerability, or make people resilient in the face of adversity. Factors which protect from episodes of disorder are not necessarily the simple obverse of factors which contribute to vulnerability – there may be entirely other factors which enhance the capacity to resist the effect of provoking agents. Rutter (1985) gives three reasons why the concept of a simple 'buffering' effect of social support could be wrong: first, the range or frequency of relationships does not appear to be as important as the individual's satisfactions with them; second, social support does not always produce a positive effect, with interdependence in particular causing hostility and bitterness over time;

third, a greater amount of social contact can have adverse effects in some social groups, such as single parents where it can contribute to problems with children.

A further difficulty with protective factors is that they may have no discernible effect in the absence of a stressor, making protected individuals indistinguishable from others. Finally, as Rutter points out:

> ... characteristics that serve a protective function need not be pleasant or desirable traits ... thus, people who appear most immune to stress often have a rather 'sociopathic' flavour ... in terms of their self-centredness and shallow, easily changeable relationships.
>
> (Rutter 1985)

We are concerned here not with those factors which enable symptoms to be lost (restitution) but with those factors which might act to protect the otherwise vulnerable individual from episodes of destabilisation or of illness. Rutter (1985) identified some of these in women who transcended the difficulties of being raised in institutions. Such women who made successful marriages turned out to have had some form of good experience at school, in social relationships, athletics or music. Good experiences made it more likely that the woman would exert 'planning', either in her choice of marital partner or work. Experience of success in one field led to feelings of enhanced self-esteem. Notarius and Pellegrini (1984) observed that successful marriages seemed to reduce the level of stressful life events.

Different factors may be protective in relation to different types (or combinations) of adversity. In the case of parental discord for example, an important protective factor appears to be the ability to maintain a good relationship with one spouse. In Rutter's view (1985) 'resilience' is characterised by some sort of action with a definite aim in mind and some sort of coping strategy involving: a sense of self-esteem and self-confidence; an ability to deal with change and adaptation; and a repertoire of social problem-solving approaches. In order to develop resilience, an individual needs experience of secure stable affectionate responses, and experience of success and achievement. He argues that 'the way in which parents themselves deal with life stresses is likely to influence how the children themselves respond to such challenges'.

## SUMMARY

A wide range of factors, from physiological to social adversity, make people more vulnerable to the onset of common mental illness, and this effect is observed most clearly after severe and threatening life events occur. Life events increase the likelihood of an episode of disorder

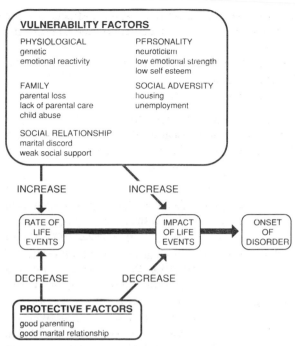

*Figure 6.1*  The relationship of vulnerability factors to one another

occurring, although it should be remembered that some episodes do happen in the absence of events. The volume of work reviewed in this chapter is substantial, and we have attempted to summarise it in Figure 6.1.

Figure 6.1 shows the range of factors which make some people vulnerable to the impact of life events, and some of the factors which make people less vulnerable. There are far more of the former than the latter, and more research is needed into the sort of circumstances which protect people from disorder. The figure also shows that most of the factors which modify the effect of a life event are correlated with the rate of events themselves. The quality of the evidence for this association is variable, but fairly reasonable evidence exists for physiological factors (McGuffin *et al.* 1988a and b), family factors (Rutter 1985; Harris *et al.* 1987), social relationships (Miller *et al.* 1976; Lin and Enscl 1984) and social adversity (Harris 1988; Champion 1990). The evidence that personality factors increase the rate of life events, while intuitively reasonable is reported less frequently (Costello 1982), and with less conviction (McKeon 1984). Protective factors which reduce the impact of life events also appear to be associated with a reduced rate of life events (Notarius and Pellegrini 1984).

# 7   Destabilisation

Destabilisation refers to the process of beginning to experience symptoms, whether or not the individuals concerned eventually reach services, and whether or not the symptoms last long enough to satisfy research criteria for being a 'psychiatric case'. We have seen in the previous chapter that there are certain factors which make individuals vulnerable to the onset of illness which then develops when certain provoking agents occur. Whether or not symptoms begin is determined by the severity of the provoking agent(s) on the one hand, and the degree of vulnerability of a particular individual on the other. We now propose to review the factors which act to bring about an episode of disorder. We shall review two important classes of provoking agent: stressful life events – which have been extensively researched in recent years – and the effects of physical illness, which have been relatively neglected. We will close the chapter by considering the evidence that different social circumstances favour the development of depression on the one hand, or anxiety on the other.

## METHODOLOGICAL PROBLEMS

In any community sample there will be individuals who have had previous episodes of illness. We have seen that previous episodes of depression (treated or untreated) might themselves act as a vulnerability factor. It is possible that the provoking agents for people with previous episodes differ from those which provoke onset in vulnerable individuals without previous onset. There might for instance be a 'repetition effect' in which a similar but less threatening event provokes another onset, something akin to the 'anniversary effect' in suicide and parasuicide. Individuals are sensitised to certain sets of circumstances which produced the original episode. A variant of this type of effect is the *additive model*, in which destabilisation occurs not in relation to a single event, but occurs only when a number have accumulated. It may be that each of these provoking agents is related in some way, or that the events arise out of a long-standing social problem. Brown and Harris (1989) have shown that events leading to onset in their community samples are often related to similar long-term social difficulties in the working-class woman's background. For middle-class women provoking events do not arise in the context of ongoing difficulties and it is therefore easier for them to draw upon personal and social assets in a way that is impossible when a long-standing difficulty is present. Thus they may either not destabilise at all, or restitute spontaneously.

A second consideration is that specific types of provoking agent may lead to specific forms of disorder. Evidence will be presented that certain types of events are more likely to be associated with illnesses which have primarily depressive symptomatology, while others are associated primarily with symptoms of anxiety. There might be a *specific effect* with loss events leading to depression and threat events leading to anxiety.

There may also be a *matching effect* in which early events which make someone vulnerable are matched by similar events which eventually produce destabilisation. There may be a *weakening effect* in which some forms of support are temporarily unavailable or removed, or in which physical debility reduces resistance to the provoking agent. A final consideration is the degree to which a relationship exists between a complex set of social factors and specific forms of disorder.

In the individual case, the exact sequence of events in the development of symptoms of anxiety and depression may arise through complex combinations of events and reactions to them. Anxiety may arise first in the context of a threat of loss, and then depressive symptoms are predominant when the loss occurs. Anxiety may arise again as the changes, challenges and opportunities occasioned by the loss have to be addressed, and depression may arise again in so far as the person becomes hopeless in the face of continued failure to meet these challenges and adjust to the changes required by the loss or by the crisis in their lives.

## THE ROLE OF LIFE EVENTS

In an interesting study of patients at levels 4 and 5, Dolan and others (1985) show that episodes of illness are more severe after severe life events. For first episode depressions the frequency of life events was 62 per cent, but in those having a second episode the rate was 29 per cent. This supports the assertion that an episode of depression becomes a vulnerability factor for some people. (It should be noted that no such difference has been observed in schizophrenia – Birley and Brown 1970.) Dolan and others say that their findings may indicate that 'social factors are more important in the onset of depression, but that once a patient has developed depression, other factors assume greater importance'. Patients with severe life events had higher urinary cortisols than those without (p<.05). 'A stress hypothesis might suggest that in some patients these changes are adaptive responses to environmental stressors, rather than manifestations of purely internal biological processes.'

Brown has consistently argued that the individual meaning of an event is of central importance; on occasion the rigorous definition of severe events has precluded consideration of some lesser but equally meaningful event as important (Brown and Harris 1978a,b). It is also the case that a severe event can be the source of both stress and support at the same time. Threatening events which have negative consequences can also have positive ones, and even long-standing social difficulties can have their redeeming features: 'even a strained marriage can provide stability, economic security and a sense of identity' (Lennon 1989).

The effect of life events may be more dramatic in neurotic rather than other types of depression. Bebbington *et al.* (1988) show that both severe and non-severe life events are more frequent in the month before onset in both types of depression. For males and females there were no differences in the rates of events for neurotic depressions but far more women had events before endogenous depressions – 66.7 per cent compared with 26.7 per cent for males, and women had higher rates of events than men. Half of the cases in a community sample (Tennant *et al.* 1981a) contacted one month later had recovered within the month.

Finlay-Jones (1988) reports that, with one exception, studies have reported that the number and type of life events experienced by those suffering from endogenous and neurotic depression do not differ. Roy (1987) compared 300 non-endogenous depressives and 46 endogenous depressives seen by the mental health service (levels 4 and 5) with similar numbers of non-depressed controls. In the non-endogenous group there were significant control/index differences on each of the items: unemployment, poor marriage in the previous year, a first degree relative treated for depression, separation from parent for more than one year before the age of 17, and three or more children at home. However, for the endogenous group the first degree relative treated for depression and the poor marriage were the only significant differences. These results indicate that social variables may have a greater role to play in causing neurotic depression than in the more severe variety of the illness, where genetic factors are undoubtedly more important. It should be noted that this was not a community study, and this may account for the discrepant results.

Costello (1982), in a partial replication of Brown (Brown and Harris 1978a), found that lack of intimacy and life events and difficulties are associated with depression, but that social class and children at home, loss of mother and unemployment were not. Those suffering from depression are likely to suffer life events and other social circumstances for which they have every reason to believe that they are partly to blame. Similar results were found by Campbell and others (1983).

### Special groups

In children the rate of disorder is increased three to six times in the presence of life events, and multiple events are likely to produce a quicker onset of disorder. Life events are thought to be additive (Goodyer *et al.* 1987).

Working-class depressed elderly people had a higher incidence of depression due to poorer health and greater social difficulties (Murphy 1982). Those without a confidante were more vulnerable. The lack of a confidante reflects life-long personality traits. Severe life events, major social difficulties and poor physical health predict onset of depression. This study suggests the existence of 'weakening' circumstances which reduce resistance to the effect of events. Poor physical health may be one of the major 'weakening' factors.

## SPECIFIC EVENTS CAUSING SPECIFIC ILLNESSES

At its most general, the specificity hypothesis relates anxious symptoms to threat and danger, and depressive symptoms to loss. Uhlenhuth and Paykel (1973) found that losses which were beyond control were as frequent in those suffering anxiety as in those suffering depression, but that the anxious people had twice as many events involving a severe threat. Barrett (1979) reported that anxiety sufferers had experienced fewer exit events, fewer undesirable events and fewer uncontrollable personal disruptions than people suffering depression.

Finlay-Jones and Brown (1981) showed that severe danger events were more common before anxiety disorders, loss events before depressive

*Table 7.1* Percentage in each row that had experienced a life event in the previous 12 months (after Finlay-Jones and Brown 1981)

|  | *1 + Loss* | *Both* | *1 + Danger* |
|---|---|---|---|
| Depression n = 17 | 65 | 35 | 47 |
| Anxiety and depression n = 15 | 80 | 60 | 73 |
| Anxiety n = 13 | 15 | 8 | 77 |
| Non-cases n = 119 | 10 | 2 | 12 |

illnesses, and a combination of both types of event before cases of mixed anxiety–depression. Harris and Brown (1989) argue that a specific relationship between types of events and difficulties and types of symptom pattern 'is intuitively as easily acceptable [in respect of anxiety symptoms] as with depression, possibly because anxiety disorders constitute, as it were, the other wing of affective disorder, and are thus found frequently enough to be easily studied'.

Cooke and Hole (1983) use the concept of *population attributable risk* to argue that 32 per cent of male cases and 41 per cent of female cases are due to life events. They confirm the relationship between loss and danger and anxiety and depression suggested by Finlay-Jones and Brown (1981).

*Table 7.2*  The relationship between loss and depression, and danger and anxiety (after Cook and Hole 1983)

|            | Loss | Danger |
|------------|------|--------|
| Anxiety    | 5    | 72     |
| Depression | 58   | 37     |

Miller and Ingham (1983, 1985) classify events into six types: loss events, threat events, anti-social events, hopeless events, events involving choice of action and uncertain outcome. They placed backache, tiredness, anxiety and depression in an ascending hierarchy and showed that the higher up illness is associated with more severe events. Anxiety is associated with a threat event plus any two of the others, whereas tiredness is associated with combinations of either choice, uncertainty and hopelessness, or choice and hopelessness, or uncertainty and hopelessness.


## Matching events

So far we have seen that there is some suggestion that specific events are associated with the development of specific disorders. Brown and Harris (1989) have examined the nature of the relationship between onset of depression and the type of event experienced. Women with events which *matched* an area of their lives in which they had made a commitment and which therefore in some way was frustrated by the occurrence of the event were three times more likely to develop depression than those who did not have an event which matched a commitment.

In Brown and his colleagues' (1987) study of 400 women, 20 per cent with long-term severe threatening life events develop 'onset' depression. In those in whom the event 'matches' a prior difficulty then 46 per cent of women develop onset, and if it matches a prior commitment then the rate is

40 per cent. If negative evaluation of self is taken together with these two types of matching event rates of 63 per cent to 100 per cent onsets were found. They examined the nature of the link between events occurring in the context of similar ongoing *difficulties* (*D-events*). The presence of matching D-events was related to a three-fold greater risk of depression. Of women who experienced D-events 38 per cent responded with profound hopelessness, compared with only 9 per cent of those with other sorts of events. This type of matching may represent an 'additive' or cumulative effect. Similarly *R-events* were observed, relating to *role conflict*, and because of the overlap between D and R events a combined category of D/R-events was created. The concept of *D- and R-events* has a lot in common with Pearlin and colleagues' concept of role strains (1981) and Lazarus and DeLongis's (1983) view of 'hassles' in the immediate social environment.

The negativity of core relationships (negative interaction with children and husband together with 'security-diminishing characteristics of housewife role'), plus 'inner states' (low self-esteem or chronic sub-clinical symptoms) predicted onset. This combination (of negative core relationships and 'discomfiture') is called the *conjoint index*. D/R-events did not contribute much on their own to the raised risk of depression. The conjoint index acted as a vulnerability factor, and in association with D/R-events (with which the conjoint index was directly associated) produced onset. In other women experiencing severe events other than D/R-events, the conjoint index also produced onset. Inadequate support mediates the vulnerability and event-production effects of the conjoint index. The conjoint index predicted reasonably well those who were let down. Seventy-five per cent of onsets occurred in the 25 per cent of the whole sample who were positive on the conjoint index.

Brown finds that inadequate parenting is not associated with D/R-events 'unless there was also the relevant life-producing structure represented by the Conjoint Index. This, of course, suggests the current environment provides the vital intervening link between inadequate parenting and depression.' He also recognises (1991) that ongoing difficulties are often the source of severe events, and that they undoubtedly tend to generate events throughout their course. Two-thirds of depressive conditions in Islington were preceded by a severe event and three-quarters by a severe event or major difficulty.

A personality factor may be involved since women with inadequate parental care were more likely than others to turn to unsuitable or inappropriate others for support once a crisis had occurred (Andrews and Brown 1988). Those who did so tended to romanticise close relationships and to deny incipient problems.

'Borderline' depressive conditions (as defined by Brown and Harris 1978a) are also provoked in the same way, but often in the absence of vulnerability factors. In the Islington study there was only a small difference in the onset of a borderline condition in women who were positive on the conjoint index (5 cases out of 50; 10 per cent) and those who were not (12 cases out of 80; 15 per cent). Brown (1991) suggests that the most probable explanation is that 'women who are well-supported are not protected from depression altogether but are more likely to develop a borderline case than a case disorder in response to a major loss or disappointment'. We will return to this point when we consider restitution.

## THE EFFECTS OF PHYSICAL ILLNESS

We have seen in Chapter 2 that the level of mental illness is high among patients in primary care settings; among medical and surgical in-patients surveys using research interviews linked with operational criteria for mental illness yield rates between one-quarter and one-third of all patients (Goldberg 1989). It is also true that medical conditions are frequently found in psychiatric in-patient (Morris *et al.* 1983) and out-patient populations (Hoffman and Koran 1984).

It is possible to use community surveys to compute a *relative risk* of psychological disorder in the presence of physical ill-health: Weyerer (1990) summarises ten recent surveys, and shows that psychological illness is between 1.5 and 3 times more likely when physical ill health is present. These findings apply to both children and adults, and to both sexes. In a community study in rural Spain where physical morbidity was assessed by the family doctors, and mental disorders by a research psychiatrist, the association between physical illness and psychological morbidity was shown to be at its strongest among the illiterate and the socially isolated (Vazquez-Barquero *et al.* 1981). Wells and others (1988) have considered the risk of common mental disorder in a large community sample in those with chronic physical disease by bodily system: they show that whereas high blood pressure and diabetes are associated with rates only just higher than chance, that heart disease and neurological disorders are associated with very high rates, and disorders like arthritis and cancer are intermediate between them.

There are several possible mechanisms at work when physical and mental illness are found in the same person. Schulberg *et al.* (1987a,b) report that there are continuing ambiguities in the literature about the nature and the extent of the association. It is possible that there are causal associations, or a joint vulnerability mechanism, or processes whereby emotional problems are manifested through somatic symptoms (Kessler *et al.* 1983). Disentangling cause from effect is particularly difficult, even in longitudinal studies.

Aneshensel and her colleagues (1984) suggest that 'findings to date may reflect operational confounding in the two distinct domains of depressive and organic morbidity. Positive associations may be spurious if both domains share a common aetiology.' They assessed a community sample of 744 people four times in one year in an attempt to sort out the direction of the relationship between physical illness and depression. They used a 'latent variable causal model' to separate error-free unobserved variables from the error present in each of the observed variables. They constructed a *depression factor* from scores on four self-report scales dealing with well-being, depression, hopelessness and thoughts of death; and a *physical illness factor* from the number of disability days, and the number of episodes of physical illness in the previous two weeks. They concluded that physical illness has a large immediate effect in increasing depressive symptomatology over previous levels, and depression has a smaller '4 month lagged effect' of increasing levels of physical illness. The authors considered that the conjunction between physical morbidity and depression was self-perpetuating and mutually reinforcing, using both biological and social mechanisms.

### Physical illness causing psychological disorder

There are five distinct ways in which physical disorder can cause psychological ill-health. First, the patient may be distressed because of the implications of their physical symptoms. This can be a new and disturbing symptom – a woman may have felt a lump in her breast, or a smoker may have coughed up some blood – or the patient may be depressed because of the serious nature of an established disease – perhaps a malignant tumour, or a severe progressive disease.

Second, the psychological symptoms may be a direct consequence of the physical disease process – as in several neurological diseases; or it may be related to hormonal disturbances, as in thyroid disease, Cushing's disease, and depressive illnesses following childbirth. Some infective illnesses are also often followed by depressive illnesses and states of fatigue, like glandular fever, infectious hepatitis, brucellosis and influenza. Here the chain of causation is more complex, and there is good evidence that personality factors are also important in determining who is likely to develop such disorders, and how quickly they remit.

Third, multiple physical diseases may be associated with multiple pains. Dworkin and others (1990) have shown that patients with a single acute pain do not have an increased relative risk of depression, but those with severe and persistent pains have more than twice the risk, and those with multiple pains have a greatly increased risks of depression.

Fourth, are depressive illnesses that are directly caused by medical treatment of physical diseases – these may be hormones like steroids, drugs to prevent epilepsy like phenobarbitone, several of the drugs used to treat high blood pressure, among others.

Finally, chronic physical disease is often associated with marked disability, and loss of mobility may make it more difficult to contact relatives, or to engage in previously pleasurable activities. When disability is compounded by poverty, social circumstances get progressively worse, and the expectancy of states of anxiety and depression correspondingly higher.

While only a small minority of new cases of mental disorder (about 4 per cent) are secondary to physical disease in primary care settings, about half of all cases of mental disorder seen on the medical wards are in this category (see Goldberg 1989), and a large proportion of those with established chronic mental disorders seen in general medical settings will be found to have a combination of chronic physical disease and social disadvantage: we shall therefore return to physical ill-health as a cause of delayed restitution.

There is evidence that 'familial' factors are less important when depression follows episodes of physical illness. Pollitt (1972) considered 142 new cases of depression seen in a general hospital, and divided his sample into 67 patients whose illness followed a physical illness and 77 patients whose illness did not. He measured the risk of depression in first degree relatives, and found that in those depressive illnesses immediately following physical illness the incidence of depression in first degree relatives was very much lower than in those whose depression was not related to physical illness. In the latter group, the rate in first degree relatives was lower if the depression followed hard upon the heels of a stressful life event. Thus 'familial' factors are least important when there is either a clear life event, or when depression follows a physical illness.

Murphy (1982) compared 200 elderly depressives with 200 controls, and found that working-class subjects had a higher incidence of depression due to poorer physical health and greater social difficulties. In general, severe life events, major social difficulties and poor physical health predict the onset of depression in the elderly.

Winokur and his colleagues (1988) studied 401 patients with depressions secondary to medical illnesses, and those where the depression was secondary to a psychiatric illness (substance abuse disorders or somatoform, anxiety, or personality disorders). They found that the former patients had less alcoholism in their families, a later age of onset, were less likely to have suicidal thoughts or actions, but more likely to have memory disorders and to be improved by treatment. The latter point is disputed by Popkin and others (1985), who found that depressions associated with physical illness respond poorly to treatment.

## Psychological disorder followed by physical disorder

There are also studies which indicate that psychological disorder may be followed by an onset of physical disease. An early study by Schmale and Iker (1966) examined women with cervical smears and found that those reporting depressive symptoms were more likely to be shown subsequently to have malignant disease. Davies and his colleagues (1986) confirmed that women with high depression scores were more likely to have malignant tumours at subsequent investigation. Haines and his colleagues (1987) have shown that phobic anxiety measured on the Crown–Crisp experiential index is an antecedent of myocardial infarction.

A number of studies have related stressful life events to the onset of various physical diseases, sometimes invoking a mood disturbance as an intervening variable. Murphy and Brown (1980) studied 81 women with a recent onset of physical disease causing admission to hospital. Among those below the age of 55, severe life events were commoner before the onset, and these in turn were followed by an episode of affective disturbance which antedated the onset of the physical disease. Specific physical diseases that have been investigated in this way include rheumatoid arthritis (Baker and Brewerton 1981) and multiple sclerosis (Grant *et al.* 1989).

Craig and Brown (1984) show that while functional gastrointestinal disorders (dyspepsia, irritable bowel syndrome, etc.) resembled cases of depression in having high rates of severe life events and major social difficulties, those with a variety of proven organic gastrointestinal disorders (ulcers, pancreatitis, ulcerative colitis, etc,) had a high rate of events which obstructed the goals and ambitions of the subject, and which were referred to as 'goal frustration'.

## SOCIAL CIRCUMSTANCES AS DETERMINANTS OF SPECIFIC DISORDERS

The possibility that specific types of social difficulties are related to specific types of disorder has been referred to as 'the specificity hypothesis' (Harris and Brown 1989). Much of Brown's work referred to above links circumstances associated with loss to depression and circumstances associated with danger to anxiety, and Miller and Ingham's (1985) findings can be interpreted in the same way.

The relationships described earlier in the chapter are summarised in Table 7.3, with possible intervening variables included. The evidence for the second row – 'less severe events of uncertain outcome' is sketchy, and it should be emphasised that mixed states of anxiety/depression may occur because social factors often do not group themselves together in simple ways.

*Table 7.3*   Possible relationships between types of event and types of symptoms. (Mixed states may also occur because of combinations of social circumstances)

| Types of life event | Possible intervening mechanisms | Predominant symptoms |
|---|---|---|
| THREAT | stress emotional reactivity | ANXIETY |
| LESS SEVERE EVENTS OF UNCERTAIN OUTCOME | poor coping ability | MIXED |
| MATCHED (with chronic social difficulties) | negative self-evaluation | DEPRESSION |
| LOSS | poor support generalised hopelessness | DEPRESSION |

Goldberg and his colleagues (1990) considered a wide range of social variables as possible determinants of the scores that each patient had on anxiety and depression scales that had been derived from latent trait analysis. Each patient was measured with the Social Interview Schedule (Clare and Cairns 1978), the Social Stress and Support Schedule (Jenkins *et al.* 1981), certain personality scales and ratings made both by the GP and the research psychiatrist making the clinical assessment of the patient. It emerged that the social co-variates of depressive symptoms were completely distinct from those of anxiety. Depression was predicted by high levels of trait anxiety, lack of support from confidante or other family members, and dissatisfaction with interaction with relatives; whereas anxiety was predicted by an assessment by the psychiatrist that the patients presenting complaints were entirely psychological, or that there were a mixture of organic and psychological factors at work. Higher levels of anxiety were seen among those who had had their symptoms for a long time, or were experiencing stress at work or in their social life.

The possibility that there are specific links between types of social circumstances and the development of specific disorders is, therefore, a very real one, and one which demands the attention of social science research workers. We understand more about the relationship between life events and social difficulties and the development of depression than we do about the circumstances which lead to anxiety rather than depression, and so attention could usefully be addressed to the pattern of relationships which exist between social circumstances which embody 'danger' and the subsequent development of anxiety. It would also be of interest to study groups of patients who had been subjected to a uniform threat (for example: held as hostages; or told that they had cancer) to elucidate the social characteristics and coping mechanisms of those who did, and those who did not, experience symptoms of anxiety.

# 8 Restitution

Restitution refers to the process of losing symptoms. The factors that determine restitution are therefore concerned with the duration of symptoms and the process of recovery. It might be thought that the same processes that determine acquisition of symptoms (destabilisation) also determine how long they last. Thus those with more vulnerable personalities, and with more severe environmental stressors, would be both more likely to destabilise and slower to restitute. There is undoubtedly some overlap between the two processes, but a recent study indicates that rather different social factors determine the duration of episode from those that determined initial acquisition of symptoms (Goldberg *et al.* 1990).

In this chapter we will first of all describe factors which are associated with very short-term episodes of symptom experience: such disorders often do not last long enough even to reach minimal research criteria for mental illnesses, since they restitute spontaneously in a week or so. We will then consider factors which determine the length of episode of the very large group of illnesses which reach research criteria for diagnosis but which last for less than one year; and finally we will summarise what is known about factors which determine failure to restitute: which we will define arbitrarily as illnesses which last for longer than one year.

## SPONTANEOUS RESTITUTION

Investigators who have carried out validity studies of psychiatric screening questionnaires invariably discover a substantial group of patients who are 'false positives' on the test: that is to say, they have high scores but they do not reach research criteria for a diagnosis. Such patients are usually experiencing the symptoms which they have reported on the test, but either the disorder has not yet lasted long enough to satisfy the minimum duration required for a diagnosis, or the patient does not have quite enough symptoms for a diagnosis. These patients are often thought to be experiencing understandable minor adjustment reactions to stresses, or to be mildly defensive people who are reluctant to discuss their psychological symptoms with another person (see description in Goldberg *et al.* 1976a).

Considerable numbers of patients with disorders that just reach criteria for a diagnosis will in fact remit over the next month. Thus Goldberg and Williams (1988) have analysed validity studies of the GHQ by the delay which elapsed between the screening test and the second-stage interview: validity coefficients are equally high after one week as they are if there is no delay at all, but they drop considerably if there is a delay of one month, since the symptom-status of many patients will change over the course of one month. Several longitudinal studies have swept the same population on repeated occasions with the GHQ and have confirmed this. If the case material is stratified by initial GHQ score, it can be shown that those with higher scores will lose their symptoms more slowly than those with scores just above threshold.

*Table 8.1* Scores of patients in primary care who had scores above threshold on their index consultation, and who completed the GHQ-30 on four occasions over six months (from Brodaty 1983)

| Group | Initial | 2 months | 4 months | 6 months |
|-------|---------|----------|----------|----------|
| Score 5–10 | n = 255 100% | n = 116 45.4% | n = 71 27.8% | n = 42 16.5% |
| Score >11 | n = 211 100% | n = 151 71.6% | n = 117 55.5% | n = 86 40.1% |

Brodaty (1983) administered the GHQ-30 to patients attending primary care physicians in Sydney, Australia at two-month intervals over 6 months. During this time only 36 per cent of the patients had a score below threshold on all four occasions. Table 8.1 shows the scores of the group with scores above threshold on the first occasion, and shows that the remission rate is very much higher for the group with intermediate scores than the group with very high scores.

Johnstone and Goldberg (1976) assigned patients with unexpectedly high GHQ scores at initial consultation to an index group in which the GP discussed the high score with them, and a control group which had no intervention. The behaviour of this control group over the next 12 months is of great interest, since they were not recognised as ill and received no treatment. There was a steady improvement with time, so that by 12 months they had improved as much as the group whose illnesses were detected. As in the study by Brodaty, those with intermediate scores (between 12 and 19 on the GHQ-60) improved dramatically with time, whereas those with really high scores (>20) contained a substantial group who were still symptomatic one year later at follow-up.

Tennant and his colleagues (1981) followed up 'cases' ascertained in the Camberwell survey one month after initial diagnosis, and showed that almost one-half of them were no longer cases. Remission was unrelated to medical consultation, whether psychotropic medication was prescribed, to severity as assessed by ID level, to syndrome type as assessed by Catego, or to sociodemographic variables. However, remission *was* predicted by a recent onset, a recent 'peak' of the disorder (i.e., they were already improving!), by recent threatening life events, and by 'neutralising' experiences. They report that 80 per cent of 'onset' cases following a threatening life event will have remitted one month later.

Lin and Ensel (1984) carried out a prospective community survey for depression at two time-points. They found that 73 per cent of respondents were free from depression on both occasions ('normals'), and 7 per cent were depressed on both occasions (chronics). There were 10 per cent in each of the other two categories which the authors call the 'recovered' and 'deteriorating' categories. Of those depressed at time 1, 43 per cent were depressed at time 2. The 'normals' had less than average frequency of undesirable life events and high social support at times 1 and 2, whereas the chronic group had high levels of undesirable life events and low levels of social support at inception and at follow-up. For the recovered there was a significant decrease of undesirable events from time 1 to time 2.

Surtees and Miller (1990) have studied medical students at Edinburgh University with the GHQ, and are able to identify a group of students who were initially symptomatic but who improved, and to compare these with students who were always well on the one hand, and those who were initially symptomatic and remained so on the other. As might have been predicted from the previous chapter, the two sick groups were differentiated from the always well by having more vulnerable personalities, having worse memories of maternal care on the PBI, and by having fewer supportive relatives. However, the students who remitted (without treatment) were distinguished from the always ill by having less suspicious personalities, fewer rows with others, better memories of maternal care and more supportive relatives.

The high rate of spontaneous remission of common disorders helps to explain some of the discrepancies about social support between the findings of Scott Henderson's group in Canberra and George Brown's group in London. Henderson and Moran used the GHQ as their indicator of caseness in their longitudinal surveys, and showed that neuroticism accounted for almost 70 per cent of the variance in illness, but 'with personality and background factors ... controlled, ... availability of social relationships make quite negligible contributions to the variance of illness'. Henderson and Moran find that for those who become symptomatic there is no difference between them and 'normals' in the availability or adequacy of close or diffuse ties: 'we conclude that when neurotic symptoms arise, there is no evidence that the social network is affected, but rows with close others increase. When neurotic symptoms improve, there is no significant change in social relationships at 4 and 8 months' (Henderson and Moran 1983: 471). Thus Henderson and Moran have been predicting the tendency to have a high GHQ score: that is, the tendency to destabilise readily. However, there are many false positives when the GHQ is used in community settings, as the positive predictive value of a GHQ score falls in community settings due to the lower prevalence of illness (see Goldberg and Williams 1988 for explanation). We have also seen that many of those with high GHQ scores will normalise over the next month or so, so that Henderson's groups will inevitably contain many individuals who will restitute spontaneously. Thus, Henderson has shown that the tendency to destabilise readily is largely accounted for by neuroticism, which is consistent with data in the previous chapter.

Brown's group (Brown and Harris 1978a), on the other hand, use the PSE as their case-finding instrument, and where depression is concerned they attach major importance to social relationships (see pp 97–9 and 106–8). They have been concerned with confirmed cases of depression (thus no false positives, and clear criteria for caseness), and they have reported remission rates for his overall data-sets which are much lower than those reported for a high GHQ score. As we shall see, social variables are shown to be important in determining the duration of depressive illness, although these are not identical with those discussed previously for the onset of illness.

## SHORT-TERM RESTITUTION

### Studies in the community (level 1)

According to Norris and Murrel (1984) the perception of the availability of resources was related to reduced depressive symptoms in older people (n=1402) over a six-month period. Strong resource persons maintained their advantage in terms of lower symptoms at all levels of undesirable events. The presence of stronger resources reduced the possibility of depression developing.

Pearlin and others (1981) examine the extent to which coping and social support measures act by reducing the effect of job disruption on the economic strain felt by the individual as a consequence, or by sustaining their sense of mastery and self-esteem, by directly inhibiting the development of symptoms, or some combination of all three. Both coping and social support measures were unrelated to measures of depression, but they did reduce the effect of changes in economic strain since the job disruption, and helped to buttress the sense of mastery and self-esteem when changes in economic strain and job disruption are held constant. Coping does blunt some of the effect of job loss, social support on the other hand seems to act by helping job losers to avoid the lowering of positive self-concepts, and by doing this they indirectly rather than directly act to prevent an increase in depression scores over time.

Essentially similar findings are reported by Lin and Ensel (1984, see pp.96, 101). The 'normals' in their sample had less than average frequency of undesirable life events and high social support at times 1 and 2. On both occasions the chronics had high levels of undesirable life events and low levels of social support.

For the recovered there was a significant decrease of undesirable events from time 1 to time 2 and for the deteriorating group there was a significant increase in these events between the two assessments. There was an insignificant increase in strong ties support for the recovered and a significant decrease in strong ties support for the deteriorated. Change in social support from inception to follow-up has a greater effect on clinical change than change in undesirable life events. Together, however, they only accounted for 14 per cent of the variance in clinical change. The 'interaction term' of change in support and events was not related to change in depression, but the combination of the two factors was related to depressed status at time 2 in the following ways: the increase in undesirable events had a less marked effect on the not depressed group at time 1, increasing their rate from 10 per cent to 16 per cent. For those who were depressed at time 1, had increased events and decreased social support, the depression rate at time 2 was 72 per cent. For those who were not depressed at time 1, had no increase in events and no decline in support, their rate was 7 per cent. Although we do not know the exact sequence of changes in support and events, there appears to be no doubt about their overall effect.

McFarlane *et al.* (1983) found that a reciprocal relationship existed between social supports and stressful events in that those who suffered from symptoms were more likely to experience stressful events subsequently, and the impact of life events was to increase the size but reduce the perceived helpfulness of the social network.

Lin and others (1985) attempted to see whether, once an event occurs, those receiving help from strong and homophilous (sharing similar characteristics) social ties had lower rates of depression than those whose help came from heterophilous ties. Access to strong homophilous ties may be important in maintaining mental health through the reduction of depression. They predicted that access to such ties alleviates the deterioration which is consequent upon the life event, and the absence of such ties or the use of heterophilous ones does not prevent decline in mental health. Life events over the past six months were ascertained from a check list and most important events identified. Subjects were then asked about help from close friends and the characteristics of the ties were then obtained. In general, help from closer ties was associated with lower levels of depression, but this result applied only to individuals in stable marriages. For those experiencing marital disruption the social network is disrupted and cannot act in this way. The greater the similarity between the married person's helper in terms of age and, to a lesser extent, education the fewer the depressive symptoms. For the unmarried the greater the similarity in occupational prestige the lower the level of depression.

## Crisis support

Crisis support is defined as that which involves confiding about the event, receiving moderate social support from the same person, and the lack of negative reaction at some point in the crisis. In Brown and others (1986) women with no support before or after a crisis had a high rate of depression (a number received a protective effect from someone very close – usually a woman – but only if they had been let down by their husband); women who did have a confiding relationship before but who failed to obtain it in crisis also had a high rate. Only those women who received support both before and after the crisis were at low risk. Single mothers practically always received support from those whom they had named as very close; their high rate of depression was due to inadequate levels of support to begin with (Brown *et al.* 1986).

Brown has suggested that 'women who are well-supported are not protected from depression altogether but are more likely to develop a borderline case than a case disorder in response to a major loss or disappointment'. So the role of social support may be more important for restitution of borderline rather than case depression. A *protective factor* for middle-class women may be that their provoking events do not arise in the context of ongoing difficulties and it is therefore easier for them to draw upon personal and social assets in a way that is impossible when a long-standing difficulty is present. They may therefore have shorter episodes of destabilisation. A further consideration is that the occurrence of subsequent positive events makes it easier for people to lose symptoms after they have begun to be ill or destabilise.

*Fresh-start and neutralising life events*

Some studies have observed a relationship between the occurrence of positive life events and a better outcome. Brown and his colleagues (1988) describe fresh-start events as those which represent 'an important change in the subject's life and ... that appeared to herald new hope – an indication that there might be a way forward'. In people who had been depressed for more than a year a reduction in their difficulties did not relate to improvement, but the occurrence of fresh-start events did. For those who did not have fresh-start events, improvement only occurred in those whose initial difficulties were low, thus supporting the idea that long-term difficulties do make restitution less likely. Brown and Harris (1989) have observed that when worsening, improvement or recovery of an established depression are concerned, the picture of social–clinical influence that emerges is more compatible with an 'additive' model. In other words, in long-term cases, chronic social difficulties and severe events can accumulate in ways which prevent restitution from occurring.

The occurrence of 'fresh-start' events has been shown to be related to improvement in community cases of depression, but improvement in longer standing social difficulties was not associated with the remission of symptoms in those who had been ill for more than twelve months (Brown *et al.* 1988). The figures for chronic cases and those lasting between three and twelve months were almost exactly comparable. For those women who recovered without becoming chronic there was no evidence for difficulty reduction or fresh-start events playing a part. Brown and Harris (1989) suggest that 'it is therefore possible that future research should concentrate on psychosocial factors in the recovery of individuals whose depression has lasted at least three months'. Recovery in cases of depression in women in the community does occur despite the presence of continuing difficulties, and even in the face of threatening events. On some occasions though, the threatening event also included an element of hope, which may contribute to the person's ability to recover. Parker and others (1988) in an examination of outcome at 20 weeks found that the breaking of an intimate relationship in the previous 12 months predicted outcome, perhaps because such an incident was related to the occurrence of a later positive event. This result parallels one in the study by Huxley and others (1989) in which family break-up in a social services population of cases was related to a better outcome at twelve months.

In summary, it can be seen from Table 8.2 that the factors which are associated with restitution in the community can be sub-divided into three types. The first is changes in life events, either in the rate at which they occur, or in the type of event. Remission is more likely when the rate of recent life events is declining, and (or) when positive or hopeful life events occur. The second is the level of social support perceived by the individual, and here close confiding relationships that provide help at times of need ('core crisis support') are especially important. Where this perceived level is high and where there is no actual falling off in support at the time of crisis, then restitution is more likely. The third type is the absence of physical illness and long-standing social difficulties, since the presence of one or the other appears to hinder the remission process.

*Table 8.2* Summary table of factors shown to be important in producing restitution in community settings

| Factors predicting remission in the community | | |
| --- | --- | --- |
| *Life events:* | | |
| Lin and Ensel | 1984 | Decrease in life events |
| | | No decline in social support |
| Brown *et al.* | 1988 | Fresh-start events |
| Tennant *et al.* | 1981 | Recent onset, recent life events |
| | | Recent 'peak' and 'neutralising' experiences |
| *Social support:* | | |
| Brown *et al.* | 1986 | 'Core crisis support' |
| Lin *et al.* | 1985 | Married persons – homophilous ties |
| Henderson | 1981 | Perceived available resources |
| Norris and Murrel | 1984 | Perceived available resources |
| Pearlin *et al.* | 1981 | Better coping mechanism |
| | | Better social support |
| *Physical illness:* | | |
| Aneshensel *et al.* | 1984 | No physical illness |

## Studies among care-seekers (level 2)

### General practice attenders

Kedward (1969) showed that at three-year outcome 73 per cent of 422 primary care patients were symptom free. Those who failed to restitute had many attendant social problems including chronic housing problems, bereavement, chronic physical illness and the adverse financial consequences of caring for a disabled relative: 'the reality had not changed'. In contrast, those who recovered went to their doctor at a time of social crisis, and they were worried about money, work, housing or children. Their recovery took place after the crisis had been resolved.

A later study by Johnstone and Shepley (1986) found that treatment by the GP or the social worker produced equivalent outcomes for high GHQ scorers in a general practice setting. Restitution was associated with treatment of a physical illness, resolution of the original life-problem and job satisfaction. Poor outcome was associated with a past history of psychiatric illness and problems with neighbours, children and other household members.

Physical illness was also associated with a failure to remit in Cooper's (1965) study of 100 chronic patients. Twenty-six cases had a definite physical disease and twelve had a psychological illness with an important physical component. Fifty-two of the cases had emotionally disturbed childhoods, and twenty-four had parental loss before 15 years of age. Thirty-eight cases had current or recent environmental stress. Mann *et al.* (1981) found physical ill health predicted outcome in patients in general practice. Hankin and Locke (1982) show that chronic physical disease is more prevalent among medical patients who continue to have many depressive symptoms than among patients with fewer symptoms. Although Schulberg *et al.*'s (1987a,b) study involves only small numbers, their findings confirm the association between physical illness and failure to restitute. As the number of physical disorders recorded in the patient's chart increases from none to eight, the probability of those depressed at time 1 being depressed six months later rises from 10 per cent to 78 per cent.

Goldberg and his colleagues (1990) found that restitution was correlated with housing (owner occupiers and those satisfied with their housing did better): these variables might have acted as proxies for a wide range of social advantages. As might have been expected, those with a high score on an index of hypochondriasis lost fewer symptoms. Loss of depressive symptoms was best predicted by having entirely psychological presenting symptoms and a low score on 'locus of control' (meaning that they did not consider that what happened to them was due to chance); those dissatisfied with their housing and with restricted opportunities for social interaction also had relatively greater loss of depressive than anxious symptoms. Loss of anxiety symptoms was best predicted by getting on well with the neighbours, and being rated by the GP as having either a psychological causation, or a physical disorder exacerbated by psychological distress; while a relatively greater loss of anxiety than depressive symptoms was predicted by those who were rated as defensive or who were somatising and who reported adequate opportunities for interacting with their relatives.

The finding that variables related to housing and social links with neighbours is broadly in line with previous work, and the finding that those having no restrictions in opportunities for interactions with relatives had relatively greater loss of anxious symptoms fits well with Brown's finding that those with increased integration in the community had increased anxiety and decreased depression.

In an attempt to predict case outcome at twelve months in a general practice setting, Mann *et al.* (1981) identified initial severity as a predictor. One of the other variables which made a contribution in the correct classification of 70 per cent of case outcomes was problems in the patient's social life.

*Studies in social services departments*

A series of studies of the clients of social services departments have been reported by one of us (Huxley and Fitzpatrick 1984; Huxley *et al.* 1987, 1988). Using the PSE we were able to identify as cases (ID of 5 or more) 53 per cent of a sample of cases allocated to social workers for investigation. Factors which were associated with a better outcome at 12 months follow-up for this group were time 1 variables: having a 'family break-up' problem and being younger. A worse outcome was associated with a high initial GHQ score and poor ratings of coping ability. Huxley and his colleagues (1989) found that failure to restitute over a twelve-month period was associated with problems with children, and unresolved housing problems. These findings are strikingly similar to those reported by Mann in general practice, and this may have been due to the fact that a proportion of the cases in our study were referred to GP-attached social workers. Those clients in our study who were still psychiatric 'cases' at time 2 had more unresolved problems concerning their housing and their children, unresolved parental problems, unresolved problems in their social lives, and were more often in contact with a CPN.

It would appear that short-term acute social crises, involving relationship problems are associated with prompt restitution, whereas longer-standing social problems, and poor coping abilities and the presence of physical illness are associated with delayed restitution.

**Studies with patients referred to the mental illness services (level 4)**

Huxley and Goldberg (1975) found that outcome at 6 months was predicted by material circumstances such as housing problems and Huxley and others (1979) produced similar findings with regard to twelve-month outcome for psychiatric out-patients. The percentage change in symptom levels in the latter study was predicted by housing, social class, restrictions on leisure, genetic risk, and contact with social agencies. Huxley (1978; Huxley *et al.* 1979) followed up an out-patient sample over 12 months. Of this sample 10 per cent had been ill for 12 months, and 27 per cent for less than one month,

*Table 8.3*  Summary table of factors predicting restitution among consulting samples

| Factors predicting remission among care-seekers | | |
|---|---|---|
| Cooper | 1965 | No physical illness |
| Kedward | 1969 | Resolution of social problems<br>No physical illness |
| Mann *et al.* | 1981 | Initial severity; age<br>Social life score<br>No physical illness |
| Johnstone and Shepley | 1986 | Resolution of original problem<br>Job satisfaction |
| Huxley *et al.* | 1989 | Family break-up problem; age<br>Low initial GHQ score;<br>Good coping ability<br>Resolution of problems |
| Goldberg *et al* | 1990 | (depression symptoms)<br>Low locus of control;<br>Entirely psychiatric complaints<br><br>(anxiety symptoms)<br>Few difficulties with neighbours<br>Satisfaction with housing<br>Entirely psychiatric complaints; or<br>Organic exacerbated by psychiatric |

21 per cent for less than 3 months and a further 23 per cent for less than 6 months; 17 per cent were ill for 7–9 months. The predictors of symptom loss were: fewer housing problems; lower genetic risk; more social assets; better material circumstances; and higher income.

It is interesting to note that additional variables were related to another outcome measure – the number of months during the year in which symptoms were present and affected functioning. The additional variables were lack of concentration, abnormalities manifest in interview at time 1, fatigue, previous history and total clinical severity score. Additional social variables related to the months ill outcome measure were social class, neighbourhood characteristics, total social dysfunction score and role dissatisfaction.

Social support appears to have a major effect on recovery of level 4 and 5 depressed patients (Brugha *et al.* 1990). The size of their primary group, the number contacted and their satisfaction with help are all related to better outcome. George and others (1989) in a study of 150 middle-aged and elderly depressed in-patients over a 6–32-month follow-up, also identified social support (subjective) as an important predictor of outcome. Those with impaired support at onset (controlled for depression scores) had the highest mean depression score at follow-up. Higher baseline depression scores, a diagnosis of dysthymia, a small social network and impaired social support were all associated with the failure to lose symptoms.

Mitchell and Moos (1984) found changes in level of strain and in positive life events were associated with changes in family support over a one-year period. There was less evidence of an effect of social support on negative life-change events, ongoing strain or positive life-change events. Cross-sectionally lower levels of strain were associated with greater levels of family support (controlled for sociodemographic variables and depression).

The outcome for patients at levels 4 and 5 (Sims 1975) is predicted by poor marital relationships and poor sexual relationships, poor material management and a poor early environment. Hooley and others (1986) adapted work with schizophrenia sufferers and examined the rates of expressed emotion in the spouses of treated depressed patients, and found that almost 60 per cent of those with high EE relationships relapsed whereas none of those with low EE relationships did.

In Parker and his colleagues' study (1988) a good outcome for level 4 patients and some 'volunteers' was predicted by the break-up of an intimate relationship. This shows again that what might sometimes appear to be a negative life event or an adverse social experience can be a positive factor in restitution, and probably that it is the meaning attached to the event which is important.

Williams and others (1990) follow Teasdale in distinguishing between 'onset vulnerability' – by which they mean a predispositon to suffer a new episode of depression – and 'persistence vulnerability' – by which they mean the tendency to restitute more slowly. They show that negative self-concepts during the episode of depression in patients admitted to psychiatric beds predict the tendency to take longer over recovery, but not the tendency to relapse at follow-up six months later.

Brugha and his colleagues (1990) showed that the main effect of social support (in women) was through the number of group members named and contacted and the satisfaction with the support given. For men, 'the main affect was through negative social interaction, living as married and the number of primary group social contacts named as acquaintances or friends'. Kurdek (1988), on the other hand, failed to find any evidence for gender related trends in the relation- ship between social support dimensions and psychological adjustment.

In summary, among those who reach psychiatric care, restitution is associated with various social advantages, such as better housing and

*Table 8.4* Summary table of factors predicting restitution among patients referred to mental illness services

| | | Factors predicting remission among psychiatric patients |
|---|---|---|
| Huxley *et al.* | 1979 | Better material circumstances; more social assets; higher income; fewer housing problems; lower genetic risk |
| Hooley *et al.* | 1986 | Low EE relationships |
| Parker *et al.* | 1988 | Relationship break-up |
| George *et al.* | 1989 | Lower initial symptom scores; absence of dysthymia; small social network; social support satisfaction; female; younger |
| Williams *et al.* | 1990 | Lack of negative self-concepts |
| Brugha *et al.* | 1990 | Size of primary group; number contacted; satisfaction with contact |

higher income, with less severe disorders, and with the availability of social support. Physical health is less important in this setting, probably because physically ill people are less likely to pass the third filter.

## FACTORS WHICH INFLUENCE LONGER TERM OUTCOME

Before looking at some specific relationships in more detail a 12-year follow-up study reported by Sims (1975) identified a host of factors related to outcome for 146 in- and day-patient first admissions. Sims also reviewed the outcome literature and found some support for the influence of each of the following factors on outcome (the review covered the period 1934 to 1972 and 32 studies): diagnosis and the nature of symptoms (16 studies); premorbid personality (11); age, sex and marital status; duration of symptoms; social adjustment (including work record) (9 each); precipitating factors (4); intelligence (3); early environment; treatment; insight; and sibship (2 each).

In his 12-year follow-up he found the following associated with a good outcome: precipitants independent of patient; normal personality; absence of somatic symptoms; presence of social (mixing) problems; and a tendency for psychotherapies to have a better outcome (due to selection factors). The following factors are associated with a poor outcome: disturbed parental relations; unhappy childhood; length of illness greater than six years; aged under 20 when illness began; pathological and immature personality; poor work record over the 3 years before admission; unemployed for more than 3 months before admission; frequent change of job; poor marital relationship; behavioural problems in spouse; accommodation and finance problems; referral for social work help; previous psychiatric history; drug or alcohol abuse; and abnormalities of appearance or behaviour.

Huxley (1978) reviewed a further eighteen studies, and he and Sirois (1975) both identify similar factors to those identified by Sims, which can be summarised as: clinical factors, in particular the length of previous illness and the presence of somatic factors; material problems and relationship problems; and a constitutional factor which has an influence through personality, family history and early childhood.

## Characteristics of the initial episode

Lee and Murray (1988) conducted a long-term 18-year follow-up of Kendell's (1968) sample of 89 patients' primary depressive illnesses at level 5 and located 98 per cent of his subjects. First admissions had a 50 per cent chance of readmission during their lifetime, but those who had had previous admissions had a 50 per cent chance of readmission over the next three years. Less than one-fifth of the surviving patients had remained well, and over one-third had suffered either unnatural death or severe chronic distress and handicap. Patients at the psychotic end of the continuum were more likely to be readmitted and had very poor outcomes compared to those with more 'neurotic' presentations. Almost two-thirds of the patients developed other psychiatric disorders or had major complications such as alcohol dependence or bulimia.

A 15-year follow-up study of 145 depressed patients at level 5 by Kiloh and others (1988) confirmed most of these findings except the high frequency of other diagnoses developing in the follow-up period. They also found only 20 per cent continuously well, and 12 per cent incapacitated by illness. Endogenously depressed patients were readmitted more often than neurotically depressed patients.

Andrews and others (1990) found that personality measures taken at initial admission 15 years earlier predicted outcome. For those suffering from an endogenous type depression the explained variance in outcome was only 2 per cent, but it was 20 per cent for the neurotic groups. In a study of 119 level-4 depressed patients Brugha and others (1990) report that the severity and duration of previous episodes predicted outcome.

## THE EFFECTS OF MEDICAL TREATMENT

### Non-specific effects

Those who work in hospital settings will have seen patients who have not improved on anti-depressants prescribed by their family doctor get better on anti-depressants prescribed by the hospital. Yet hospital drugs are no stronger than those available outside, and the idea that hospital doctors prescribe them better is an understandable piece of vanity only partly supported by evidence (Johnson 1974). The cathedral is just a more effective place for prayer than a wayside shrine: when the hospital is more effective it may indicate that healing is a matter of hope and expectancy, that cannot be entirely reduced to chemistry.

Thomas (1987) assigned 200 patients with symptoms for which there was no organic cause to a 'positive' consultation in which the doctor gave the patient a firm 'diagnosis' and predicted that the patient would get better in a few days; and a 'negative' consultation in which the doctor said that he couldn't be sure what the matter was, but that if there was no improvement in a few days the patient should come back. Improvement occurred in 64 per cent of those given the positive prediction, but only 39 per cent of those given the negative prediction. The prescription of a placebo made no difference to outcome.

### Specific effects of treatment

#### Social work

Four studies have addressed the efficacy of interventions by social workers. An early study by Cooper and his colleagues (1975) using a randomised controlled design found that there was some benefit from social intervention with long-standing neuroses in primary care, but a later more detailed sub-study failed to show a relationship between changes in outcome and degree of activity by the social worker (Shepherd *et al.* 1979) – although there was a relationship between improvement and short-term intervention. Corney (1984b) then studied the effects of social work intervention on a group of women with either an acute or an 'acute-on-chronic' depressive illness, and found that beneficial effects were confined to the latter group. Finally Johnstone and Shepley (1986) randomised patients with high GHQ scores to intervention by doctor or intervention by social worker: both groups of patients did equally well.

*Intervention by nurses*

Marks and his colleagues (1977) developed special training for psychiatric nurses in behavioural psychotherapy, and demonstrated the efficacy of treatments for chronic neurotic disorders seen in the community (Ginsberg *et al.* 1984). Mangen and others (1983) extended these findings by demonstrating that trained nurses did as well as psychiatrists in the treatment of depressive illnesses at level 4. Both of these studies used methods of economic analysis. In the latter study, the total expenditure on patients treated by nurses was about the same as the group treated by psychiatrists, but the direct psychiatric treatment costs were somewhat less.

*Psychotherapy*

Brodaty and Andrews (1983) carried out an evaluation of the efficacy of psychotherapy in primary care settings, using a design intended to minimise the effects of spontaneous restitution. Patients who scored above threshold on the GHQ on four consecutive occasions were randomly assigned to brief problem-orientated psychotherapy consisting of eight half-hourly sessions with a psychotherapist in the GP's office, to eight half-hourly sessions with their usual doctor, or to usual treatment by the family doctor. Patients were interviewed by an independent researcher, and recordings were blind-rated. All three groups improved equally both at 4-month and at one-year follow-up assessment.

*Specialist treatment*

Balestrieri and his colleagues (1988) reviewed the published work on referral of patients for specialist mental health treatment, and show that such treatment gives a 10 per cent advantage over control treatment. The effect is somewhat greater than this for the eight studies reviewed that used a random design.

**Psychotropic drugs**

Mapother wrote that among the successes claimed for any new treatment are those that never had the illness, those who never received the treatment, and those who would have got better without the treatment. Had he lived to see the era of psychotropic drugs, he might have added 'and those who managed to get better despite having received the treatment'. All these groups are well represented among those deemed to need psychotropic drugs in general medical settings, which makes it especially important to pay attention only to those studies that have used double-blind controlled designs.

### Drug treatment of those who have not sought care (level 1)

Khan and his colleagues (1986) examined the effects of psychotropic drugs on patients who had not passed the first filter. They assigned 242 people answering a newspaper advertisement and scoring highly on symptoms of anxiety and depression (more than two standard deviations above the mean on the 'Symptom Check List') to three treatments: benzodiazepines, imipramine or placebo for eight weeks. Anti-anxiety effects of the anti-depressant were better than those of either of the others by the second week of treatment, and became stronger thereafter. If patients with panic disorder and phobias were excluded, this eliminated the superior anti-depressant effect of imipramine.

### Drug treatment in primary care settings (level 3)

Mann *et al.* (1981) studied the determinants of course of neurotic illness over 12 months in a cohort of 100 patients with neurotic illnesses confirmed by an independent psychiatric assessment. Although the main determinants of a favourable course were low initial severity, young age, normal social life and absence of physical illness, a further increase in accurate prediction could be made by adding a fifth variable: receipt of psychotropic medication during the year.

Two studies have used a rigorous methodology and have confirmed that anti-depressant drugs are effective in primary care settings, provided that the severity of depressive illness is confirmed. Thomson and his colleagues (1982) assigned 115 patients in five group practices selected by GPs as having depression of more than two weeks duration and confirmed with high scores on the Hamilton Depression Scale to active treatment (amitrip-tyline, amitriptyline and tryptophan, or tryptophan alone) or to treatment with an inactive placebo. The active treatments were all as effective as each other, and all were more effective than the placebo.

Hollyman and her colleagues (1988) assigned depressed patients to either amitriptyline or placebo, and showed that a significant drug/placebo difference occurs at severities greater than a score of 13 on the Hamilton Depression Scale, which is approximately equivalent to the criteria for the *DSM-III* concept of 'major depressive episode'. This work therefore constitutes a partial validation of the diagnostic concept, in that the less severe RDC concept of 'minor depression' did equally well whether the patient had an active preparation or a placebo (Paykel *et al.* 1988). Outcome was not affected either by symptom-pattern, or by whether or not the depressive illness had been precipitated by a life event.

## Specialist mental health drug treatment (level 4)

For those with severe mental disorders – such as psychotic illnesses and severe depressive illnesses – there is abundant evidence from double-blind controlled trials that psychotropic drugs are highly effective. However, it is unreasonable to generalise from these results to the many patients with anxiety states and less severe depressive illnesses that are commonly referred to specialist services.

Johnstone and her colleagues (1980) assigned 240 anxious and depressed patients referred by their doctor to a specialist clinic to four drug treatment conditions: amitriptyline and diazepam, amitriptyline and placebo, diazepam and placebo, or placebo and placebo, for a four-week treatment trial. The outcome was good irrespective of medication, but significant drug effects were due to amitriptyline and concerned measures of anxiety as well as depression. She concluded that the distinction between anxiety and depression among neurotic out-patients was without practical value as regards drug treatment.

Tyrer and his colleagues (1988) randomly assigned 210 patients with minor neurotic illnesses to a variety of treatments. The formal diagnoses of the patients were generalised anxiety disorder (n=71), panic disorder (n=74) and dysthymic disorder (n=65). There were five possible treatments: benzodiazepines, tricyclic anti-depressants, placebos, cognitive behaviour therapy or self-help. Assessments of progress were made at regular intervals over ten weeks. Tricyclic anti-depressants, cognitive behaviour therapy and self-help were equally effective and better than placebos; whereas those on benzodiazepines did less well than those on placebos. About one-third of those on placebos eventually needed active medication given in a non-blind way, to be compared with only 7 per cent of those on tricyclics, and 18 per cent of those allocated to self-help. The effects of treatment were independent of specific diagnoses, thus removing 'one of the main planks supporting the distinction between the alleged categories of illness'. Since 'self-help' did as well as the more elaborate and demanding cognitive behaviour therapy, it is of interest to note that it consisted of a relaxation tape, self-help instructions, and regular brief sessions with a therapist 'which may have enhanced morale and determination'.

## SUMMARY

There are interesting differences between the factors which promote restitution at the different levels of our model. For instance, there are differences in the importance of subjective social support between levels 1, 3 and 5. A positive view of subjective social support is important for the community group, and less so for the others. For psychiatric patients the *actual* level rather than the perceived level seems to be more important in restitution. In comparison to community samples, the care-seekers are likely to restitute when they do *not* have an associated physical illness. Studies of care-seekers in social services settings do not report the absence of physical illness as a predictor of restitution, but the effect of physical illness upon restitution is a very real one, and only likely to be seen in general medical settings where care-seekers get a detailed assessment of their physical health status.

Subjects at level 2 more commonly experience acute social crises of one sort or another, so that these short-term crises figure as factors which are likely to lead to restitution, especially when they are responsible for subsequent positive or hopeful events which enhance the process of restitution. By the time one reaches psychiatric care, even though there is some evidence for restitution from a social crisis (Parker *et al.* 1988) in short-term outcome, long-term outcome is heavily influenced by long-term factors, such as the length of previous illness history, personality and constitutional factors, and long-standing social difficulties in work and social relationships, perhaps reflected in a history of social services as well as health service care.

# 9 Mind and body

## HOW SOCIAL EVENTS INFLUENCE BODILY PROCESSES

We have considered some possible biological underpinnings for common symptoms, and reported that the functions of neurotransmitters correspond to concepts which are meaningful to psychologists (like incentive, fear and arousal) but hardly at all to the many different categories of common illness described in conventional taxonomies. Although there is still controversy about the way in which neurotransmitters are related to anxiety and depression, we have described a possible model which would relate the two major dimensions described to disruptions in biological sub-systems.

In Chapter 5 we considered a simple model in which loss events were related to depression, and threat events were related to anxiety. However, such a model does not help us to understand the complex and important relationships that evidently exist between our physical health and our psychological health. It now seems clear that stressful life events are not merely important in determining onsets of anxiety and depression, but also release episodes of physical illness.

In this chapter we will consider what is known about the way in which our social environment can affect the fragile homeostasis upon which our health depends. We will then restate our model, and consider both its strengths and its weaknesses.

## INDIVIDUAL AND ENVIRONMENT

Perez and Farrant (1988) have pointed out that three independent yet related systems – the central nervous system (CNS), the neuroendocrine system, and the immune system – are involved in the adaptation of the individual to his environment. In order to maintain a reasonable homeostatic balance, these systems must be in constant dialogue with one another at different levels.

The CNS acts as the major controller, translator and integrator of stimuli arriving from the environment, and it also controls the adaptive response to the environment. Within the CNS, the *limbic system* is the major central system involved in adaptation, and in the neuroendocrine and emotional response to stressful signals. The limbic system serves as an important connection between the cerebral cortex and the hypothalamus, and evaluates stressful stimuli and compares them with past experience. For many years it has been thought to be the part of the brain involved in disorders of emotion. The hypothalamus acts as the efferent arm of the visceral brain, receiving information from the periphery, integrating it with the internal milieu, and adjusting important functions such as sympathetic activity and endocrine secretions. It does this by means of its intimate connections with the pituitary gland, sometimes referred to as the 'hypothalamo-pituitary axis'. The hypothalamus thus controls the hormone adrenocorticotrophin (ACTH) which is released in response to stressful stimuli (see Figure 9.2). Thus the CNS modulates the relationship between the social environment and the internal milieu. It influences the endocrine system by the secretion of pituitary hormones, and influences the immune system by neuropeptides such as encephalin and endorphin and by autonomic nervous control of lymphoid tissue. The CNS is itself influenced by the endocrine system by various hormones, and by the immune system by substances called immunotransmitters.

The endocrine system and the immune system are also capable of directly influencing one another: thus hormones like cortisol and prolactin influence immune function; and the endocrine system is itself influenced by immunotransmitters. The relationship between the three systems and the social environment is depicted in Figure 9.1.

Khansari and his colleagues (1990) point out that stress affects not only steroid hormones like cortisol but also other hormones such as growth hormone, gonadotrophins, prolactin and even thyroid hormone. They also list 16 hormones that are now known to have effects upon our immune system. The activation of both sympatho-adrenal and hypothalamo-pituitary axes leads to complex processes that have negative effects upon immune function. This negative effect of stress upon immune function tends to be transient, which favours an effect upon the feedback regulation of the systems crudely depicted in Figure 9.1.

We show the relationship between the CNS and the adrenal glands in the somatic mediation of stress responses in Figure 9.2. Whereas the relationship between pituitary and adrenal cortex is completely hormonal, the relationship between hypothalamus and adrenal medulla is partly through the sympathetic nervous system, and partly through the peripheral effects of adrenaline.

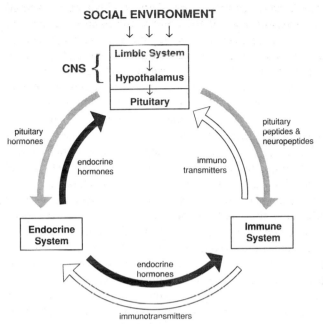

*Figure 9.1* Relationship between social events and three bodily systems

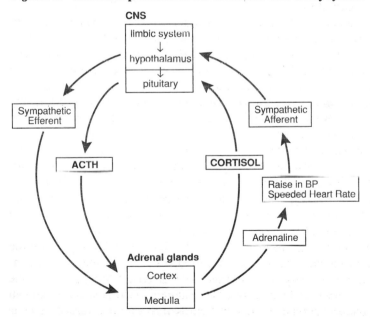

*Figure 9.2* How stress affects bodily systems: the hypothalamo-pituitary adrenal system

Perez and Farrant (1988) make a striking comparison between failure of communication at cellular level and at an emotional level leading to alienation: the failure of lymphocytes to recognise changes in cellular identity may lead to them ignoring cancer cells, and those cells therefore surviving; just as lapses in emotional communication may lead to an individual denying stress and internalising emotions, thus exposing himself to further stress.

## SOCIAL FACTORS AND THE IMMUNE RESPONSE

The immune system, like the CNS, must discriminate between self and non-self, and protect the integrity of the self from intrusions of the non-self. It is responsible for protecting us not only against intrusions from outside us, by viruses and bacterial toxins, but also against intrusions from within ourselves, by our own altered proteins or cancerous cells. Indeed, Blalock (1984) considers the immune system to be an internal sense organ that recognises non-cognitive stimuli such as bacteria, viruses and foreign proteins, and relays information to the neuroendocrine system by hormones derived from lymphocytes.

Immune responses constitute an important link between social factors and mental disorders. The immune response can be modified by hypnosis and by meditation (Black *et al.* 1963; Smith *et al.* 1985), and in experimental animals stress and separation in early life can be shown to influence the immune response in later life (Laudenslager *et al.* 1983).

Many studies of the immune responses have concentrated upon a white blood cell called a *T-lymphocyte*, which is largely concerned with cellular immunity. These can in turn be divided into helper cells (which amplify immune responses), suppressor cells (which down-regulate them) and 'natural killer (NK) cells' which are important in the defence against tumours and viruses.

### Depression and the immune response

Bartrop and others (1977) were the first workers to show a convincing relationship between an emotional state in man and the immune response by demonstrating that during bereavement the responses of lymphocytes to mitogens (a substance which causes cells to divide) was significantly impaired when compared with a control group, and Schleifer and others (1983) confirmed this in a prospective study on the husbands of 15 women dying of advanced breast cancer. The same group (1984) then showed that severe depressives (level 5) also had depressed immune responses, but it is important to note that the same effects were not seen for less severe depressives, at level 4 (Schleifer 1985). Irwin and others (1988) showed that NK activity is reduced in bereaved women and in those anticipating bereavement when compared with normal controls, but that raised cortisol levels were only seen in the bereaved women.

Irwin and others (1990) showed that in both depressed subjects and normal controls, the presence of threatening life events is associated with a 50 per cent reduction in NK activity. The decrease in NK activity was found to be significantly associated with depressive symptoms but not with age, alcohol consumption or tobacco smoking.

## Cancer, psychological factors and the immune response

There is an increased risk of cancer developing in the six months following a bereavement, probably related to the suppression of NK activity referred to above. It has been shown that depression in patients with cancer is associated with impairment of cell-mediated immunity (Linn *et al.* 1982). Brown and Paraskevas (1982) consider the possibility that antibodies formed to malignant cells may bind to 5HT receptors and block them, thus causing depression directly.

However, there are reasons for suspecting that causal links may work in the other direction as well. Shekelle and his colleagues (1981) studied 2020 men between the ages of 40 and 50 with a psychological inventory (the MMPI). All subjects were followed up for 17 years. Among 18.8 per cent who had high depression scores there were twice as many cancer deaths as among those with low scores.

## STRESS, CORTISOL AND NEUROTRANSMITTERS

The emotional and behavioural response to stress is anxiety, and cortisol emerges as a hormonal factor which accounts for changes in both the behavioural and the immune response. There is a direct relationship between the severity of anxious and depressive symptoms and the levels of cortisol found in the blood (Melzer *et al.* 1984), possibly because cortisol enhances the activity of the 5HT pathways (Cowen and Anderson 1985). There is also a relationship between high levels of cortisol and a decrease in the immune response (Fauci and Dale 1974), which we shall discuss in the next section.

In Chapter 5 we reviewed evidence that arousal and fear are mediated in the brain by noradrenaline and $5HT_2$ systems, and suggested that resilience might be related to $5HT_1$ systems, and that failure of these systems resulted in depression. Psychosocial stressors activate $5HT_2$ systems, related to anxiety and fear. Prolonged social stress was shown to lead to chronic increases in blood levels of cortisol, and this, together with long-term $5HT_2$ over-stimulation, may lead to breakdown of resilience system and thus depression.

A possible mechanism for reduced $5HT_1$ receptor function in depression is chronic hypercortisolaemia, which may itself result from chronic adverse social conditions. Thus Deakin *et al.* (1990) show that depressed patients with chronic social difficulties have higher basal cortisol levels than those without them, and Dolan *et al.* (1985) showed that depressives seen on a community survey with life events and chronic difficulties had higher urinary cortisol than those without; finally Sapolsky (1989) shows that wild baboons low in dominance hierarchies have chronically elevated cortisol levels compared to those above them. Deakin and his colleagues (1990a, b) showed that hormonal measures of $5HT_1$ functions were impaired in depressives and that this was related to increased secretion of cortisol. There is evidence from experiments with animals that cortisol impairs $5HT_1$ receptor functioning. Thus the $5HT_1$ resilience system may break down either because of hypercortisolaemia, or perhaps because of chronic or intense stimulation of $5HT_2$ aversion/fear receptors.

## BODILY CONSEQUENCES OF SOCIAL ISOLATION AND SOCIAL SUPPORT

It is not merely that man is a social animal: loneliness can kill. Berkman and Syme (1979) carried out a prospective study of nearly 7000 adults over nine years in California, and calculated age-adjusted relative risks for those most isolated compared with those with most social ties. Social isolation increased the mortality of males by 2.3 times, and of females by 2.8 times. Similar results were reported by Blazer (1980) in a study of 326 elderly patients observed over 2.5 years. Khansari and his colleagues (1990) assert that lonely medical students have low NK cell activity. Thomas and others (1985) showed a significant correlation between lack of social support and impaired lymphocyte response to mitogens in elderly women between the ages of 60 and 90, and this relationship was independent of age, weight, use of tobacco or alcohol and perceived psychological stress.

On the other hand, animal work suggests that social support may promote $5HT_1$ function, and so increase resilience. Rats which are socially isolated sometimes become extremely aggressive, and this has been shown to be related to a decreased activity of brain $5HT_1$ receptors (Popova and Petkov 1990). On the other hand, group housing reverses the effects of immobilisation stress in rats, producing effects similar to anti-depressants or drugs which stimulate $5HT_1$ receptors.

Knowledge about social processes and their relationship to biological processes is expanding rapidly, and the above review can only give a thumbnail sketch of the field as it was developing in 1990. However, it is clear that there are many possible bridges between the two universes of discourse, and it is a certainty that others will be elucidated in the near future.

## THE MODEL PROPOSED

The purpose of the model proposed in this book is to provide an alternative way of conceptualising the common varieties of mental disorder from the orthodoxies offered by traditional taxonomy. Instead of the myriad sub-divisions of minor illness to be found in the *ICD* or the *DSM-III* classifications, we assert that there are only a very limited number of ways that the human frame responds to psychological stress, and that these are defined by two underlying dimensions of symptomatology: anxious symptoms on the one hand, and depressive symptoms on the other. These two dimensions are themselves correlated, and combinations of the two sets of symptoms are more common than either set on its own.

The apparent diversity of common illnesses is because there are a number of ways of responding to the experience of symptoms of anxiety or depression, and each of these ways is associated with a cluster of highly characteristic symptoms which have attracted the various 'categories' contained in official taxonomies. Some of these are ways of dealing with anxiety – either by avoiding particular situations or things, or by the adoption of various anxiety-reducing inner stratagems – and some seem to be ways of reducing one's own sense of responsibility for the predicament that one happens to be in, as in somatised forms of mental disorder. This cannot wholly explain the phenomenon of somatisation, since some patients do experience severe depressive symptoms during their illness: it is likely that depression also serves to heighten the experience of pre-existing pains and discomforts.

It is possible that later work will demonstrate that it is useful to think of a third dimension representing neurasthenic symptoms, but at present this does not appear to be justified, and such symptoms seem to represent a chronic, mild form of symptom experience, with symptoms that load on both anxiety and depression. Similarly new constructs like 'dysthymic disorder' seem to refer to chronic, mild symptom experience, while old constructs like 'adjustment disorders' represent individuals who have developed symptoms, but who are thought to be about to lose them without specific treatment. Instead of thinking about such disorders as a separate category of human illness, the present model regards such people as those who are similar to other patients in every way except that they are about to restitute spontaneously.

### The triad of vulnerability, destabilisation and restitution

It is argued that common mental disorders are provoked either by stressful events in one's personal life, or by new episodes of physical illness, and this process has been termed destabilisation. However, it is a matter of common observation that an event that causes one person to experience symptoms will hardly cause a ripple with someone else. Indeed, the sort of 'severe life event' that has been incriminated in depressive illness and anxiety states occurs in the normal population without provoking the same responses. There appears to be an understandable relationship between the type of provoking event and the type of symptoms developed, but the relationship is a loose one.

Thus, vulnerability to provoking agents becomes almost of greater interest than the processes by which individuals destabilise. This vulnerability has been considered at four levels: genetic, experiences of parenting and experiences during childhood, personality variables and current social situation. There is strong evidence that genetic factors are important, but they do not seem to determine the exact pattern of common symptoms developed. They appear to be related to 'neuroticism', which is one of the more important personality variables, but the evidence strongly favours the notion that most common disorders are familial rather than genetic. The common form of depressive illness seen in community settings is an excellent example of a disorder that tends to run in families, but is probably not determined by specific genes. There are many things that are part of the culture of a family other than the genes that are passed within it, and these include patterns of parenting, patterns of interpersonal behaviour, learned patterns of coping and ways of responding to physical discomforts and pains. All these appear to be relevant in helping to determine the particular set of symptoms developed by a particular individual at a particular time.

We have reviewed the evidence that all these factors are relevant to a consideration of vulnerability to destabilise under stress, and laid special emphasis upon parental neglect, 'affectionless control' by parents, parental discord and sexual abuse as important factors. Where personality is concerned, it is likely that apart from neuroticism, scales like 'interpersonal dependency' and 'external locus of control' are themselves reflecting experiences during childhood and should not be thought of as independent causal factors in their own right. This does not imply that they should not be measured, as their attraction lies in the fact that they can be readily measured in surveys, whereas the quality of childhood experiences is more difficult to measure in a reproducible and valid way.

The final group of vulnerability factors relates to current social circumstances, and includes chronic social adversity and various measures of social support. There are compelling reasons for supposing that the former are important in sensitising individuals to aversive life events, but the latter are more controversial. We have argued that much of the apparent disagreement about the importance of social support stems from a failure to appreciate that a distinction should be made between transient episodes of destabilisation (where Scott Henderson's group have shown that such factors are not of great importance) and episodes that do not remit spontaneously, where Brown's group have shown that social support seems to be of great importance.

Although it has not been much studied, it is of great interest to ask how some people come to be resilient in the face of life stress. We suspect that good experiences of parenting are important here, but have been unable to quote any convincing figures to buttress our belief. It appears that those with more active and satisfying social relationships may be at an advantage, and we pointed out that some undesirable characteristics like sociopathic traits may be protective.

The final part of the triad refers to those factors that determine the length of an episode. We are arguing that it is not sufficient to develop a theory to explain why some individuals in a population become ill at particular times; the theory must include explanations of why some illnesses last much longer than others, and why some do not get better at all.

One of the disadvantages of a crude categorical model for mental disorder is that it distracts attention from the wide variations that exist in the duration of episodes of distress. Most episodes of distress are self-limiting and have remitted in less than two weeks. Since research criteria require two weeks as the minimum length of time that symptoms must be experienced before they are 'diagnosable', such episodes are either not recorded, or are referred to as 'adjustment disorders'. Yet, from the epidemiological standpoint, we need to come to terms with these episodes as well, which are responsible for much time off work, and for much distress. We have argued that the factors that determine duration of illness are not the same as those that determine the onset of symptoms.

We described three ways in which symptomatic individuals try to restitute: psychological, chemical and neurotic. The first set depend upon the availability of social support, and are assisted by intimate, confiding relationships. The occurrence of further, positive life events (whether termed 'neutralising' or 'fresh-start') will clearly supplement efforts made by each individual to reduce distress within their immediate social group. Chemical methods of restitution are resorted to by most people in distress, either in the form of alcohol and recreational drugs, of self-medication, or of psychotropic agents prescribed by a doctor. Chemical restitution is maladaptive when it produces dependence. We have mentioned that the various forms of 'neurotic' restitution have been responsible for diseases being named after what are basically anxiety-relieving or responsibility-removing symptoms or behaviours. Neurotic restitution is maladaptive when it interferes with one's life (as in phobic avoidance or hysterical paralysis) or leads to forms of symptomatology which are themselves distressing (as in fixed somatic pains, dysfunctional organs or obsessive-compulsive phenomena).

It seems likely that a combination of psychological restitution and self-medication with anxiety-relieving substances are used initially, with women tending more frequently to talk through the problem with others, and men a greater tendency to take alcohol and avoid discussion. If short-term methods of restitution are effective, it is not necessary to resort to neurotic methods of restitution, and one can stop anxiety-reducing substances before dependence has developed. However, it is possible that constitutional factors make some people more likely to develop particular patterns of symptom formation, or they may have been learned as part of the culture of the family. Obsessional traits, for example, may be learned patterns of behaviour that develop into obsessional symptoms at times of life stress.

It is evident that there may be a number of different explanations for restitution not occurring: an insoluble life problem in a personal life that allows no 'fresh-starts'; dependence upon a chemical method for reducing distress; or being stuck in an over-learned habit like a compulsion. However, the above by no means exhaust the reasons for staying symptomatic, which include physical disease and social disadvantage. Both of these serve to trap individuals in situations which offer no hope of improvement, so that hopelessness becomes an understandable response. It is clear that these factors are by no means specific to particular diagnoses, so that it becomes plausible to conceptualise restitution in a general way, across 'diagnoses'.

### Natural disasters

A disaster – whether it be forest fire, hurricane or flood – provides an interesting example for considering whether the model provides a useful framework. The disaster itself can be thought of as an extremely severe stressful life event which affects an entire population at the same time.

Studies with the GHQ have shown that a much higher proportion than usual of the population become symptomatic in the weeks immediately following, but the rate of loss of symptoms is very rapid. Most people, for example, lose their symptoms without specialised mental health treatments. However, there will be a relatively small group who will develop long-standing symptoms, and these can be thought of as vulnerable people who might otherwise have not become symptomatic, but whose unremitting symptoms reflect partly the severity of the provoking agent, but more often the experience of loss of family members and home that prevent full restitution.

McFarlane (1987) administered the GHQ to 469 fire-fighters after the Adelaide forest fires of 1983, and showed that distress measured by the GHQ was related to property loss and other recent stressful life events, and there was a significant relationship between degree of adversity experienced and GHQ score. He concluded that effects of the disaster were separate and additive in determining distress. He described some examples when the failure to restitute is because events during the disaster represent a 'match' between a pre-existing personality trait and a stressful event. During the forest fires officers in the fire service witnessed harrowing scenes, which included seeing children burned alive. Sometimes they had advised people to travel in a particular direction, but the wind had changed and people would suffer because they had followed advice given in good faith by the officers.

It is hardly surprising that some officers should have destabilised in the weeks following the fire, complaining of severe anxiety, poor sleep with recurrent nightmares, and various other symptoms of depression. What is of interest is that many officers were able to deal with their symptoms after discussion, and eventually returned to work. However, some officers with rigid traits to their personality, who tended to respect authority, had special difficulty coming to terms with what had happened, and in some cases had to leave the service. The traumatic events were no worse, but they had traits that made them especially vulnerable to what had occurred (McFarlane, personal communication).

## STRENGTHS OF THE MODEL

The model seeks to bring common mental disorders into a unifying framework, and relate them to advancing knowledge in biological psychiatry. In order to do this, it is thought essential to abandon a categorical model of disease, and to explore a model which has been empirically derived from patients, and which directly corresponds to possible biological derangements that occur in common disorders.

The model proposed has no difficulty in accounting for 'co-morbidity' of anxious and depressed states; and indeed, would have predicted them on two grounds. First, the associations between the biological sub-systems which underlie these common disorders; and second, the associations between the social factors and each dimension of symptomatology are themselves correlated, so that a mixture of the two states would be expected.

The development of different types of symptom is seen as being determined by early childhood events, the present social circumstances and the kind of provoking event, and not at all by genetic factors. Genetic factors are seen as being very important in determining overall vulnerability towards common mental disorders, and are responsible for some of the specific vulnerability to major mental disorders such as schizophrenia and bipolar illness; but they do not determine why one person will become depressed and another anxious.

By making a distinction between factors determining the onset of disorder and those that determine the speed of recovery, the model is able to account for the many individuals encountered on community surveys who complain of many symptoms, but whose symptoms soon remit. It is possible that transient disorders represent the effects of stressful life events in relatively resilient people, who possess personal qualities that enable them to restitute spontaneously and quickly. It is also true that the onset of symptoms is determined by the magnitude of the provoking event, so that many disorders will be only just at threshold, and would be predicted to remit quickly.

However, once symptoms of depression have become established those with good social support and the availability of confiding relationships would be predicted to restitute more quickly. The distinction between spontaneous remission within two weeks and slower rates of remission helps to explain the discrepancy between findings on social support, which were described in Chapter 8.

Finally, by directing separate attention to processes of restitution the model directs attention to common factors between patients with long-standing disorders.

## IMPLICATIONS FOR RESEARCH

### Vulnerability research

It is time for research to move away from its current emphasis upon stressful life events, and to turn attention to vulnerability. Stressful events help us to understand why an individual destabilises at a particular time, but they represent only a rather small part of causation. Some individuals destabilise with very small stressors, and some even develop symptoms in the absence of discernible acutely stressful events.

Researchers naturally carry out projects that are feasible for them, and it is not hard to see why progress has been so slight. If we carry out research only on populations that have destabilised but failed to restitute (in simple language, 'cases'!) then we never learn about factors that have helped others to surmount equally severe life problems. If we try to elucidate early life experience by asking 'cases' how they remember their childhoods we obtain information of doubtful validity and in any case never learn much about how such people differ from others who did not destabilise.

Longitudinal, prospective surveys are clearly of great potential importance, especially if they collect information about styles of parenting and methods of family-coping that might be important in understanding the development of disorder in adult life. However, the researchers who carry out such work typically have other concerns, and in any case tend not to follow their sample far enough into adult life. However, exceptional datasets do exist, and we can expect better information to accumulate in the future – providing that we wait long enough.

An alternative design offers quicker returns, although it has problems of its own. This is to study populations who have all endured some specified stress, and to concentrate on individuals who have had severe stress but not destabilised, those who have destabilised but managed to restitute spontaneously, and others who have become 'cases'. The death of a child, the death or imprisonment of a spouse, suffering a natural disaster, becoming a refugee are all natural test beds for such research. One needs to study factors such as coping styles, asthenic traits and locus of control. It is of great interest to document the methods of psychological restitution that spontaneous restituters have used, as these may be useful for others.

## Destabilisation

We predict that factors responsible for destabilisation are not the same across diagnoses, and that this will be especially true if one includes vulnerability as well as symptom-releasing factors. This prediction follows from our belief that genetic factors are not of importance in determining specific symptoms.

Depressive illnesses following physical illnesses are not a homogeneous group. Some may possibly be directly related to the physical disease process itself, but the majority are probably due to the physical illness acting as the 'life event' and releasing depression in a vulnerable individual. Studies need to be carried out which are addressed to those factors which favour the development of depression in the physically ill.

## Restitution

This needs to be studied in its own right, rather than having to be disembedded – as we have done to prepare this book – from studies that were planned with other ends in mind. The hypothesis that we are advancing here is that the factors that determine medium- and long-term restitution tend to be constant across diagnoses, and that social factors are of great importance.

## Taxonomy

While it is encouraging that Wilmink (1989) has been able to replicate our work on the dimensions of neurosis in Holland, it is important to discover how robust our model is across cultures, and across research interviews. Provided that the research interview gives reasonable coverage of the symptom area, one would expect similar results to our own to emerge, provided that similar methods of analysis were used.

For the forseeable future, it seems likely that official taxonomies will continue to use categorical models and earnestly to report 'co-morbidity'; but we would hope that a start could be made in experimenting with a system that did two things: gave a score on two dimensions, and mentioned any particular forms of symptom formation (such as somatisation, agoraphobia, panic or obsessional symptoms) that suggested particular therapeutic approaches.

## *Social factors*

The model proposed in this book, and our review of that literature which is relevant to the model, have shown the central relevance of social circumstances to vulnerability, destabilisation and restitution. A good deal of work needs to be done on the improvement of the measurement of social circumstances so that we are better able to answer questions about the relationships between specific social factors and the different dimensions of morbidity. Further research, using the bio-social model, is needed into the relationship between the social circumstances, and mental and physical health status of those who seek care from social care agencies.

## SHORTCOMINGS OF THE MODEL

The data given in this book only provide preliminary pointers to an eventual model for common mental disorders. It is likely that many modifications will be made to the model as more data become available.

The most serious weakness in the model is that there is considerable overlap between the factors responsible for vulnerability, destabilisation and restitution. For example, high neuroticism scores and adverse social conditions not only make individuals more vulnerable, but they also delay restitution to some extent. The same is probably true of people with asthenic traits, with high scores on hypochondriasis scales, and with low ego-strength.

There is also common ground between the factors responsible for destabilisation and restitution, although each appears relatively more important for one than for the other. For example, the severity of a provoking event is probably related to both, although more to destabilisation; while chronic social adversity and physical illness are also related to both, but more so to delayed restitution.

# 10 Public health implications of the model

## IMPLICATIONS OF THE ANALYSIS AT 'FIVE LEVELS AND FOUR FILTERS'

There are important public health implications of the rates for mental disorders at the five levels described by us in Chapter 2. Despite the fact that mental illness services are treating the most severe cases, the majority of disordered patients are seen in primary care settings. However, many of these disorders will not be detected by the clinician seeing them. Providing that it can be shown that detection of such disorders actually helps the patient, training general practitioners and internists and surgeons in the detection and management of the common forms of mental disorder becomes an important public health task.

Since a substantial proportion of the more severe forms of mental disorder will in fact be referred to specialist mental illness services, the next implication is that it is of great public health importance to organise such services so that they are most cost-effective, and so that chronic disability due to severe mental disorder is minimised. It is quite wrong to think of 'mental disorder' as a homogeneous entity, so that all resources are funnelled into primary care; the spontaneous remission rate of disorders seen in general medical settings is high, and those referred to levels 4 and 5 are much more likely to have special treatment needs. However, the figures do argue for better co-ordination of services between primary care and specialised services. It becomes important to consider the best ways in which specialist mental illness services can integrate with primary care services.

This leaves unanswered the problem of what to do with the large numbers of disordered people consulting care-givers, at level 2. Since the numbers of consultant psychiatrists and clinical psychologists can never be sufficient to meet needs on this scale, it becomes reasonable to design treatment packages which can be administered by less expensive staff in community and general medical settings. Thus, an important part of many training programmes for community workers is to give them therapeutic skills which can be used for certain targeted groups. Examples of such skills would be behavioural treatments for agoraphobia, anxiety management packages, and methods of bereavement counselling, in addition to any general counselling skills that were taught.

## Implications of our dimensional model

### *Primary prevention*

It is unlikely that common disorders can ever be completely prevented: there will always be vulnerable people, and the kinds of life events that release episodes of illness are part of being alive. However, much real preventive work can nonetheless be carried out. It follows that it only really makes sense to try primary prevention with groups of patients who are known to be vulnerable. This has generally been done by thinking in terms of the environmental factor that is potentially releasing disorder: thus, preventive work has been described with those recently bereaved, with women who have had breast cancer operated upon, with survivors of some natural disaster, or with young wives whose husbands have just been imprisoned. However, it would actually make better sense to identify patients within such groups who are known to be vulnerable, either because of previous episodes of illness or because of personality traits like high 'neuroticism'. An example of such a group would be pregnant women who have had an episode of depression after a previous baby was born (see Holden *et al.* 1989).

### *Secondary prevention*

Even without treatment, the majority of disorders seen in consulting settings will eventually restitute spontaneously. The importance of case detection is to help people to restitute more quickly than they would have done on their own. This constitutes secondary prevention by early case detection. The evidence that early case detection is helpful to the patient is not as overwhelming as one would wish, but the weight of evidence favours a positive effect (see Chapter 3).

The dimensional view of anxiety–depression that we have proposed is consistent with the view that long-standing minor anxiety symptoms act as vulnerability factors towards the development of common forms of depressive reaction, so that the depressive symptoms are often secondary to the anxiety symptoms. If this is so, teaching community workers simple anxiety management procedures for use with chronically anxious people might be expected to have a preventive effect on the development of depressive illnesses. This possibility awaits future research.

### Tertiary prevention: treating established illnesses

Another aim of teaching doctors to detect mental disorders is to identify the minority of patients with disorders that are unlikely to restitute without help. Agoraphobia, obsessional neurosis and chronic schizophrenia are all examples of disorders that have negligible spontaneous remission rates, while acute schizophrenia, severe (psychotic) depression and mania are examples of disorders that will probably remit eventually, but whose course can be modified dramatically by medical treatment. However, the common forms of mental disorders are not like this: they take the form of mixed states of anxiety and depression, often accompanied by somatic symptoms. We have seen that there is evidence favouring the effectiveness of 'anti-depressants', which in fact have both anxiety-reducing and mood-elevating effects, and that it is probable that mere detection of disorder, followed by non-specific counselling treatment, has an effect in shortening the course of such disorders. Teaching simple skills of detecting disorder, and helping patients to 're-attribute' their somatic symptoms (Goldberg *et al.* 1989) are therefore important components of skills packages for doctors working in general medical settings. Social workers and specialised nurses carrying out work in the community need to be taught counselling skills, special skills for helping families to cope with schizophrenic members, and other focused therapeutic interventions.

In the remainder of the chapter we will address these problems by first considering the ways in which mental illness services might best work with primary care and general medical services, and then considering the effect that such changed patterns of working have on the hospital-based mental illness services. We then consider the organisation of social work services. The final section of the chapter is devoted to the need for training courses, with sections on the training needs of medical practitioners, social workers and community psychiatric nurses.

## PSYCHIATRIC SERVICES IN THE COMMUNITY

### Psychiatrists in primary care clinics

A survey of British consultant psychiatrists showed that by 1984 20 per cent were working in primary care, and the number had been rising sharply with each year that passed (Strathdee and Williams 1985). Younger psychiatrists were more likely to carry out this work, which they usually did in addition to their hospital duties, rather than instead of some of them. By 1988, fully 56 per cent of Scottish psychiatrists were occupied in the same way (Pullen and Yellowlees 1988).

The commonest pattern of work was described as the *shifted out-patient* model, in which the psychiatrist carries out what is effectively an out-patient clinic, except that it is located in the community in a group practice – often during a flat time, when the GPs are not using all their offices. The psychiatrist is mainly seeing discharged hospital patients, and his or her contact with the GP is minimal. This model accounted for almost two-thirds of the psychiatrists.

The *consultation* model accounts for another quarter: here the psychiatrist spends much of his time with the GP, trying to advise him or her or improve his or her therapeutic skills, but also sees patients when asked to do so. If the first model is like sending food to starving countries in the developing world, the second is like sending irrigation equipment and seeds.

The least prevalent model, which accounted for only 5 per cent of the respondents, is *the liaison-attachment* model, where the psychiatrist rarely sees patients, but forges links with other members of the primary care team.

Tyrer *et al.* (1984) gave an early description of the 'shifted out-patient' model in five general practices, and showed that the patients preferred to see a psychiatrist in this setting because it was more convenient and had less stigma and was less formal. He argued that there was better communication with the GP and that there were advantages in having access to the GP's notes. He made the penetrating observation that those practices that required most input from him were the least welcoming. Tyrer used case register data to compare the effects of the new service with areas in Nottingham where such clinics were not being offered at the time, and shows that more ex-hospital psychiatric patients come back into care, although fewer new patients are seen.

A modification of the consultation model is the *consultation-liaison* model, where the psychiatrist attends the primary care team meeting and discusses the management of several problem patients with members of the primary care staff, after which s/he sees several patients, often in conjunction with the GP (Mitchell 1983; Creed and Marks 1989). This model effectively reaches a much wider set of patients than the 'shifted out-patient' model, since in addition to the patients who are prepared to see the psychiatrist, the GP can seek advice about the group of psychotic patients who prefer not to be seen by the psychiatrist, as well as gaining advice about many patients with common disorders who have been seen but not referred. A comparison between the two models reported by Goldberg

(1991) showed that the psychiatrist barely saw the GPs at all in the 'shifted out-patient' model, and less than 5 per cent of patients seen were new patients; in contrast, the psychiatrist spent between 30 per cent and 60 per cent of the session with the GPs, and 45 per cent of the patients seen were new patients. Most (87 per cent) patients seen in the former clinics were those with schizophrenia or bipolar illness, whereas over half of those seen in the latter suffered from common disorders.

*Table 10.1* A comparison between sessions by psychiatrists in primary care using two types of approach (Goldberg 1991)

| Average number of patients | Shifted out-patients | Consultation-liaison |
| --- | --- | --- |
| Seen by psychiatrist | 5.3 | 1.8 |
| Discussed with CPNs | 3–4 | zero |
| Discussed with GPs and nurses | zero | 4–6 |

Strathdee and her colleagues (1990) compared patients referred to them in primary care clinics with those referred to out-patient departments, and showed that the two groups were similar in terms of their social adjustment and their psychological and physical health. They saw more women in primary care, and more personality disorders in out-patients, and they confirmed that the patients preferred to be seen in primary care settings.

## Effects of community services on need for hospital services

Williams and Balestrieri (1989) have shown a statistical association between the number of psychiatrists working in primary care and reductions in admission rates to hospital; however, the direction of the causal link is less clear than the authors suggest. Did the move by psychiatrists into primary care enable a reduction to be made in admissions, or did they move into primary care in response to bed closures and restrictions in the hospital service – in other words, did the psychiatrists jump, or were they pushed?

Tyrer and his colleagues (1984, 1989) claim that community services in Nottingham – which include a heavy component of primary care clinics – do have such an effect, although the decrease seems to be achieved by a reduction in admissions for depressive illness, neurosis and personality disorders, since no reduction occurs in respect of admissions for schizophrenia and organic states, and admissions for 'other' diagnoses actually show a consistent rise. It is clearly appropriate to use beds for the most severe disorders, and to observe others with more complex problems.

However, it appears from this study that hospital beds will still be needed despite the development of community services.

Stefansson and Cullberg (1986) used a case register to assess the impact of the introduction of community mental health centres with substantial emphasis on out-patient care on the 'Nacka Project' in Sweden. There was an overall increase of about 30 per cent in the total number of patients seen, with a reduction of 22 per cent in admissions to hospital. However, a similar study in Mannheim by Hafner and Klug (1982) confirmed the overall increase in total number of patients seen, but showed an actual increase in the numbers of patients requiring short-term admission.

A controlled study of introducing community psychiatric services to primary care was carried out in the Norwegian city of Tromso by Hansen (1987). A new team, not affiliated to the mental hospital, and dedicated to avoiding admission, attached itself to primary care teams throughout the city. The mental health services for the city are divided between two sectorised teams, one of which was critical about the new service, because it was not integrated into the rest of the mental health service. No change in admission rates occurred in this sector, despite the activities of the team. However, a substantial reduction took place in the other sector, which could be entirely attributed to changed professional behaviours of the mental hospital staff in this team, rather than any changed behaviour of primary care physicians.

In Manchester we have investigated the effects of randomising primary care physicians to an index group which received regular liaison from members of a multi-disciplinary community mental health team, and a control group who continued to relate to the mental illness service by means of traditional doctors' referral letters. In this way we built up two groups of 20,000 people at risk, and compared their utilisation of mental illness services (Jackson *et al.* 1991).

The community service resulted in almost three times as many people coming into care. Many of these additional cases were common disorders such as anxiety–depressions and adjustment disorders: but we also treated almost twice as many schizophrenics, and three times as many cases of depression. However, there was only a negligible reduction in morbidity treated in hospital, possibly because we had already reduced hospital treatment to a minimum before the study started.

## ORGANISATION OF SOCIAL WORK SERVICES

By now it must be obvious to the reader that common mental disorders are sometimes caused by, sometimes exacerbated by, and sometimes ameliorated by, social events and circumstances. We have argued elsewhere

(Goldberg and Huxley 1980; Huxley 1990) that health care and social care ought to be delivered together for maximum effectiveness and efficiency. Bringing health and social care together in organised western health care systems is a challenge, and we appear to be, if anything, getting further away from achieving joint approaches to patient care than we were ten years ago when we wrote our original book (Goldberg and Huxley 1980).

A particular problem in the UK is the attempt to separate health and social care in the White Papers (Department of Health 1989a and b). If the thinking in the White Papers is followed slavishly then increasing fragmentation of services is likely to result. Over the past ten years, while there has been an increase in the recognition that much of the work done by social workers in social services settings does constitute mental health social work, and the 1983 Mental Health Act did create the Approved Social Worker, there have been problems with the role of social workers within the specialised mental health services (levels 4 and 5). In general medical clinics there appears to have been very little progress in finding ways of enabling GPs and social workers to work more closely together on common mental disorders. Although there are some individual examples of good practice where community mental health teams have enabled GPs to make referrals and undertake joint work, the general picture is one in which the social aspects of care are neglected. This is unfortunate, because, as we have pointed out elsewhere (Huxley *et al.* 1990) to withhold social care at the time of presentation to the general practitioner means that social workers are missing one of the best opportunities for early inter- vention, and thus secondary prevention.

Within the mental illness service there has been a reduction in the contribution from hospital social workers who have largely been withdrawn to work in community settings. Hospital patients almost certainly have a poorer assessment as a result, and in some places the withdrawal of hospital social workers is not compensated for by continuing multi-disciplinary work from the new community base. As a result there may be more work being undertaken with common mental disorders, but more severe disorders are being neglected. In 1974 hospital social workers became the responsibility of social service departments in the UK, and since then the progressive with- drawal of social workers from hospital settings to work in the community has effectively undermined multi-disciplinary teamwork in both settings.

It is hard to sustain the argument that by locating social workers in the community there has been a net increase in the amount of mental health social work undertaken with psychiatric patients by local authorities. Social workers in existing community teams must, as we have seen, already have been dealing with mental health problems and undertaking mental health social work, but calling it something else. Removing social workers from health-care settings to work in the community not only weakens the contribution which can be made by social workers to the care of people who are in states of acute distress, but carries with it the risk that unless it is targeted on people with long-term problems the overall care of those with the most severe disabilities will be weakened as a result.

The growth of community mental health centres and teams (Sayce 1990) has gone some way to correcting the tendency for social workers to be withdrawn from multi-disciplinary teams, but social services contributions to the creation, staffing and management of community teams have tended to follow rather than lead the health service contribution. In many ways this is understandable because over the past ten years local authorities have been faced with decreasing budgets. It is also true to say, however, that there continues to be a 'child care officer' hegemony in local authority social services departments in the UK, in spite of the fact that child care social workers are not in a majority in SSDs, the child care budget is frequently smaller than the budget for elderly people, and most of the public scandal about practice has been in the child care field. Child care nevertheless dominates the thinking in social services departments. The local authorities' statutory child care responsibilities are indeed burdensome, and the increases in statutory responsibilities combined with the shrinking budget do raise the question of whether social services' contribution to mental health care and to psychiatric social work is ever going to be discharged properly.

## A combined mental health service

One solution, which would not be popular with the child care lobby, would be to remove care for patients at levels 2, 4 and 5 from local authority responsibility and discharge them through the health service, or better still through a combined health and local authority funded 'mental health service'. This would leave social services with responsibility for preventive mental health social work in existing child care cases, and with the statutory functions of mental health legislation. This has many disadvantages (mostly for professionals), but in terms of the efficiency and effectiveness of the care provided the patient/client would almost certainly benefit. Such an arrangement would enable us to combine health and social care and provide both at the points where they are most needed, in primary care (and social services) at the early stages of destabilisation, and at levels 4 and 5 when those with more serious disorders need social assessment and social care to prevent the development of a chronic course.

A combined service has been advocated by Kathleen Jones (1988) who identifies the need for a common base for professional staff working in the community so that services avoid fragmentation, save travelling time and encourage face-to-face communication. She suggests that community services should be operated from large rather than small 'centres' (serving populations of up to 200,000) so that they have a real impact, can include a range of services and discharge research and training functions.

A similar solution may be necessary in relation to child psychiatry, where the same problems (between health and social services) in joint work can be found. These problems probably reflect genuine differences in the philosophies of care of different professional groups, but the conflict does not serve the best interests of children and families. It is crucial to get the balance of social and health care correct, and to make sure that the only social care which is provided is not simply reduced to the statutory function, but includes social assessment and preventive work. We have seen the relevance of disturbance in childhood for depression and anxiety in later life. A genuinely preventive contribution can be made where child psychiatry and social care work together.

However services come to be organised in future, the requirements of a joint approach will remain the same. Among these are the need to have a genuine multi-disciplinary assessment and to include the user's views in a systematic way. Assessment will include clinical and social aspects – details of family composition, previous history, childhood problems and present material difficulties and recent life events as well as an assessment of social relationships and network support. Treatment goals will be established for both clinical and social circumstances, and where possible these will be agreed with the patient/client. We know that there will be circumstances where joint goals are not possible, and in these cases the professionals must understand who is responsible for which aspect of care with each patient/client. Regular review of these goals is necessary and will need to be recorded in a suitable format. Assessments of outcome need to be built into the system so that progress can be assessed in a systematic way and related to measures obtained at the outset. There are many competing systems of assessment and outcome, but we feel that structured assessments of 'quality of life' have an important part to play, not only because they cover the relevant life domains outlined above, but because they are acceptable to users, give them a systematic input to the assessment process, and can be administered in a short time. It may also be possible to make use of the vast amount of relevant material developed by Brown and his colleagues (Brown and Harris 1989) to produce a more systematic social assessment of life events and difficulties which can be used in a social work context.

It is apparent from work in the USA (Huxley *et al.* 1990) and in the intentions of the UK White Paper *Caring for People* that case management can play a central role in the care of people with long-term disabilities. The core functions of case management are assessment, counselling, linkage/ brokerage (enabling the client to establish contact with other agencies providing needed services), monitoring and evaluation, and these are the functions which are essential to maintain people in the community. It is possible that the monitoring function is of most significance with people with long-term disability, and is related to their 'quality of life' whereas brokerage may not be (Huxley and Warner, 1990). In order to make a difference to the effectiveness of services, case management needs to be properly organised, and to include direct service provision by the 'case manager'. For case management services to be as effective as they appear to be in the USA (Huxley et al. 1990), it is of vital importance to arrange for adequate training for case managers and adequate support services for them.

## THE NEED FOR TRAINING

### Courses for family doctors

In recent years there has been much interest in devising training courses in mental health skills for family doctors which can be shown to be effective in changing their professional behaviours. Courses that are too general may not alter observed behaviour with patients: an example of this would be Zabarenko and others' (1968) demonstration that Balint seminars did not improve the professional behaviours of family doctors. Bensing and Sluijs (1985) exposed GPs to a three-month course of Rogerian training, and recorded live consultations before and after training. Although the doctors' behaviour changed in the expected way, the patients' behaviour didn't change, in that they did not talk more about their problems.

In general it is more effective if training focuses on specific skills, and if trainees are provided with feedback (either audio or video) of their actual behaviour with patients. Lesser (1985) produced his 'problem-based interviewing' which focuses on specific skills to be acquired by trainees, and McWhinney's group (Levenstein et al. 1986; Brown et al. 1986) have also done the same, with operational descriptions of desirable and undesirable behaviours.

Video feedback has been shown to be effective by Verby et al. (1979) and by Goldberg and his colleagues (1980a). Gask and her colleagues (1988) show that GP trainees can be taught Lesser's 'problem-orientated' model using group video feedback of interview skills at a weekly supervision session lasting two hours, given over six months.

Established general practitioners can also benefit from teaching using feedback. Gask and others (1987) showed that such skills could also be learned, using group feedback of audiotaped consultations, in two-hour sessions spaced over 18 weeks. Gask and McGrath (1989) advocate a skills-sharing approach, in which primary care physicians are helped to acquire the necessary skills first from interested psychiatrists and psychologists, but eventually from their own trainers.

## Special skills packages

Goldberg *et al.* (1989) describe a special treatment package to help GPs deal with sub-acute somatisation, while Gask and her colleagues (1989) show that this model can be effectively taught. Andrews and Brodaty (1980) describe an extended training course for GPs in psycho-therapeutic skills extending over 26 sessions, including instruction in behaviour therapy, marital and sexual counselling. Gath and Mynors-Wallis (1991) describe a problem-solving package for the treatment of anxiety disorders by family doctors, and show that it is effective for patients with persistent anxiety. It is likely that such specific training packages will continue to be developed as services expand for patients in general medical settings.

## Training implications for social workers and community nurses

Since we know that health and social care workers will very frequently encounter patients and clients with common mental disorders then we should aim to provide all such workers with some basic understanding. All basic trained nurses and social workers need to have an understanding of the relationship between health and social circumstances, health and social care systems, and health and social assessment and intervention. In addition they need to grasp the difference between problems which they can handle without specialist help and those where they will need the assistance of others.

It is essential that students in training, in whatever discipline, encounter people with common mental illnesses. While there is room for training packages which develop a degree of familiarity with the problem at a distance, there is usually no substitute for a period of direct work with service users. This in turn means that the practice teacher or supervisor of the student should have had a similar exposure, and the development of training packages for practice teachers and supervisors could be a useful first step. The psychiatric or mental health component in basic social work and nurse education should enable the learner to become acquainted with the techniques of recognition of states of anxiety and depression. In both professions this experience will best be gained by working in community settings where common disorders are most likely to be seen, in general practice and in social services teams.

## Social work training

In basic social work and probation training (Diploma in Social Work level) recognition training is probably most appropriately given at an early stage rather than reserving consideration of anxiety and depression for specialist mental health modules at a later stage of the programme. This means that, just as in the same way that the Central Council for Education and Training in Social Work (CCETSW) requires anti-racist and anti-sexist teaching to permeate the curriculum in social work education, so a common mental disorder awareness should permeate basic social work and nurse training. An introduction, again preferably through practice, to more severe and rarer disorders should accompany this teaching, but, for those who intend to specialise, prolonged exposure to work with people with severe disorders, preferably in a multi-disciplinary context is required. In both cases, of rare and common disorder, there has to be a recognition that the clinical and social aspects of the patient's situation are going to be almost inextricably bound together. Physical and mental illness will coexist with serious social difficulties in both material circumstances and relationships, and a collaborative approach involving several professional disciplines, the carer if there is one, the user, and other agencies will almost always be required.

The training of social workers should enable them to make a preliminary assessment of the health care needs of their clients, not least because we know that a substantial proportion, if not the majority of clients in contact with social services have physical health problems. Part of this induction training should include some consideration of the difficult area of personality because, as we have seen, personality does appear to play a part in the vulnerability to common mental disorder. This is not easy teaching, but it is necessary to include personality because it is probably one of the main indicators that the individual worker is going to need the help of others to handle the problem. Where personality difficulties are present it is often hard for workers to form an opinion whether help should be kept to a minimum or whether it is appropriate to enter into a long-term helping role. These things are best decided (by doctors as well as social workers) with the assistance of other workers.

Social workers need to be taught basic counselling skills in order to undertake the kind of assessment work which is required, and on the whole teaching these skills is still a core part of the training of both disciplines. Although individuals suffer from common mental illnesses, disturbances in their social networks are intimately connected as cause or consequence. A basic understanding of interpersonal, familial and social relationships is essential, although this need not be at the level of understanding or competence required to undertake family group work or expressed emotion counselling with families of patients. These could be left to post-qualifying education for those who intend to specialise in work with more severely ill people.

Social workers could benefit from practical experience in crisis work. Some understanding of the nature and stages of a 'crisis' and training, perhaps within a specialist crisis team, would enable them to be more effective at dealing with the acute social problems which are associated with increased symptom levels. Our finding that family 'break-up' is associated with a better outcome in social services clients after one year, emphasises the point that effective help at this time of crisis may be important in enabling restitution to take place. As Lin *et al.* (1985) point out, people going through a marital disruption also have their social network support disrupted and outside help may be necessary to prevent or relieve depressive tendencies. These findings confirm that work with this sort of family problem can appropriately be thought of as mental health social work.

The ability to seek out resources which are necessary to ameliorate the poverty of patients' social circumstances is an essential for the worker in this field. This ability has been subsumed under a variety of headings such as 'linkage', 'brokerage' and sometimes 'advocacy'. Clearly there is the potential for positive events associated with this type of help to promote restitution, although Brown's work (Brown *et al.* 1988) did not provide support for this thesis in people who had been depressed for over a year. For those with more acute difficulties social workers, nurses or case managers, or whoever undertakes this task, can, however, probably make a major difference to the course of the disorder, if circumstances can be ameliorated through the use of income maintenance and housing agencies. Kedward (1969) argued that restitution was associated with the amelioration of the person's material problems. This type of work is also legitimately called mental health social work.

For those who are going to specialise in work in health care and in work with mental illness specifically then there must be formal post-basic education which develops skills and abilities beyond the basic level and over time (Huxley and Oliver 1990). Staff development is enhanced if credit accumulation and transfer schemes are available so that credits acquired can be used to gain further qualifications or open up avenues of further or higher education which would otherwise be unavailable. Transfer of learning from one discipline to another also becomes a possibility under CAT schemes. Multi-disciplinary training which provides credits acceptable to several disciplines is very attractive, and even more attractive if it is offered in modular form, and part time, to enhance access.

There is a need for training in the statutory functions associated with compulsory admission to hospital, currently discharged by the Approved Social Worker (ASW) in the UK. This statutory responsibility should remain with the social services department to ensure the independence of the judgement from that of health service workers. A need also exists, however, to organise training on a wider basis than within-authority courses, which is probably the most common practice. There is evidence that the psychiatry teaching is best undertaken by academic psychiatrists with the resources to do it (Huxley and Oliver 1990), and that there are considerable benefits for ASWs in training if their programme is organised across several authorities rather than within the same authority (however large). Among the benefits are the avoidance of an unthreatening comfortable view of one's own practices and procedures because one can be challenged by workers who use different approaches, and, conversely, multi-agency training enables examples of good practice in different authorities to be more widely disseminated.

## Courses for nurses

White (1990) has documented the history of community psychiatric nursing education in the UK, and shows that, like psychiatric social work education, it has survived a chronic shortage of central funding, poorly organised post-basic education, and rampant and ultimately misplaced genericism in the rest of professional nurse education. The curriculum of specialist community nurse training changed radically during the 1980s to become focused on a more practical ('skills-oriented') training, in line with developments elsewhere in professional and vocational education for social care professionals. The latest curriculum (ENB c.c.no 812) aims to produce a worker who can function autonomously and as a member of a team providing care to people in community settings. The curriculum for the Mental Health Branch of Project 2000 courses continues the same trend, preparing nurses for working in community settings. The increasing emphasis upon the acquisition and practice of therapeutic skills in work with people with specific illnesses is to be welcomed.

Given the considerable similarities, particularly at the post-basic level, in the knowledge and skills required by nurses and social workers for work with mentally ill people in the community, it is logical for the training bodies (CCETSW and ENB) to be considering the provision of some common post-basic education. Candidates which immediately spring to mind are the acquisition of specific techniques, such as in work with schizophrenia sufferers or their relatives (Brooker 1990; Wolsey 1990), or preparation for the provision of reorganised community 'case management' services.

White (1990) has lamented the absence of a nationally agreed education strategy for post-registration psychiatric nurses but, given the similarities identified above, the case for a comprehensive post-basic strategy in the whole mental health field would seem to be required. The diversity and inadequacy of most post-qualifying education as it is presently organised surely supports the argument for an integrated mental health service with responsibility for the development, coordination and provision of approved programmes. The separation of different disciplines in training is a handicap to successful work in the community, and has probably contributed to our present level of difficulty. Persuading professional and training interests to give up entrenched positions is, of course, another matter.

## CONCLUDING COMMENT

During the asylum era we knew next to nothing about the causes of mental disorder, and the proportion of the population who could expect to receive care from a mental health professional was very low. However, our predecessors had a very clear notion of the structures – both administrative and architectural – that were required, and these structures secured resources to maintain services.

There is now an explosion of knowledge about mental disorder, and it at last becomes possible to discern the outlines of a model for mental disorder which takes account of findings in both social psychiatry and molecular biology. However, we have not made corresponding progress in refining the administrative and architectural requirements for meeting the needs of the mentally ill, and in most countries of the world services for the mentally ill survive on the crumbs left from the banquet of general health care. At times of scarce resource, our services are very easy to prune. The liberation of others – clinical psychologists, nurses and social workers – from domination by the medical profession has occurred in many countries, and has been the enemy of a united service which offers the best to patients, and which commands adequate resources from society.

The lack of unity of service has been accompanied by a rather narrow view of training by each profession. In England, clinical psychologists know very little about social psychiatry and epidemiology; social workers know very little about either psychology or the biological basis of mental disorders; and our psychiatrists all too often adopt either a narrowly biological approach to their subject, or an approach heavily emphasising dynamic psychiatry which is relatively uninfluenced by recent advances in either biological or social psychiatry.

We offer this book in hopes that it will answer a need felt by those who require a broad-based, eclectic approach to their subject which takes account of advances in knowledge across a wide front. It will certainly be overtaken by advances in knowledge almost before it appears, but we offer it as a rough sketch rather than as a finished picture.

# References

Abrahams, M. and Whitlock, F. (1969) 'Childhood experiences of depression', *British Journal of Psychiatry*, 115, 883–888.

Alloway, R. and Bebbington, P. (1987) 'The buffer theory of social support – a review of the literature', *Psychological Medicine*, 17, 91–108.

American Psychiatric Association (1987) *Diagnostic and Statistical Manual of Mental Disorders* (Third Edition – Revised). Washington: American Psychiatric Association.

Andersen, A. and Laake, P. (1983) 'A causal model for physician utilisation: analysis of Norwegian data', *Medical Care*, 21, 266–278.

Andersen, R. and Aday, L. (1978) 'Access to medical care in the US. Realised and potential', *Medical Care*, 16, 533–546.

Andersen, R., Kravits, J. and Anderson, O. (1975) *Equity in Health Services: Empirical Analyses in Social Policy*. Cambridge, Mass.: Ballenger.

Andrews, G. and Brodaty, H. (1980) 'General practitioner as psychotherapist', *Medical Journal of Australia*, 50, 655–659.

Andrews, G. and Brown, G.W. (1988) 'Social support, onset of depression and personality: An exploratory analysis', *Social Psychiatry*, 23, 99–108.

Andrews, G., Kiloh, L. and Kehoe, L. (1978) 'Asthenic personality, myth or reality', *Australian and New Zealand Journal of Psychiatry*, 12, 95–98.

Andrews, G., Tennant, C., Hewson, D. and Vaillant, G. (1978) 'Life event stress, social support, coping style and risk of psychological impairment', *Journal of Nervous and Mental Disease*, 166, 307–316.

Andrews, G., Neilson, M., Hunt, C., Stewart, G. and Kiloh, L. (1990) 'Diagnosis, personality and the long-term outcome of depression', *British Journal of Psychiatry*, 157, 13–18.

Andrews, G., Stewart, G., Morris-Yates, A., Holt, N. and Henderson, A.S. (1990) 'Evidence for a general neurotic syndrome', *British Journal of Psychiatry*, 157, 6–12.

Aneshensel, C., Frerichs, R. and Clark, V.A., (1981) 'Family roles and sex differences in depression', *Journal of Health and Social Behaviour*, 22, 379–393.

Aneshensel, C., Frerichs, R. and Huba, G. (1984) 'Depression and physical illness: a multi-wave, non-recursive causal model', *Journal of Health and Social Behaviour*, 25, 350–371.

Angst, J. (1990) 'Depression and anxiety: a review of studies in the community and in primary care', in *Psychological Disorders in General Medical Settings* (ed.

N. Sartorius, D. Goldberg, G. de Girolamo, J. Costa e Silva, Y. LeCrubier and H.-U. Wittchen). Bern: Huber-Hogrefe.

Angst, J. and Clayton, P. (1986) 'Premorbid personality of depressive, bipolar and schizophrenic patients with special reference to suicidal issues', *Comprehensive Psychiatry*, 27, 511–532.

Angst, J. and Dobler-Mikola, A. (1984) 'The Zurich Study. II. The continuum from normal to pathological depressive mood swings', *European Archives of Psychiatry and Neurological Science*, 234, 21–29.

Angst, J. and Dobler-Mikola, A. (1985) 'The Zurich Study. VI. A continuum from depression to anxiety disorders?', *European Archives of Psychiatry and Neurological Science*, 235, 179–186.

Angst, J., Dobler-Mikola, A. and Binder, J. (1984) 'The Zurich Study. A prospective epidemiological study of depressive neurotic and psychosomatic syndromes', *European Archives of Psychiatry and Neurological Science*, 234, 13–20.

Angst, J., Vollrath, M., Merikangas, K. and Ernst, C. (1987) 'Co-morbidity of anxiety and depression in the Zurich Study', unpublished paper given at NIMH Conference on Symptom Co-morbidity in Anxiety and Depression. Tuxedo, New York.

Arreghini, E., Agostini, C. and Wilkinson, G. (in press) 'GP referral to specialist psychiatric services. A study comparing GPs' practices in North and South Verona', *Psychological Medicine*.

Atkinson, T., Liem, R. and Liem, J.H. (1986) 'The social costs of unemployment: implications for social support', *Journal of Health and Social Behaviour*, 27, 317–331.

Baker, G. and Brewerton, D. (1981) 'Rheumatoid arthritis: a psychiatric assessment', *British Medical Journal*, 282, 2014–2016.

Balestrieri, M., Williams, P. and Wilkinson, G. (1988) 'Specialist mental health treatment in general practice: a meta-analysis', *Psychological Medicine*, 18, 711–718.

Barrett, J.E. (1979) 'The relationship of life events to the onset of neurotic disorders', in *Stress and Mental Disorders* (ed. J.E. Barrett) (pp. 87–109). New York: Raven Press.

Bartrop, R., Luckhurst, E., Lazarus, L., Kiloh, L. and Penny, R. (1977) 'Depressed lymphocyte function after bereavement', *Lancet*, 1, 834–836.

Bebbington, P. (1987) Personal communication.

Bebbington, P. (1988) 'The social epidemiology of clinical depression', in *Handbook of Social Psychiatry* (ed. S. Henderson and G. Burrows). Amsterdam: Elsevier.

Bebbington, P., Hurry, J., Tennant, C., Sturt, E. and Wing, J. (1981) 'Epidemiology of mental disorders in Camberwell', *Psychological Medicine*, 11, 561–581.

Bebbington, P., Hurry, J., Tennant, C. and Sturt, E. (1984) 'Misfortune and resilience: a community study of women', *Psychological Medicine*, 14, 347–363.

Bebbington, P., Brugha, T., MacCarthy, B., Potter, J., Sturt, E., Wykes, T., Katz, R. and McGuffin, P. (1988) 'The Camberwell Collaborative Depression Study: I. Depressed probands: adversity and the form of depression', *British Journal of Psychiatry*, 152, 754–765.

Beck, A. (1967) *Depression: Clinical, Experimental and Theoretical Aspects*. New York: Hoeber.

Becker, J. (1974) *Depression: Theory and Research*.Washington: Winston.

Bensing, J. and Sluijs, E. (1985) 'Evaluation of an interview training course for general practitioners', *Social Science and Medicine*, 20, 737–744.

Berkanovic, E., Telesky, C. and Reeder, S. (1981) 'Structural and psychological factors in the decision to seek medical care for symptoms', *Medical Care*, 19, 693–709.

Berkman, L. and Syme, S. (1979) 'Social networks, host resistance and mortality', *American Journal of Epidemiology*, 109, 186–204.

Bifulco, A., Brown, G.W. and Harris, T. (1987) 'Loss of parent, lack of parental care and adult psychiatric disorder: the Islington study', *Journal of Affective Disorder*, 12, 115–128.

Birley, J. and Brown, G.W. (1970) 'Crises and life changes preceding the onset of acute schizophrenia', *Archives of General Psychiatry*, 26, 123–129.

Birtchnell, J. (1988) 'Depression and family relationships', *British Journal of Psychiatry*, 153, 758–769.

Birtchnell, J., Masters, N. and Deahl, M. (1988) 'Depression and the physical environment', *British Journal of Psychiatry*, 153, 56–64.

Black, A. (1974) 'The natural history of obsessional neurosis', in *Obsessional States* (ed. H. Beech) London: Methuen.

Black, J., Humphrey, J. and Niven, J. (1963) 'Inhibition of Mantoux reaction by direct suggestion under hypnosis', *British Medical Journal*, 1, 1649–1652.

Blalock, J. (1984) 'The immune system as a sensory organ', *Journal of Immunology*, 132, 1067–1070.

Blazer, D. (1980) 'Social support and mortality in an elderly population', Unpublished PhD thesis, University of North Carolina, USA.

Blazer, D., Swartz, M., Woodbury, M., Manton, K., Hughes, D. and George, L.K. (1988) 'Depressive symptoms and depressive diagnoses in a community sample', *Archives of General Psychiatry*, 45, 1078–1084.

Boardman, A.P. (1987) 'The General Health Questionnaire and the detection of emotional disorder by general practitioners: a replicated study', *British Journal of Psychiatry*, 151, 373–381.

Bolton, P. (1984) 'Management of compulsorily admitted patients to a high security unit', *International Journal of Social Psychiatry*, 30, 77–84.

Bolton, W. and Oatley, K. (1987) 'A longitudinal study of social support and depression in unemployed men', *British Journal of Psychiatry*, 17, 453–460.

Bradshaw, C. and Szabadi, E. (1989) 'Central neurotransmitter systems and the control of operant behaviour by "natural" reinforcers', in *The Neuropharmacological Basis of Reward* (ed. J. Liebman and S. Cooper). Oxford: Oxford University Press.

Bridges, K. and Goldberg, D. (1985) 'Somatic presentation of *DSM-III* psychiatric disorders in primary care', *Journal of Psychosomatic Research*, 29, 563–569.

Bridges, K. and Goldberg, D. (1987) 'Somatic presentations of depressive illness in primary care', in *The Presentation of Depression: Current Approaches* (ed. P. Freeling, L. Downey and J. Malkin). Royal College of General Practitioners, Occasional Paper 36.

Bridges, K., Goldberg, D., Evans, B. and Sharpe, T. (1991) 'Determinants of somatisation in primary care', *Psychological Medicine*.

Brodaty, H. (1983) 'Brief psychotherapy in general practice: a controlled prospective intervention trial', unpublished MD thesis, University of New South Wales, Australia.

Brodaty, H. and Andrews, G. (1983) 'Brief psychotherapy in family practice: a controlled prospective intervention trial', *British Journal of Psychiatry*, 143, 11–19.

Brooker, C. (1990) 'The application of the concept of expressed emotion to the role of the community psychiatric nurse: a research study', *International Journal of Nursing Studies*, 27, 277–285.

Brown, G.W. (1991) 'A psychosocial view of depression', in *Community Psychiatry* (ed. D.H. Bennett and H. Freeman). London: Churchill-Livingstone.

Brown, G.W. and Andrews, B.A. (1985) 'Comparison of Camberwell and Islington intimacy rating'. Unpublished paper.

Brown, G.W. and Harris, T.O. (1978a) *Social Origins of Depression*. London: Tavistock.

Brown, G.W. and Harris, T.O. (1978b) 'Social origins of depression: a reply', *Psychological Medicine*, 8, 577–588.

Brown, G.W. and Harris, T.O. (1986) 'Stressor, vulnerability and depression: a question of replication', *Psychological Medicine*, 16, 739–744.

Brown, G.W. and Harris, T.O. (1989) 'Depression', in *Life Events and Illness* (ed. G.W. Brown and T.O. Harris). London: Unwin Hyman.

Brown, G.W. and Prudo, R. (1981) 'Psychiatric disorder in a rural and an urban population. 1. Aetiology of depression', *Psychological Medicine*, 11, 581–599.

Brown, G.W., Craig, T.K. and Harris, T.O. (1985) 'Depression: disease or distress? Some epidemiological considerations', *British Journal of Psychiatry*, 147, 612–622.

Brown, G.W., Andrews, B.A., Harris, T.O., Adler, Z. and Bridge, L. (1986) 'Social support, self-esteem and depression', *Psychological Medicine*, 16, 813–831.

Brown, G.W., Bifulco, A. and Harris, T.O. (1987) 'Life events, vulnerability and onset of depression: some refinements', *British Journal of Psychiatry*, 150, 30–42.

Brown, G.W., Adler, Z. and Bifulco, A. (1988) 'Life events, difficulties and recovery fom chronic depression', *British Journal of Psychiatry*, 152, 487–498.

Brown, J. and Paraskevas, F. (1982) 'Cancer and depression: cancer presenting with depressive illness: an autoimmune disease?' *British Journal of Psychiatry*, 141, 227–232.

Brown, J., Stewart, M., McCracken, E., McWhinney, I. and Levenstein, J. (1986) 'The patient-centred clinical method. 2: Definition and application', *Family Practice*, 3, 75–79.

Brown, R., Strathdee, G., Christie-Brown, J. and Robinson, P. (1988) 'A comparison of referrals to primary care and hospital out-patients', *British Journal of Psychiatry*, 153, 168–173.

Brugha, T., Bebbington, P., MacCarthy, B., Sturt, E., Wykes, T. and Potter, J. (1990) 'Gender, social support and recovery from depressive disorders: a prospective clinical study', *Psychological Medicine*, 20, 147–156.

Burke, A. (1976) 'Socio-cultural determinants of attempted suicide among West Indians in Birmingham: ethnic origin and immigrant status', *British Journal of Psychiatry*, 129, 261–266.

Burke, A. (1984) 'Racism and psychiatric distress among West Indians in Britain', *International Journal of Social Psychiatry*, 30, 50–68.

Burvill, P. and Knuiman, M. (1983) 'The influence of minor psychiatric morbidity on consulting rates to GPs', *Psychological Medicine*, 13, 635–644.

Campbell, E., Cope, S. and Teasdale, J. (1983) 'Social factors and affective disorder: an investigation of Brown and Harris's model', *British Journal of Psychiatry*, 143, 548–553.

Carpenter, L. and Brockington, I. (1980) 'A study of mental illness in Asians, West Indians and Africans living in Manchester', *British Journal of Psychiatry*, 137, 201–205.

Champion, L. (1990) 'The relationship between social vulnerability and the occurrence of severely threatening life events', *Psychological Medicine*, 20, 157–161.

Cheng, T.-A. (1985) 'A pilot study of mental disorders in Taiwan', *Psychological Medicine*, 15, 195–203.

Cheng, T.-A. (1988) 'A community study of minor psychiatric morbidity in Taiwan', *Psychological Medicine*, 18, 953–968.

Cheng, T.-A. (1989) 'Psychosocial stress and minor psychiatric morbidity: a community study in Taiwan', *Journal of Affective Disorders*, 17, 137–152.

Clare, A. and Cairns, V.E. (1978) 'Design, development and use of a standardised interview to assess social maladjustment and dysfunction in community studies', *Psychological Medicine*, 8, 589–604.

Cleary, P.D. and Kessler, R. (1982) 'The estimation and interpretation of modifier effects', *Journal of Health and Social Behaviour*, 23, 159–169.

Cleary, P.D. and Mechanic, D. (1983) 'Sex differences in psychological distress among married people', *Journal of Health and Social Behaviour*, 24, 111–121.

Cloninger, C.R., Martin, R. and Guze, S.B. (1985) 'Diagnosis and prognosis in schizophrenia', *Archives of General Psychiatry*, 42, 15–25.

Cooke, D. and Hole, D. (1983) 'The aetiological importance of stressful life events', *British Journal of Psychiatry*, 143, 397–400.

Cooper, B. (1965) 'A study of 100 chronic psychiatric patients identified in general practice', *British Journal of Psychiatry*, 111, 595–605.

Cooper, B., Harwin, B., Depla, C. and Shepherd, M. (1975) 'Mental care in the community: an evaluative study', *Psychological Medicine*, 5, 372–380.

Corney, R. (1984a) 'The mental and physical health of clients referred to social workers in a local authority department and a general practice attachment scheme', *Psychological Medicine*, 14, 137–144.

Corney, R. (1984b) 'The effectiveness of attached social workers in the management of depressed female patients in general practice', *Psychological Medicine Monograph Supplements*, 6.

Corney, R. and Williams, P. (1987) 'Social and familial dysfunction, general practitioner attendance, and psychiatric diagnosis', *International Journal of Family Psychiatry*, 7, 137–148.

Costello, C.G. (1982) 'Social factors associated with depression: a retrospective community study', *Psychological Medicine*, 12, 329–339.

Cowen, P. and Andersen, I. (1985) '5HT neuroendocrinology: changes during depressive illness and antidepressant drug treatment', in *Biology of Depression* (ed. J. Deakin). London: Gaskell.

Craig, T. and Brown, G.W. (1984) 'Goal frustration and life events in the aetiology of painful gastrointestinal disorder', *Journal of Psychosomatic Research*, 28, 411–421.

Creed, F. and Marks, B. (1989) 'Liaison psychiatry in general practice: a comparison of a liaison attachment scheme and the shifted out-patient model', *Journal of the Royal College of General Practitioners*, 39, 514–517.

Croft-Jeffreys, C. and Wilkinson, G. (1989) 'Estimated costs of neurotic disorder in

UK general practice 1985', *Psychological Medicine*, 19, 549–558.

Crow, T. (1973) 'Catecholamine neurons and self-stimulation. A theoretical interpretation and some psychiatric implications', *Psychological Medicine*, 3, 66–73.

Crow, T. (1986) 'The continuum of psychosis and its implication for the structure of the gene', *British Journal of Psychiatry*, 149, 419–429.

Crow, T. (1990) 'The continuum of psychosis and its genetic origins', *British Journal of Psychiatry*, 156, 788–797.

Crowe, R., Noyes, R., Pauls, D. and Slymen, D. (1983) 'A family study of panic disorder', *Archives of General Psychiatry*, 40, 1065–1069.

Davenport, S., Goldberg, D. and Millar, T. (1987) 'How psychiatric disorders are missed during medical consultations', *Lancet*, 3, 439–442.

Davies, A., Davies, C. and Delpo, M. (1986) 'Depression and anxiety in patients undergoing diagnostic investigations for head and neck cancers', *British Journal of Psychiatry*, 149, 491–493.

Deakin, J. (1989) '5HT receptor subtypes in depression', in *Behavioural Pharmacology of 5HT* (ed. P. Bevan, A. Colls and T. Archer). Hillsdale, New Jersey: Erlbaum.

Deakin, J. (1990) 'Serotonin subtypes and affective disorder', in *Serotonin – Sleep and Mental Disorder* (ed. C. Idzikowski and P. Cowen). Oxford: Blackwell Scientific.

Deakin, J., Pennell, I., Upadhaya, A. and Lofthouse, R. (1990) 'A neuroendocrine study of 5HT function in depression: evidence for biological mechanisms of endogenous and psychosocial causation', *Psychopharmacology*, 101, 85–92.

Dean, C., Surtees, P. and Sashidharan, S. (1983) 'Comparison of research diagnostic systems in an Edinburgh community sample', *British Journal of Psychiatry*, 142, 247–256.

Dean, G., Walsh, D., Downing, H. and Shelley, E. (1981) 'First admissions of native-born and immigrants to psychiatric hospitals in South-East England 1976', *British Journal of Psychiatry*, 139, 506–512.

Dent, J. and Teasdale, J.D. (1988) 'Negative cognition and the persistence of depression', *Journal of Abnormal Psychology*, 97, 29–34.

Department of Health (1989a) *Caring for People*. London: Her Majesty's Stationery Office.

Department of Health (1989b) *Working for Patients*. London: Her Majesty's Stationery Office.

Diamond, E. and Lilienfeld, A. (1962) 'Effects of errors in classification and diagnosis in various types of epidemiological studies', *American Journal of Public Health*, 52, 1137–1144.

Dilling, H. (1980) 'Psychiatry and primary health services: results in a field survey', *Acta Psychiatrica Scandinavica* Supplement No. 285, 62, 15–22.

Dohrenwend, B., Shrout, P., Egri, G. and Mendelson, F. (1980) 'Non-specific psychological distress and other dimensions of psychopathology', *Archives of General Psychiatry*, 37, 1229–1236.

Dolan, R., Calloway, S., Fonagy, P., de Souza, F. and Wakeling, A. (1985) 'Life events, depression and hypothalamic-pituitary-adrenal axis function', *British Journal of Psychiatry*, 147, 429–433.

Duggan, C., Lee, A. and Murray, R. (1990) 'Does personality predict long-term outcome in depression?' *British Journal of Psychiatry*, 157, 19–24.

Duncan-Jones, P. (1987) 'Modelling the aetiology of neurosis', in *Psychiatric*

*Epidemiology* (ed. B. Cooper). London: Croom Helm.

Duncan-Jones, P. and Henderson, P. (1978) 'The use of a two-stage design in a prevalence survey', *Social Psychiatry*, 13, 231–237.

Duncan-Jones, P., Grayson, D. and Moran, P. (1986) 'The utility of latent trait models in psychiatric epidemiology', *Psychological Medicine*, 16, 391–405.

Duncan-Jones, P., Fergusson, D., Orel, J. and Horwood, L., (1990) 'A model of stability and change in minor psychiatric symptoms: results from three longitudinal studies', *Psychological Medicine Monograph Supplements* No.18 Cambridge: Cambridge University Press.

Dunn, J. and Fahy, T.A. (1990) 'Police admissions to a psychiatric hospital: demographic and clinical differences between ethnic groups', *British Journal of Psychiatry*, 156, 373–378.

Dworkin, S., Von Korff, M. and LeResche, L. (1990) 'Multiple pains, psychiatric and psychosocial disturbance: an epidemiologic investigation', *Archives of General Psychiatry*, 47, 239–245.

Eales, M. (1988) 'Depression and anxiety in unemployed men', *Psychological Medicine*, 18, 935–946.

Eaton, W. and Ritter, C. (1988) 'Distinguishing anxiety and depression with field survey data', *Psychological Medicine*, 18, 155–166.

Eisenberg, L. (1986) 'Mindlessness and brainlessness in psychiatry', *British Journal of Psychiatry*, 148, 497–508.

Engel, G. (1977) 'The need for a new medical model: a challenge for biomedicine', *Science*, 196, 129–136.

Everitt, B., Gourlay, J. and Kendell, R. (1971) 'An attempt at validation of traditional psychiatric syndromes by cluster analysis', *British Journal of Psychiatry*, 119, 399–412.

Everitt, B. and Smith, A.M.R. (1978) 'Interactions in contingency tables: a brief discussion of alternative definitions', *Psychological Medicine*, 9, 581–583.

Faravelli, C., Webb, T., Ambonetti, A., Fonnesu, F. and Sessarago, A. (1985) 'Prevalence of traumatic early life events in 31 agoraphobic patients with panic attacks', *American Journal of Psychiatry*, 142, 1493–1494.

Fauci, A. and Dale, D. (1974) 'The effect of *in vivo* hydrocortisone on subpopulations of human lymphocytes', *Journal of Clinical Investigation*, 53, 240–246.

Fennell, M.J.V. and Campbell, E.A. (1984) 'The cognitions questionnaire: specific thinking errors in depression', *British Journal of Clinical Psychology*, 23, 81–92.

Fergusson, D.M. and Horwood, J.L. (1987) 'Vulnerablity to life events exposure', *Psychological Medicine*, 17, 739–749.

Fergusson, D.M., Horwood, J.L. and Lawton, J. (1989) 'The relationships between neuroticism and depressive symptoms', *Social Psychiatry and Psychiatric Epidemiology*, 24, 275–281.

Finlay-Jones, R. (1988) 'Life events and psychiatric illness', in *Handbook of Social Psychiatry* (ed. S. Henderson and G. Burrows). Amsterdam: Elsevier.

Finlay-Jones, R. and Brown, G.W. (1981) 'Types of stressful life event and the onset of anxiety and depressive disorders', *Psychological Medicine*, 11, 803–816.

Finlay-Jones, R. and Burvill, P. (1977) 'The prevalence of minor psychiatric morbidity in the community', *Psychological Medicine*, 7, 474–489.

Finlay-Jones, R. and Ekhardt, B. (1984) 'Psychiatric disorder among young unemployed', *Australian and New Zealand Journal of Psychiatry*, 15, 265–70.

Freeling, P., Rao, B., Paykel, E., Sireling, L. and Burton, R. (1985) 'Unrecognised depression in general practice', *British Medical Journal*, 290, 1880–1883.

Gabe, J. and Williams, P. (1987) 'Is space bad for your health? The relationship between crowding in the home and emotional distress in women', *International Journal of Health Services Research*, 17, 667–669.

Gask, L. and McGrath, G. (1989) 'Psychotherapy and general practice', *British Journal of Psychiatry*, 154, 445–453.

Gask, L., McGrath, G., Goldberg, D. and Millar, T. (1987) 'Improving the psychiatric skills of established general practitioners: evaluation of group teaching', *Medical Education*, 21, 362–368.

Gask, L., Goldberg, D., Lesser, A. and Millar, T. (1988) 'Improving the psychiatric skills of the general practice trainee: an evaluation of a group training course', *Medical Education*, 22, 132–138.

Gask, L., Goldberg, D., Porter, R. and Creed, F. (1989) 'The treatment of somatisation: evaluation of a teaching package with general practice trainees', *Journal of Psychosomatic Research*, 33, 697–703.

Gater, R., de Almeida e Sousa, R., Caraveo, J., Chandrasekar, C., Dhadphale, M., Goldberg, D., al Kathiri, A., de Llano, G., Mubbashar, M., Silhan, K., Thong, D., Torres, F. and Sartorius, N. (1991) 'The pathways to psychiatric care: a cross-cultural study', *Psychological Medicine*.

Gath, D. and Catalan, J. (1986) 'The treatment of emotional disorders in general practice: psychological methods versus medication', *Journal of Psychosomatic Research*, 30, 381–386.

Gath, D. and Mynors-Wallis, L. (1991) 'Brief psychological treatments for emotional disorders in primary care', in *Horizons in Medicine 3*. London: Royal College of Physicians.

George, L.K., Blazer, D.G., Hughes, D.C. and Fowler, N. (1989)'Social support and the outcome of major depression', *British Journal of Psychiatry*, 154, 478–485.

Gibbons, J., Jennings, C. and Wing, J. (1984) *Psychiatric Care in Eight Register Areas*. Southampton University: Department of Psychiatry.

Giel, R., Koeter, M. and Ormel, J. (1990) 'Detection and referral of primary care patients with mental health problems: the 2nd and 3rd filter', in *The Public Health Impact of Mental Disorders* (ed. D. Goldberg and D. Tantam). Bern: Huber-Hogrefe.

Ginsberg, G., Marks, I. and Waters, H. (1984) 'Cost-benefit analysis of a controlled trial of nurse therapy for neuroses in primary care', *Psychological Medicine*, 14, 683–690.

Girolamo G. de, Mors, O., Rossi, G., Grandi, L., Ardigo, W. and Munk-Jorgensen, P. (1988) 'Admission to general hospital psychiatric wards in Italy. 1. A comparison between two catchment areas with differing provision of out-patient care', *International Journal of Social Psychiatry*, 34, 248–257.

Goldberg, D. (1981) 'Estimating the prevalence of psychiatric disorder from the results of a screening test', in *What is a Case?* (ed. J. Wing, P. Bebbington and L. Robins). London: Grant, McIntyre.

Goldberg, D. (1989) 'Mental health aspects of general health care', in *Health and Behaviour* (ed. D. Hamburg and N. Sartorius). Cambridge: Cambridge University Press.

Goldberg, D. (1991) 'Integrating mental health in primary health care', in *Mental Health Evaluation in the Community* (ed. J. Henderson). London: Gaskell.

Goldberg, D. and Bridges, K. (1988) 'Somatic presentations of psychiatric illness in primary care settings', *Journal of Psychosomatic Research*, 32, 137–144.

Goldberg, D. and Huxley, P. (1980) *Mental Illness in the Community: The Pathway to Psychiatric Care*. London: Tavistock.

Goldberg, D. and Williams, P. (1988) *A User's Guide to the General Health Questionnaire*. Windsor: NFER/Nelson.

Goldberg, D., Rickels, K., Downing, R and Hesbacher, P. (1976a) 'A comparison of two psychiatric screening tests', *British Journal of Psychiatry*, 129, 61–67.

Goldberg, D., Kay, C. and Thompson, L. (1976b) 'Psychiatric morbidity in general practice and the community', *Psychological Medicine*, 6, 565–569.

Goldberg, D., Steele, J., Smith, C. and Spivey, L. (1980a) 'Training family doctors to recognise psychiatric illness with increased accuracy', *Lancet*, 2, 521–523.

Goldberg, D., Steele, J. and Smith, C. (1980b) 'Teaching psychiatric interview techniques to family doctors', *Acta Psychiatrica Scandinavica Supplement* 285, 62, 41–47.

Goldberg, D., Bridges, K., Duncan-Jones, P. and Grayson, D. (1987) 'Dimensions of neuroses seen in primary care settings', *Psychological Medicine*, 17, 461–471.

Goldberg, D., Gask, L. and O'Dowd, T. (1989) 'The treatment of somatisation: teaching techniques of reattribution', *Journal of Psychosomatic Research*, 33, 689–695.

Goldberg, D., Bridges, K., Cook, D., Evans, B. and Grayson, D. (1990) 'The influence of social factors on common mental disorders: destabilisation and restitution', *British Journal of Psychiatry*, 156, 704–713.

Goldberg, D., Jenkins, L., Millar, T. and Faragher, B. (1991) 'The ability of general practitioners to identifiy emotional distress among their patients', *Medical Education*.

Goodyer, I., Kolvin, I. and Gatzanis, S. (1987) 'The impact of recent undesirable life events on psychiatric disorders in childhood and adolescence', *British Journal of Psychiatry*, 151, 179–184.

Gore, S. and Mangione, T.W. (1983) 'Social roles, sex roles and psychological distress: additive and interactive models of sex differences', *Journal of Health and Social Behaviour*, 24, 300–312.

Gotlib, I., Mount, J., Cordy, N. and Whiffen, V. (1988) 'Depression and perception of early parenting: a longitudinal investigation', *British Journal of Psychiatry*, 152, 24–27.

Grant, I., McDonald, W., Patterson, T. and Trimble, M. (1989) 'Multiple sclerosis', in *Life Events and Illness* (ed. G.W. Brown and T.O. Harris). New York: Guildford.

Gray, J. (1971) *The Psychology of Fear and Stress*. Cambridge: Cambridge University Press.

Gray, J. (1982) *The Neuropsychology of Anxiety*. Oxford: Oxford University Press.

Gray, J. (1988) 'Anxiety and personality', in *Handbook of Anxiety. Volume 1. Biological, Clinical and Cultural Perspectives* (ed. M. Roth, R. Noyes and G. Burrows). Amsterdam: Elsevier Science Publications.

Grayson, D. (1987) 'Can categorical and dimensional views of psychiatric illness be distinguished?', *British Journal of Psychiatry*, 151, 355–361.

Grayson, D., Bridges, K., Cook, D. and Goldberg, D. (1990) 'The validity of diagnostic systems for common mental disorders: a comparison between the ID-Catego and the *DSM-III* systems', *Psychological Medicine*, 20, 209–218.

Grayson, D., Bridges, K., Duncan-Jones, P. and Goldberg, D. (1987) 'The relationship between symptoms and diagnoses of minor psychiatric disorder in general practice', *Psychological Medicine*, 17, 933–942.

Hafner, H. and Klug, J. (1982) 'The impact of an expanding community health service on patterns of bed usage', *Psychological Medicine*, 12, 177–190.

Haines, A., Imeson, J. and Meade, T. (1987) 'Phobic anxiety and ischaemic heart disease', *British Medical Journal*, 295, 297–299.

Hankin, J. and Locke, B. (1982) 'Persistence of depressive symptomatology among prepaid group practice enrollees: an exploratory study', *American Journal of Public Health*, 72, 1000–1007.

Hansen, V. (1987) 'Psychiatric service within primary care', *Acta Psychiatrica Scandinavica*, 76, 121–128.

Harding, T., De Arango, M., Baltazar, J., Climent, C.E., Ibrahim, H.H., Ladrido-Ignacio, L., Srinivasa Murthy, R. and Wig, N.N. (1980) 'Mental disorders in primary health care: a study of their frequency and diagnosis in four developing countries', *Psychological Medicine*, 10, 231–242.

Harris, T.O. (1988) 'Psychosocial vulnerability to depression', in *Handbook of Social Psychiatry* (ed. S. Henderson and G. Burrows). Amsterdam: Elsevier.

Harris, T.O. and Brown, G.W. (1989) 'The LEDS findings in the context of other research: An overview', in *Life Events and Illness* (ed. G.W. Brown and T.O. Harris). London: Hyman Unwin.

Harris, T.O., Brown, G.W. and Bifulco, A. (1986) 'Loss of parent in childhood and adult psychiatric disorder: the role of lack of adequate parental care', *Psychological Medicine*, 16, 641–659.

Harris, T.O., Brown, G.W. and Bifulco, A. (1987) 'Loss of parent in childhood and adult psychiatric disorder: the role of social class position and premarital pregnancy', *Psychological Medicine*, 17, 163–184.

Harrison, G., Ineichen, B., Smith, J. and Morgan, G. (1984) 'Psychiatric hospital admissions in Bristol. II. Social and clinical aspects of compulsory admission, *British Journal of Psychiatry*, 145, 605–611.

Henderson, S. (1981) 'Social relationships, adversity and neurosis', *British Journal of Psychiatry*, 138, 391–398.

Henderson, S. and Moran, P. (1983) 'Social relationships during the onset and remission of neurotic symptoms: a prospective community study', *British Journal of Psychiatry*, 143, 467–472.

Henderson, S., Byrne, D.G. and Duncan-Jones, P. (1981) *Neurosis and the Social Environment*. London: Academic Press.

Her Majesty's Stationery Office (1986) *Morbidity Statistics from General Practice 1981–1982*. London: HMSO.

Hesbacher, P., Rickels, K. and Goldberg, D. (1975) 'Social factors and neurotic symptoms in general practice', American Journal of Public Health, 65, 148–155.

Hirsch, S., Platt, S., Knights, A. and Weyman, A. (1979) 'Shortening hospital stay for psychiatric care: effect on patients and their families', *British Medical Journal*, 1, 442–446.

Hirsch, S. (1988) *Psychiatric Beds and Resources: Factors Influencing Bed Use and Service Planning*. Royal College of Psychiatrists, London: Gaskell.

Hirschfeld, R. and Cross, C. (1982) 'Epidemiology of affective disorders. Psychosocial risk factors', *Archives of General Psychiatry*, 3935, 46–50.

Hirschfeld, R. and Klerman, G. (1979) 'Personality attributes and affective disorders', *American Journal of Psychiatry*, 136, 67–70.

Hirschfeld, R., Klerman, G., Clayton, P. and Keller, M. (1983) 'Personality and depression', *Archives of General Psychiatry*, 40, 993–998.

Hirschfeld, R., Klerman, G., Lavori, P., Keller, M.B., Griffith, P. and Coryell, W. (1989) 'Premorbid personality assessments of first onset of major depression', *Archives of General Psychiatry*, 46, 345–349.

Hodiamont, P., Peer, N. and Syben, N. (1987) 'Epidemiological aspects of psychiatric disorder in a Dutch health area', *Psychological Medicine*, 17, 495–506.

Hoeper, E., Nycz, G. and Cleary, P. (1979) *The quality of mental health sevices in an organised primary care setting*, Final report: NIMH Contract no. DBE-77-0071. Washington: NIMH.

Hoeper, E., Nycz, G., Kessler, L., Burke, J. and Pierce, W. (1984) 'The usefulness of screening for mental illness', *Lancet*, 1, 33–35.

Hoffman, R. and Koran, L. (1984) 'Detecting physical illness in patients with mental disorders', *Psychosomatics*, 25, 654–660.

Holden, J., Sagovsky, R. and Cox, J. (1989) 'Counselling in general practice settings: a controlled study of health visitor intervention in the treatment of post-natal depression', *British Medical Journal*, 298, 223–226.

Hollyman, J., Freeling, P., Paykel, E., Bhat, A. and Sedgwick, P. (1988) 'Double-blind placebo controlled trial of amitriptyline among depressed patients in general practice', *Journal of the Royal College of General Practitioners*, 38, 393–397.

Hooley, J., Orley, J. and Teasdale, J. (1986) 'Levels of expressed emotion and relapse in depressed patients', *British Journal of Psychiatry*, 148, 642–647.

Hurry, J., Bebbington, P. and Tennant, C. (1987) 'Psychiatric symptoms, social disablement and illness behaviour', *Australian and New Zealand Journal of Psychiatry*, 21, 68–73.

Huxley, P.J. (1978) 'Social versus clinical prediction in minor psychiatric disorders', unpublished PhD Thesis, University of Manchester.

Huxley, P.J. (1990) 'Community mental health: a challenge to care', *Community Psychiatric Nursing Journal*, 10, June.

Huxley, P.J. and Fitzpatrick, R. (1984) 'The probable extent of minor mental illness in the adult clients of social workers: a research note', *British Journal of Social Work*, 14, 67–73.

Huxley, P.J. and Goldberg, D.P. (1975) 'Social versus clinical prediction in minor psychiatric disorders', *Psychological Medicine*, 5, 96–100.

Huxley, P.J. and Oliver, J.P.J. (1990) *A report on the nature of postqualifying studies in Mental Health*, Mental Health Social Work Research Unit Report for CCETSW.

Huxley, P.J. and Warner, R. (1990) 'Case management services for people with long-term mental health problems: a study of quality of life', *Project Report*, Community Mental Health Center, Boulder County, Co. USA.

Huxley, P.J., Goldberg, D., Maguire, P. and Kincey, V. (1979) 'The prediction of the course of minor psychiatric disorders', *British Journal of Psychiatry*, 135, 535–43.

Huxley, P.J., Korer, J. and Tolley, S. (1987) 'The psychiatric "caseness" of clients referred to an urban social services department', *British Journal of Social Work*, 17, 507–520.

Huxley, P.J., Korer, J. and Tolley, S. (1988) 'Psychiatric morbidity in the clients of social workers', *Journal of Psychiatric Research*, 22, 57–67.

Huxley, P.J., Raval, H., Korer, J. and Jacob, C. (1989) 'Psychiatric morbidity in the clients of social workers: clinical outcome', *Psychological Medicine*, 19, 189–198.

Huxley, P.J., Hagan, T., Henelly, R. and Hunt, J. (1990) *Effective Community Mental Health Services*. Aldershot: Avebury.

Ingham, J.G., Kreitman, N.B., Miller, P., Sashidharan, S.P. and Surtees, P. (1986) 'Self-esteem, vulnerability and psychiatric disorder in the community', *British Journal of Psychiatry*, 148, 375–385.

Ingham, J.G., Kreitman, N., Miller, P., Sashidharan, S. and Surtees, P. (1987) 'Self-appraisal, anxiety and depression in women: a prospective enquiry', *British Journal of Psychiatry*, 150, 643–651.

Irwin, M., Daniels, M., Risch, S., Bloom, E. and Weiner, H. (1988) 'Plasma cortisol and natural killer activity during bereavement', *Biological Psychiatry*, 24, 173–178.

Irwin, M., Patterson, T., Smith, T., Caldwell, C., Brown, S., Gillin, J. and Grant, I. (1990) 'Reduction of immune function in life stress and depression', *Biological Psychiatry*, 27, 22–30.

Jackson, G., Gater, R., Goldberg, D., Tantam, D., Taylor, H. and Loftus, L. (1991) 'A new community mental health team based in primary care', *British Journal of Psychiatry*.

Jarman, B. (1983) 'Identification of underprivileged areas', *British Medical Journal*, 286, 1705–1709.

Jarman, B. (1984) 'Validation and distribution of scores', *British Medical Journal* 289, 1587–1592.

Jarman, B., White, P., Hirsch, S. and Driscoll, R. (1990) Personal communication.

Jenkins, R. (1985) 'Sex differences in minor psychiatric morbidity', *Psychological Medicine Monograph Supplements*, 7.

Jenkins, R., Mann, A.H. and Besley, E. (1981) 'Design and use of a short to assess social stress and support in research and clinical settings', *Social Science and Medicine*, 158, 195–203.

Jenkins, R., Smeeton, N. and Shepherd, M. (1988) 'Classification of mental disorder in primary care', *Psychological Medicine Monograph Supplements*, 12.

Jennings, C., Der, G., Robinson, C., Rose, S., de Alarcon, J., Hunter, D., Holliday, R. and Moss, N. (1989) 'In-patient statistics from 8 psychiatric case registers, 1977–1983', in *Health Services Planning and Research* (ed. J. Wing). London: Gaskell.

Johnson, D. (1974) 'A study of the use of antidepressant medication in general practice', *British Journal of Psychiatry*, 125, 186–192.

Johnstone, A. and Goldberg, D. (1976) 'Psychiatric screening in general practice. a controlled trial', *Lancet*, 1, 605–608.

Johnstone, A. and Shepley, M. (1986) 'The outcome of hidden neurotic illness treated in general practice', *Journal of the Royal College of General Practitioners*, 36, 413–415.

Johnstone, E., Owens, D., Frith, C., McPherson, K., Dowie, C., Riley, G. and Gold, A. (1980) 'Neurotic illness and its response to anxiolytic and anti-depressant treatment', *Psychological Medicine*, 10, 321–328.

Jones, K. (1988) *Experience in Mental Health: Community Care and Social Policy*. London: Sage.

Kahn, R., McNair, D., Lipman, R., Covi, L., Rickels, K., Downing, R., Fisher, S. and Frankenthaler, L. (1986) 'Imipramine and chlordiazepoxide in depressive and anxiety disorders. II. Efficacy in anxious out-patients', *Archives of General Psychiatry*, 43, 79–85.

Kedward, H.B. (1969) 'The outcome of neurotic illness in the community', *Social Psychiatry and Psychiatric Epidemiology*, 4, 1–4.

Kendell, R. (1968) 'The classification of depressive illness', *Maudsley Monograph 18*, London: Oxford University Press.

Kendell, R. (1974) 'The stability of psychiatric diagnosis', *British Journal of Psychiatry*, 124, 352–356.

Kendell, R. (1975) *The Role of Diagnosis in Psychiatry*. Oxford: Blackwell.

Kendell, R. and DiScipio, W. (1968) 'Eysenck personality inventory scores of patients with depressive illness', *British Journal of Psychiatry*, 114, 767–770.

Kendler, K., Heath, A., Martin, N. and Eaves, L. (1987) 'Symptoms of anxiety and symptoms of depression', *Archives of General Psychiatry*, 122, 451–457.

Kessler, L., Cleary, P. and Burke, J. (1985) 'Psychiatric disorders in primary care', *Archives of General Psychiatry*, 42, 583–587.

Kessler, R., House, J. and Turner, J. (1987) 'Unemployment and health in a community sample', *Journal of Health and Social Behaviour*, 28, 51–59.

Kessler, R., Tessler, R. and Ncyz, G. (1983) 'Co-occurrence of psychiatric and medical morbidity in primary care', *Journal of Family Practice*, 16, 319–324.

Kessler, R. and Neighbours, H.W. (1986) 'A new perspective on the relationships among race, social class and psychological distress', *Journal of Health and Social Behaviour*, 27, 107–115.

Khansari, D., Murgo, A. and Faith, R. (1990) 'Effects of stress on the immune system', *Immunology Today*, 11, 170–174.

Kiloh, L., Andrews, G. and Neilson, M. (1988) 'The long-term outcome of depressive illness', *British Journal of Psychiatry*, 153, 752–757.

Kleinman, A. (1988) *Rethinking Psychiatry*. London: The Free Press.

Kohn, M. (1972) 'Class, family and schizophrenia', *Social Forces*, 50, 295–302.

Kurdek, L.A. (1988) 'Gender differences in predicting loneliness for social network characteristics', *Journal of Personality and Social Psychology*, 51, 1069–1074.

Laudenslager, M., Ryan, S., Drugan, R., Hyson, R. and Maier, S. (1983) 'Coping and immunosuppression: inescapable but not escapable shock suppresses lymphocyte proliferation', *Science*, 221, 568–570.

Lazarus, R.S. and DeLongis, A. (1983) 'Psychological stress and coping in ageing', *American Psychologist*, 38, 245–254.

Leckman, J., Weissman, M., Merikangas, K., Pauls, D. and Prusoff, B. (1983) 'Panic disorder and major depression: inceased risk of depression, alcoholism, panic and phobic disorders in families of depressed probands with panic disorder', *Archives of General Psychiatry*, 40, 1055–1060.

Lee, A. and Murray, R. (1988) 'The long-term outcome of Maudsley depressives', *British Journal of Psychiatry*, 153, 741–751.

Lennon, C. (1987) 'Sex differences in distress: the impact of gender and work roles', *Journal of Health and Social Behaviour*, 28, 290–305.

Lennon, C. (1989) 'The structural contexts of stress', *Journal of Health and Social Behaviour*, 30, 261–286.

Lesser, A.L. (1985) 'Problem-based interviewing in general practice: a model', *Medical Education*, 19, 299–304.

Levenstein, J., McCracken, E., McWhinney, I., Stewart, M. and Brown, J. (1986) 'The patient-centred clinical method. 1. A model for the doctor–patient interaction in family medicine', *Family Practice*, 3, 24–30.

Lewinsohn, P.M., Steinmetz, J.L., Larson, D.W. and Franklin, J.L. (1981) 'Depression-related cognitions: antecedent or consequence?', *Journal of Abnormal Pschology*, 90, 213–219.

Lewis, A. (1934) 'Melancholia – a clinical survey of depressive states', *Journal of Mental Science*, 80, 1–41.

Lewis, C.S. (1961) *A Grief Observed*. London: Faber.

Lin, N. and Ensel, W.M. (1984) 'Depression-mobility and its social etiology: the role of life events and social support', *Journal of Health and Social Behaviour*, 25, 176–188.

Lin, N., Woelfel, M.W. and Light, S.C. (1985) 'The buffering effect of social support subsequent to an important life event', *Journal of Health and Social Behaviour*, 26, 247–263.

Linn, B., Linn, M. and Jensen, J. (1982) 'Degree of depression and lymphocyte responsiveness', *Psychosomatic Medicine*, 44, 128–129.

Lobo, A. (1990) 'Mental health in general medical clinics', in *The Public Health Impact of Mental Disorder* (ed. D. Goldberg and D. Tantam) Bern: Huber-Hogrefe.

Low, C. (1988) 'Psychiatric clinics in different settings', *British Journal of Psychiatry*, 153, 243–245.

McFarlane, A. (1987) 'Life events and psychiatric disorder: the role of natural disaster', *British Journal of Psychiatry*, 151, 362–367.

McFarlane, A.H., Norman, G.R., Streiner, D.L. and Roy, R.G. (1983) 'The process of social stress: stable, reciprocal and mediating relationships', *Journal of Health and Social Behaviour*, 24, 160–173.

McGuffin, P., Katz, R., Aldrich, J. and Bebbington, P. (1988a) 'The Camberwell Collaborative Depression Study. II. Investigation of family members', *British Journal of Psychiatry*, 152, 766–774.

McGuffin, P., Katz, R. and Bebbington, P. (1988b) 'The Camberwell Collaborative Depression Study: III. Depression and adversity in the relatives of depressed probands', *British Journal of Psychiatry*, 152, 775–782.

McKeon, J., Roa, B., and Mann, A. (1984) 'Life events and personality traits in obsessive-compulsive neurosis', *British Journal of Psychiatry*, 144, 185–189.

Maguire, P., Fairbairn, S. and Fletch, C. (1986) 'Consultation skills of young doctors. Benefits of feedback training in interviewing as students persist', *British Medical Journal*, 292, 1573–1578.

Mangen, S., Paykel, E., Griffith, J., Burchell, A. and Mancini, P. (1983) 'Cost effectiveness of community psychiatric nurse or out-patient psychiatrist care of neurotic patients', *Psychological Medicine*, 13, 407–416.

Mann, A., Jenkins, R. and Belsey, E. (1981) 'The 12-month outcome of patients with neurotic illness in general practice', *Psychological Medicine*, 11, 535–550.

Marks, I. (1985) 'Controlled trial of psychiatric nurse therapists in primary care', *British Medical Journal*, 290, 1181–1183.

Marks, I. (1986) 'Genetics of fear and anxiety disorders', *British Journal of Psychiatry*, 149, 406–418.

Marks, I., Hallam, R., Connolly, J. and Philpott, R. (1977) *Nursing in Behavioural Psychotherapy*. London: Royal College of Nursing.

Marks, J., Goldberg, D. and Hillier, V. (1979) 'Determinants of the ability of general practitioners to detect psychiatric illness', *Psychological Medicine*, 9, 337–353.

Martin, C.J. (1982) 'Psychosocial stress and puerperal psychiatric disorder', paper presented to the Marce Society.

Mavreas, V., Beis, A., Mouyias, A., Rigoni, F. and Lyketsos, G. (1986) 'Prevalence of psychiatric disorders in Athens: A community study', *Social Psychiatry*, 21, 172–181.

Maxwell, A. (1972) 'Difficulties in a dimensional description of symptomatology', *British Journal of Psychiatry*, 121, 19–26.

Mechanic, D. (1968) *Medical Sociology: A Selective View*. New York: The Free Press.

Mechanic, D. (1980) 'The experience and reporting of common physical complaints', *Journal of Health and Social Behaviour*, 21, 146–156.

Melzer, H., Umberkoman-Wiita, B., Robertson, A., Tricou, B., Lowry, M. and Perline R. (1984) 'Effectiveness of 5HT on serum cortisol levels in major affective disorders ', *Archives of General Psychiatry*, 41, 366–374.

Meyer, A. (1955) *Psychobiology: A Science of Illness*. Springfield, Illinois: Charles Thomas.

Millar, T. and Goldberg, D. (1991) 'Determinants of the ability of general practitioners to manage common mood disorders', *Journal of the Royal College of General Practitioners* .

Miller, P. and Ingham, J. (1983) 'Dimensions of experience', *Psychological Medicine*, 13, 417–429.

Miller, P. and Ingham, J. (1985) 'Dimensions of experience and symptomatology', *Journal of Psychiatric Research*, 29, 475–488.

Miller, P., Ingham, J. and Davidson, S. (1976) 'Life events, symptoms and social support', *Journal of Psychosomatic Research*, 20, 516–522.

Miller, P., Kreitman, N., Ingham, J. and Sashidharan, S. (1989) 'Self-esteem, life stress, and psychiatric disorder', *Journal of Affective Disorders,* 157, 679–686.

Mitchell, A. (1983) 'Liaison psychiatry in general practice', *British Journal of Hospital Medicine*, 30, 100–106.

Mitchell, R.E. and Moos, R.H. (1984) 'Deficiencies in social support among depressed patients: antecedents or consequences of stress?' *Journal of Health and Social Behaviour*, 25, 438–452.

Morley, M., Bradshaw, C. and Szabadi, E. (1987) 'Effect of 6-hydroxydopamine induced lesions of the noradrenergic bundle on steady state operant behaviour', *Psychopharmacology*, 93, 520–525.

Morris, C., Ben-Arie, O. and Zabon, T. (1983) 'Physical illness in the chronic mentally ill', *South Africa Medical Journal*, 63, 896–897.

Murphy, E. (1982) 'Social origins of depression in old age', *British Journal of Psychiatry*, 141, 135–142.

Murphy, E. (1983) 'The prognosis of depression in old age', *British Journal of Psychiatry*, 142, 111–119.

Murphy, E. and Brown, G.W. (1980) 'Life events, psychiatric disturbance and physical illness', *British Journal of Psychiatry*, 136, 326–338.

Norris, F.H. and Murrel, S.A. (1984) 'Protective function of resources related to life events, global stress and depression in older adults', *Journal of Health and Social Behaviour*, 25, 424–438.

Notarius, C. and Pellegrini, D. (1984) 'Marital processes as stressors and stress mediators: implications for marital repair', in *Personal Relationships 5: Repairing Relationships* (ed. S. Duck). London: Academic Press.

Obeyesekere, G. (1985) 'Depression, Buddhism and the work of culture in Sri Lanka', in *Culture and Depression* (ed. A. Kleinman and B. Good). Berkeley: University of California Press.

Orley, J. and Wing, J. (1979) 'Psychiatric disorder in two African Villages', *Archives of General Psychiatry*, 36, 513–520.

Ormel, J. and Giel, R. (1990) 'Medical effects of non-recognition of affective disorders in primary care', in *Psychological Disorders in General Medical Settings* (ed. N. Sartorius, D. Goldberg, G. de Girolamo, J. Costa e Silva, Y. LeCrubier and H.-U. Wittchen). Bern: Huber-Hogrefe.

Parker, G. (1979) 'Parental characteristics in relation to depressive disorders', *British Journal of Psychiatry*, 134, 138–147.

Parker, G. (1980) 'Vulnerability factors to normal depression', *Journal of Psychiatric Research*, 24, 67–74.

Parker, G. (1983) 'Parental "affectionless control" as an antecedent to adult depression', *Archives of General Psychiatry*, 134, 138–147.

Parker, G., Blignault, I. and Manicavasagar, V. (1988) 'Neurotic depression: delineation of symptom profiles and their relationship to outcome', *British Journal of Psychiatry*, 152, 15–23.

Parry, G. and Shapiro, D.A. (1985) 'Social support and life events in working-class women: stress buffering or independent effects', *Archives of General Psychiatry*, 43, 315–323.

Paykel, E., Klerman, G. and Prusoff, B. (1976) 'Personality and symptom patterns in depression', *British Journal of Psychiatry*, 129, 327–334.

Paykel, E.S., Emms, E.M., Fletcher, J. and Rassaby, E.S. (1980) 'Life events and social support in puerperal depression', *British Journal of Psychiatry*, 136, 339–346.

Paykel, E., Hollyman, J., Freeling, P. and Sedgewick, P. (1988) 'Predictors of therapeutic benefit from amitriptyline in mild depression: a general practice placebo-controlled trial', *Journal of Affective Disorders*, 14, 83–95.

Pearlin, L.I. and Lieberman, M.A. (1979) 'Social sources of emotional distress', in R.G. Simmons (ed.) *Research in Community and Mental Health*. Greenwich, CT: JAI Press.

Pearlin, L.I. and Schooler, C. (1978) 'The structure of coping', *Journal of Health and Social Behaviour*, 19, 2–21.

Pearlin, L.I., Lieberman, M.A., Menaghan, E.G. and Mullan, J.T. (1981) 'The stress process', *Journal of Health and Social Behaviour*, 22, 337–356.

Perez, M. and Farrant, J. (1988) 'Immune reactions and mental disorders', *Psychological Medicine*, 18, 11–13.

Pollitt, J. (1972) 'The relationship between genetic and precipitating factors in depressive illness', *British Journal of Psychiatry*, 121, 67–70.

Popkin, M., Callies, A. and Mackenzie, T. (1985) 'The outcome of antidepressant use in the medically ill', *Archives of General Psychiatry*, 42, 1160–1163.

Popova, J. and Petkov, V. (1990) 'Changes in $5HT_1$ receptors in different brain structures of rats with isolation syndrome', *General Pharmacology*, 21, 223–225.

Price, J. (1968) 'The genetics of depressive behaviour', in *Recent Advances In Affective Disorders* (ed. A. Cooper and A. Wade). Ashford: Headley.

Prudo, R., Brown, G.W., Harris, T. and Dowland, J. (1981) 'Psychiatric disorder in a rural and an urban population: 2. Sensitivity to loss', *Psychological Medicine*, 11, 601–616.

Prudo, R., Harris, T. and Brown, G.W. (1984) 'Psychiatric disorder in a rural and in an urban population: 3. Social integration and the morphology of affective disorder', *Psychological Medicine*, 14, 327–364.

Prusoff, B. and Klerman, G. (1974) 'Differentiating depressed from anxious-neurotic out-patients', *Archives of General Psychiatry*, 30, 302–309.

Pullen, I. and Yellowlees, A. (1988) 'Scottish psychiatrists in primary health care settings: a silent majority', *British Journal of Psychiatry*, 153, 663–666.

Rand, E., Badger, L. and Coggings, D. (1988) 'Towards a resolution of contradictions – utility of feedback from the GHQ', *General Hospital Psychiatry*, 10, 189–196.

Rasch, G. (1960) *Probabilistic Models for Some Intelligence and Attainment Tests.* Copenhagen: Danish Institute of Educational Research.

Raskin, M., Peeke, H., Dickman, W. and Pinsker, H. (1982) 'Panic and generalised anxiety disorder', *Archives of General Psychiatry*, 39, 687–689.

Regier, D., Goldberg, I. and Taube, C. (1978) 'The de facto US mental health services system. A public health perspective', *Archives of General Psychiatry*, 35, 685–690.

Regier, D., Myers, J., Kramer, M. and Robins, L. (1984) 'The NIMH Epidemiologic Catchment Area (ECA) Program: historical context, major objectives, and study population characteristics', *Archives of General Psychiatry*, 41, 934–941.

Regier, D., Burke, J., Manderscheid, J.R. and Burns, B. (1985) 'The chronic mentally ill in primary care', *Psychological Medicine*, 15, 265–274.

Regier, D., Boyd, J., Burke, J., Rae, D., Myers, J., Kramer, M., Robins, L., George, L., Karno, M. and Locke, B. (1988) 'One-month prevalence of mental disorders in the United States', *Archives of General Psychiatry*, 45, 977–985.

Reich, J., Noyes, R., Hirschfeld, R., Coryell, W. and O'Gorman, T. (1987) 'State and personality in depressed and panic patients', *American Journal of Psychiatry*, 144, 181–187.

Roberts, R.E. and O'Keefe, S.J. (1981) 'Sex differences in depression re-examined', *Journal of Health and Social Behaviour*, 22, 394–400.

Robertson, N. (1979) 'Variations in referral pattern to the psychiatric services by general practitioners', *Psychological Medicine*, 9, 355–364.

Romans-Clarkson, S.E., Walton, V.A., Herbison, G.P. and Mullen, P.E. (1988) 'Psychiatric morbidity among women in urban and rural New Zealand: psychosocial correlates', *British Journal of Psychiatry*, 156, 84–91.

Rosenfield, S. (1980) 'Sex differences in depression: do women always have higher rates?' *Journal of Health and Social Behaviour*, 22, 33–42.

Rosenfield, S. (1984) 'Race differences in involuntary hospitalization: psychiatric versus labelling perspectives', *Journal of Health and Social Behaviour*, 25, 14–23.

Rosenfield, S. (1989) 'The effect of women's employment: personal control and sex differences in mental health', *Journal of Health and Social Behaviour*, 30, 77–91.

Roy, A. (1978) 'Vulnerability factors and depression in women', *British Journal of Psychiatry*, 133, 106–110.

Roy, A. (1980) 'Early parental loss in depressive neurosis compared with other neuroses', *Canadian Journal of Psychiatry*, 25, 503–505.

Roy, A. (1981) 'Vulnerability factors and depression in men', *British Journal of Psychiatry*, 138, 75–77.

Roy, A. (1987) 'Five risk factors for depression', *British Journal of Psychiatry*, 150, 536–541.

Rucker, L., Frye, E., and Cygan, R. (1986) 'Feasibility and usefulness', *Archives of Internal Medicine*, 146, 729–731.

Rutter, M. (1985) 'Resilience in the face of adversity', *British Journal of Psychiatry*, 147, 598–611.

Rutter, M. and Quinton, D. (1984) 'Parental psychiatric disorder: effect on children', *Psychological Medicine*, 14, 853–880.

Rwegellera, C.G.C. (1980) 'Differential use of psychiatric services by West Indians, West Africans and English in London', *British Journal of Psychiatry*, 137, 428–432.

Sapolsky, R. (1989) 'Hypercortisolaemia among socially subordinate wild baboons originates at the CNS level', *Archives of General Psychiatry*, 46, 1047–1051.

Sashidharan, S., Surtees, P., Kreitman, N., Ingham, J. and Miller, P. (1988) 'Hospital treated and general population morbidity from affective disorders: comparison of prevalence and inception rates', *British Journal of Psychiatry*, 152, 499–505.

Sayce, L. (1990) 'The development of community mental health centres', paper presented at the Research and Development in Psychiatry Day Conference, London, 30 April.

Schein, L. (1977) 'Psychiatric illness in general practice: agreement and disagreement on the affirmation of illness', unpublished PhD thesis, Ann Arbor, Michigan. Obtainable from University Microfilms International.

Schleifer, C., Derbyshire, L. and Martin, J. (1968) 'Clinical change in jail referred mental patients', *Archives of General Psychiatry*, 18, 42–46.

Schleifer, S., Keller, S., Camerino, M., Thornton, J. and Stein, M. (1983) 'Suppression of lymphocyte stimulation after bereavement', *Journal of the American Medical Association*, 250, 374–377.

Schleifer, S., Keller, S., Meyerson, A., Raskin, M., Davis, K. and Stein, M. (1984) 'Lymphocyte function in major depressive disorder' *Archives of General Psychiatry*, 41, 484–486.

Schleifer, S., Keller, S., Siris, S., Davis, K. and Stein, M. (1985) 'Lymphocyte function in ambulatory depressed patients', *Archives of General Psychiatry*, 42, 129–133.

Schmale, A. and Iker, H. (1966) 'The affect of hopelessness and the development of cancer', *Psychosomatic Medicine*, 28, 714–721.

Schulberg, H., McClelland, M. and Burns, B. (1987a) 'Depression and physical illness: the prevalence, causation and diagnosis of co-morbidity', *Clinical Psychology Review*, 7, 145–167.

Schulberg, H., McClelland, M. and Gooding, W. (1987b) 'Six-month outcomes for medical patients with major depressive disorders', *Journal of General Internal Medicine*, 2, 312–317.

Seligman, M. (1975) *Helplessness: On Depression, Development and Death*. San Francisco: W.H. Freeman.

Shapiro, S., Skinner, E., Kessler, L., Von Korff, M., German, P., Tischler, G., Leaf, P., Benham, L., Cottler, L. and Regier, D. (1984) 'Utilisation of health and mental health services', *Archives of General Psychiatry*, 41, 971–978.

Shapiro, S., Skinner, E., German, P., Kramer, M. and Romanowski, A. (1986) 'Need and demand for mental health services in an urban community: an exploration based on houshold interviews', in *Mental Disorders in the Community: Progress and Challenge* (ed. J.E. Barrett and R.M. Rose). London: Guilford.

Shapiro, S., German, P., Skinner, E., Von Korff, M., Turner, R., Klein, L., Teitelbaum, M., Kramer, M., Burke, J. and Burns, B. (1987) 'An experiment to change detection and management of mental morbidity in primary care', *Medical Care*, 25, 327–339.

Shekelle, R., Raynor, W., Ostfeld, A., Garron, D., Bielauskas, L., Liu, S., Maliza, C. and Paul, O. (1981) 'Psychological depression and 17-year risk of death from cancer', *Psychosomatics*, 43; 117–125.

Shepherd, M., Cooper, B., Brown, A. and Kalton, G. (1966) *Psychiatric Illness in General Practice*. Oxford: Oxford University Press.

Shepherd, M., Harwin, B., Depla, C. and Cairns, V. (1979) 'Social work and the primary care of mental disorder', *Psychological Medicine*, 9, 61–669.

Shortell, S. and Daniel, R. (1974) 'Referral relationships between internists and psychiatrists in a fee-for-service practice: an empirical examination', *Medical Care*, 12, 229–240.

Sims, A. (1975) 'Factors predictive of outcome in neurosis', *British Journal of Psychiatry*, 127, 54–62.

Sirois, F. (1975) 'The natural history of neuroses: problems of methods and substance', *Canadian Psychiatric Association Journal*, 20, 273–280.

Slater, E. (1943) 'The neurotic constitution: A statistical study of 2000 neurotic soldiers', *Journal of Neurology and Psychiatry*, 6, 1–16.

Slater, E. (1966) 'Diagnostic similarity in twins with neurosis and personality disorders', in J. Shields and I. Gottesman (eds) *Man, Mind and Heredity*. London: Johns Hopkins Press, pp. 252–258.

Slater, E. and Slater, P. (1944) 'A heuristic theory of neurosis', *Journal of Neurology and Psychiatry*, 7, 49–55.

Smith, G., McKenzie, J., Marmer, D. and Steele, R. (1985) 'Psychological modulation of the human immune response', *Archives of Internal Medicine*, 145, 2110–2112.

Spitzer, R., Sheehy, M. and Endicott, J. (1977) '*DSM-III*: guiding principles', in *Psychiatric Diagnosis* (ed. V. Rakoff, H. Stancer and H. Kedward). London: Macmillan.

Stefansson, C. and Cullberg, J. (1986) 'Introducing community mental health services', *Acta Psychiatrica Scandinavica*, 74, 368–378.

Stewart, G., Andrews, G. and Henderson, S. (1990) 'Genetics of anxiety and depressive neuroses: a study of twins in the community', *Journal of Affective Disorders*, 19, 23–31.

Strathdee, G. and Williams, P. (1985) 'Patterns of collaboration', in *Mental Illness in Primary Care Settings* (ed. P. Williams, G. Wilkinson, and M. Shepherd). London: Tavistock.

Strathdee, G., King, M.B., Araya, R. and Lewis, S. (1990) 'A standardised assessment of patients referred to primary care and hospital psychiatric clinics', *Psychological Medicine*, 20, 219–224.

Sturt, E. (1981) 'Hierarchical patterns in the distribution of psychiatric symptoms', *Psychological Medicine*, 11, 783–794.

Surtees, P.G. and Miller, P. (1990) 'Title to follow', *British Journal of Psychiatry*, 157, 679–686.

Surtees, P.G., Dean, C., Ingham, J.G., Kreitman, N., Miller, P. and Sashidharan, S.P. (1983) 'Psychiatric disorders in women from an Edinburgh community: associations with demographic factors', *British Journal of Psychiatry*, 142, 238–246.

Sydenham, T. (1682) 'Dissertatio epistolaris ad Gulielmum Cole, M.D.... de affectione hysterica', in *The Entire Works of Dr Thomas Sydenham* (ed. J. Swan) 1742. London: Cave.

Tansella, M. and Williams, P. (1989) 'The spectrum of psychiatric morbidity in a defined geographical area', *Psychological Medicine*, 19, 765–770.

Tennant, C. and Bebbington, P. (1978) 'The social causation of depression: a critique of the work of Brown and his colleagues', *Psychological Medicine*, 8, 565–575.

Tennant, C., Bebbington, P. and Hurry, J. (1980) 'Parental death in childhood and risk of adult disorders: a review', *Psychological Medicine*, 10, 289–300.

Tennant, C., Bebbington, P. and Hurry, J. (1981a) 'The short-term outcome of neurotic disorders in the community: the relationship of remission to clinical factors and to "neutralising" life events', *British Journal of Psychiatry*, 139, 213–220.

Tennant, C., Bebbington, P. and Hurry, J. (1981b) 'The role of life events in depressive illness: is there a substantial causal relation?' *Psychological Medicine*, 11, 379–390.

Tennant, C., Bebbington, P. and Hurry, J. (1982) 'Social experiences in childhood and adult psychiatric morbidity: a multiple regression analysis', *Psychological Medicine*, 12, 321–328.

Thoits, P.A. (1983) 'Conceptual, methodological and theoretical problems in studying social support as a buffer against life stress', *Journal of Health and Social Behaviour*, 23, 145–159.

Thomas, K. (1987) 'General practice consultations: is there any point in being positive?' *British Medical Journal*, 294, 1200–1202.

Thomas, P., Goodwin, J. and Goodwin, J. (1985) 'Effect of social support on stress-related changes in cholesterol level, uric acid level, and immune function in an elderly population', *American Journal of Psychiatry*, 142, 735–773.

Thomson, J., Rankin, H., Ashcroft, G., Yates, C., McQueen, J. and Cummings, S. (1982) 'The treatment of depression in general practice: a comparison of L-tryptophan, amitriptyline and a combination', *Psychological Medicine*, 12, 741–751.

Tischler, G., Henisz, J., Myers, J. and Boswell, P. (1975) 'Utilization of mental health services', *Archives of General Psychiatry*, 32, 411–418.

Torgersen, S. (1983a) 'Genetic factors in anxiety disorders', *Archives of General Psychiatry*, 40, 1085–1089.

Torgersen, S. (1983b) 'Genetics of neurosis', *British Journal of Psychiatry*, 142, 126–132.

Torgersen, S. (1985) 'Hereditary differentiation of anxiety and affective neuroses', *British Journal of Psychiatry*, 146, 530–534.

Torgersen, S. (1986) 'Childhood and family characteristics in panic and generalised anxiety disorder', *American Journal of Psychiatry* 143: 630–632.

Tweed, L., Schoenbach, V., George, L. and Blazer, D. (1989) 'The effects of childhood parental death and divorce on six-month history of anxiety disorders', *British Journal of Psychiatry*, 154, 823–828.

Tyrer, P. (1984) 'Psychiatric clinics in general practice. An extension of community care', *British Journal of Psychiatry*, 145, 9–14.

Tyrer, P. (1985) 'Neurosis divisible', *Lancet*, 1, 685–688.

Tyrer, P., Seivewright, N. and Wollerton, S. (1984) 'General practice psychiatric clinics: impact on psychiatric services', *British Journal of Psychiatry*, 145, 15–19.

Tyrer, P., Seivewright, N., Murphy, S., Ferguson, B., Kingdon, D., Barczak, P., Brothwell, J., Darling, C., Gregory, S. and Johnson, A. (1988) 'The Nottingham Study of neurotic disorder: comparison of drug and psychological treatments', *Lancet*, 2, 235–240.

Tyrer, P., Turner, R. and Johnson, A. (1989) 'Integrated hospital and community psychiatric services and use of in-patient beds', *British Medical Journal*, 299, 298–300.

Uhlenhuth, E.H. and Paykel, E.S. (1973) 'Symptom configuration and life events', *Archives of General Psychiatry*, 28, 744–748.

Ulbrich, P.M., Warheit, G.J. and Zimmerman, R.S. (1989) 'Race, socio-economic status and psychological distress: an examination of differential vulnerability', *Journal of Health and Social Behaviour*, 30, 131–146.

Van den Brink, W., Koeter, M., Ormel, J., Dikstra, W., Giel, R., Schoemacker, J., Slooff, C. and Staal, J. (1990) 'Psychiatric diagnosis in an out-patient population'.

Vazquez-Barquero, J.L. (1990) 'Mental health in primary care settings', in *The Public Health Impact of Mental Disorders* (ed. D.P. Goldberg and D. Tantam). Bern: Huber-Hogrefe.

Vazquez-Barquero, J., Munoz, P. and Madoz Jauregi, V. (1981) 'The interaction between physical illness and neurotic morbidity in the community', *British Journal of Psychiatry*, 139, 328–335.

Vazquez-Barquero, J., Diez-Manrique, J.F., Pena, C., Aldama, J., Samaniego Rodriguez, C., Menendez Arango, J. and Mirapeix, C. (1987) 'A community mental health survey in Cantabria: a general description of morbidity', *Psychological Medicine*, 17, 227–241.

Verby, J., Holden, P. and Davies, R. (1979) 'Peer review of consultations in primary care: the use of audio-visual recordings', *British Medical Journal*, 1, 1686–1688.

Von Korff, M., Shapiro, S., Burke, J., Teitlebaum, M., Skinner, E., German, P., Turner, R.W., Klein, L. and Burns, B. (1987) 'Anxiety and depression in a primary care clinic', *Archives of General Psychiatry*, 44, 152–156.

Weissman, M., Prusoff, B. and Klerman, G. (1978a) 'Personality and the prediction of long-term outcome of depression', *American Journal of Psychiatry*, 135, 797–800.

Weissman, M., Myers, J. and Harding, P. (1978b) 'Psychiatric disorders in a US urban community: 1975/1976', *American Journal of Psychiatry*, 135, 459–462.

Wells, K., Golding, J. and Burnam, M. (1988) 'Psychiatric disorder in a sample of the general population with and without chronic medical conditions', *American Journal of Psychiatry*, 145, 976–998.

Wetherington, E. and Kessler, R.C. (1986) 'Perceived support, received support and adjustment to stressful events', *Journal of Health and Social Behaviour*, 27, 78–89.

Weyerer, S. (1990) 'Relationships between physical and psychological disorders', in *Psychological Disorders in General Medical Settings* (ed. N. Sartorius, D. Goldberg, G. de Girolamo, J. Costa e Silva, Y. LeCrubier and H.-U. Wittchen). Bern: Huber-Hogrefe.

Wheaton, B. (1980) 'The sociogenesis of psychological disorder: an attributional theory', *Journal of Health and Social Behaviour*, 21, 100–124.

Wheaton, B. (1983) 'Stress, personal coping resources and psychiatric symptoms: an investigation of interactive models', *Journal of Health and Social Behaviour*, 24, 208–230.

White, E. (1990) 'The historical development of the educational preparation of CPNs', in C. Brooker (ed.) *Community Psychiatric Nursing: A Research Perspective*. London: Chapman & Hall.

Wilhelm, K. and Parker, G. (1989) 'Is sex necessarily a risk factor to depression?' *Psychological Medicine*, 19, 401–413.

Williams, A.W., Ware, J.E. and Donald, C.A. (1981) 'A model of mental health, life events, and social supports applicable to general populations', *Journal of Health and Social Behaviour*, 22, 324–336.

Williams, P. and Balestrieri, M. (1989) 'Psychiatric clinics in general practice: do they reduce admissions?', *British Journal of Psychiatry*, 154, 67–71.

Williams, P., Tarnopolsky, A., Hand, D. and Shepherd, M. (1986) 'Minor psychiatric morbidity and general practice consultations: the West London Survey', *Psychological Medicine Monograph Supplements*, 9.

Williams, P., Wilkinson, G. and Arreghini, E. (1990) 'The determinants of help-seeking for psychological disorders in primary care settings', in *Psychological Disorders in General Medical Settings* (ed. N. Sartorius, D. Goldberg, G. de Girolamo, J. Costa e Silva, Y. LeCrubier and H.-U. Wittchen). Bern: Huber-Hogrefe.

Wilmink, F. (1989) *Patient, Physician, Psychiatrist. An Assessment Of Mental Health Problems In Primary Care*. Glimmen, The Netherlands: Phais.

Wilmink, F., Ormel, J., Giel, R., Krol, B., Lindeboom, E., van der Meer, K. and Soetsman, J. (1990) 'General practitioners' characteristics and the assessment of psychiatric illness', unpublished manuscript.

Wing, J. (1989) *Contributions to Health Services Planning and Research: Comparative Studies from Eight Psychiatric Case Registers*. London: Gaskell.

Wing, J., Mann, S., Leff, J. and Nixon, J. (1978) 'The concept of a "case" in psychiatric population surveys', *Psychological Medicine*, 8, 203–217.

Wing, J., Bebbington, P., Hurry, J. and Tennant, C. (1981) 'The prevalence in the general population of disorders familiar to psychiatrists in hospital practice', in *What is a Case?* (ed. J. Wing, P. Bebbington and L. Robins). London: Grant, McIntyre.

Winokur, G., Black, D. and Nasrallah, A. (1988) 'Depression secondary to other psychiatric disorders and medical illness', *American Journal of Psychiatry*, 145, 233–237.

Wolinsky, F. (1978) 'Assessing the effects of predisposing, enabling and illness-morbidity characteristics in health service utilisation', *Journal of Health and Human Behaviour*, 19, 384–396.

Wolsey, P. (1990) 'The training needs of CPNs in relation to work with schizophrenic clients', in C. Brooker (ed.) *Community Psychiatric Nursing: A Research Perspective*. London: Chapman & Hall.

WONCA (World Organisation of National Colleges, Academics and Academic Associations of General Practice) (1979) ICHPPC-2 (International Classification of Health Problems in Primary Care – 2nd edn), Oxford: Oxford University Press.

World Health Organisation (1988) 'Mental, behavioural and developmental disorders', Chapter 5 in *International Classification of Disease*. Geneva: World Health Organisation.

Zabarenko, L., Pittenger, R. and Zabarenko, R. (1968) *Primary Medical Practice: A Psychiatric Evaluation*. New York: Warren, Green Incorporated.

Zung, L., Magill, M. and Moore, J. (1983) 'Recognition and treatment of depression in a family medicine practice', *Journal of Clinical Psychiatry*, 4, 1–9.

# Name index

# Subject index